Legal Essentials for California Couples

By **Ed Sherman** & **Susan Cameron**
California Attorneys

Nolo Press
occidental
501 Mission Street, Suite 2
Santa Cruz, CA 95060
(831) 466-9922

THIS BOOK WAS PRINTED IN
JANUARY 2005
Do not use an old edition!
Out-of-date information can cause trouble

FREE UPDATE NOTICES
look for new laws & fixes at
www.nolocouples.com

© 2005 by Charles E. Sherman

ISBN: 0-944508-54-5

Library of Congress Card Number: 2004110642

Design and graphics:	Ed Sherman
Art:	Linda Allison
Cover design:	Ben & Shirley Thompson
Photo credits:	IFC: Todd Tsukushi

About the authors

Ed Sherman, a family law attorney since 1970, founded Nolo Press with *How to Do Your Own Divorce in California*. Through his several books on divorce and relationships, creation of the independent paralegal movement, and his co-founding of Divorce Helpline and Couples Helpline, he has made it his life's work to keep family problems out of the adversarial court system by making the legal process understandable, affordable and accessible for all.

Susan Cameron, an attorney since 198, has experience in family law, business law, conflict management and mediation. She joined Divorce Helpline in 1990, and in 1996, she co-authored *California Marriage Law* with Ed Sherman. Since 1997, she has practiced family mediation in Southern California, where she also teaches business law and conflict management at the University of Phoenix. She is now working on her Master of Divinity degree at Fuller Theological Seminary.

Acknowledgments

We are amazed and moved by the number of outstanding professionals who pitched in so generously to help make this a better book. It is impossible to rank them, so they appear alphabetically. Our heartfelt thanks and gratitude to:

Mahmoud Abdel-Baset, PhD, Director of Religious Affairs, Islamic Center of Southern California

Pamela Adams, MA, MFT, Carlsbad, couples counselor, management consultant

Ellyn Bader, PhD, Menlo Park, co-founder of The Couples Institute

Dr. Mackenzie Brooks, Victoria, BC, couples coach, counselor, trainer

Prof. Michael Broyde, Emory University School of Law, Director of the Law and Religion program

Prof. Robert F. Cochran, Jr., Pepperdine University School of Law, Straus Institute for Dispute Resolution, founder of the Institute on Law, Religion and Ethics

J. Steven Cowen, La Jolla, Certified Financial Planner

William C. Cuthbertson, MBA, CFP, San Juan Capistrano, The Fiscalis Group

Mary Dee Dickerson, PhD, CFP, San Diego, author of *Grow Your Goals*

Betty Goldwater, Santa Barbara, family counselor (retired)

Randi Gottlieb, MFT, Tehama County Department of Social Services

Jill D. Hollander, MBA, CFP, Berkeley, Financial Connections

Elaine R. Kiernan, CFP, Santa Cruz, Financial Resource Associates

Lauren S. Klein, CFP, EA, MBA, Irvine, Klein Financial Advisors

J. Jeffrey Lambert, CFP, Sacramento, Program Director, UC Davis Extension, Lighthouse Financial Planning

David Olsen, PhD, co-author of *The Couples Survival Workbook*

Peter Pearson, PhD, Menlo Park, co-founder of The Couples Institute

Jonathan Rich, PhD, Irvine, author of *The Couples Guide to Love and Money*

Nancy J. Ross, San Jose, therapist, couples counselor, collaborative law

Prof. Duane Ruth-Heffelbower, MDiv, JD, Center for Peacemaking and Conflict Studies, Fresno Pacific University

Susan Schreiner, La Mesa, Schreiner Financial Solutions

Robin Seigel, San Diego, National Mediation Center

Prof. Megan Sullaway, PhD, El Segundo, UCLA Deptartment of Psychology, Pacific Psychological Associates

Sylvia Weishaus, PhD, Sherman Oaks, co-founder of Making Marriage Work

and

Couples Helpline attorneys: Peggy Williams, Anne Lober, Janet Thompson, Charma Pipersky, and Allison Hardin—outstanding attorneys, great colleagues!

Nolo staffers: Joe Cosentino and Sandra Borland

Table of Contents

PART THREE ~
HOW THE LAW GOVERNS YOUR RELATIONSHIP
WHEN THERE'S NO AGREEMENT

PART FOUR ~ ENDINGS

Appendix A—Nolo Supplementary Family Arbitration Rules

Appendix B—Relationship Agreement Resources

INDEX

Introduction

The book in a nutshell

This book is about the vast body of rules that silently and invisibly go into effect when you say "I do" or move in together. It explains when you need to know the rules, when you should tailor the rules by written agreement and how to do it. And—fanfare!—it marks the introduction of a new approach to marital and living-together agreements, developing positive and constructive features in them that no couple should be without. The result is a relationship agreement, which is a document that is so different from what has gone before that it deserves a new name to distinguish it from others, so we call it the Couples Contract.

There are sound reasons why some couples, even of modest means, should redefine their financial relationships; but every couple—yes, every single one!—should make the basic Couples Contract found in this book and (so far) nowhere else. Going far beyond money and property, our agreement is written in positive and loving language that underscores the couple's commitment to a lasting relationship. It will keep the couple forever out of the adversarial legal system and it introduces concepts that will someday help solve problems if any arise.

Marriage contracts developed a dark past. They have typically been legalistic, money-grubbing things, often used when a woman marries a wealthy man, to strip her of property, support and inheritance rights. But now they have a bright future when applied for the benefit of every couple to an important new purpose.

You might find it surprising that agreements that can rescue relationships are the logical extension of more than thirty years' experience helping thousands of people get through divorces more smoothly with less cost and pain. Breaking up is a very dicey business, so emotionally charged that a misstep can produce the stereotypical nightmare divorce, yet we found that a few specific changes in how couples go about breaking up will make a huge difference in the degree and duration of conflict, often alleviating most of it. We also learned that the earlier we can get involved in a case, the more effective we can be at smoothing things out, helping people avoid missteps before too much damage is done. Well, guess what? The best time to begin is before there is any sign of trouble at all, or at least before it becomes entrenched. If we can introduce our principles *that* early, why, there might not be any breakup at all. Principles very similar to those that enable a smooth breakup can resolve issues before they destroy the relationship and can, in fact, open lines of communication and strengthen ties. Experience and statistics show that couples who follow these steps have better relationships and a far lower rate of breakup.

*　*　*

This is a book you can talk to. If you have questions to ask or problems to solve, or if you want a friendly, reliable family law attorney to act as your coach, advisor, mediator or arbitrator, call Couples Helpline. Tell them Ed Sherman sent you.

CHAPTER 1

How the law governs your relationship —and when it matters

In our family law practices, one of the most common things we hear over and over from clients who have just had the law explained to them is, "I wish I had known that a long time ago!" Or, "If only I had known that before (whatever) happened."

People entering any form of long-term relationship, whether married, domestic partners,[1] or just living together, are typically unaware that their relationship to each other—and to third parties, like creditors or government agencies—are defined and governed by rules of law, often in ways they did not expect or would not have agreed to had they known. They are not aware of what can happen when events force these rules into play.

Another surprise is that new laws can come along at any time and change your legal relationship in significant ways without you knowing or agreeing to it. And that's nothing compared to what can happen when you move to another state. Rights and duties that you might or might not have been aware of will suddenly become entirely different. Law books are filled with the cases of unhappy people who found out after the fact that things were not as they had thought or wished.

Here are two more things that couples should know. First, couples can make written agreements that change the rules of their relationship to suit their own needs and preferences. And, second, a relationship agreement (like the one in this book) can be a positive and constructive thing that reinforces your commitment to one another and creates a foundation for working out problems that might arise in the future, possibly saving your relationship.

It is much better if you do not wait in ignorance for some defining event to spring up and force the rules to your attention. We encourage every couple to know where they stand and learn how and to what extent they can tailor their legal relationship to more closely suit their personal wishes.

Above all, we recommend that every couple enter into at least the basic Couples Contract (chapter 5) and give themselves the invaluable advantages that can be had just for spending a little effort to do it. These advantages are described more fully in the next chapter.

---

[1] **Note to domestic partners.** Everything said in this book about marriage, spouses, husbands and wives applies equally to registered domestic partners unless we clearly state otherwise. Domestic partnership, who can register and how to register is discussed in chapter 11A, C and D.

A. Your legal relationships have already been defined

If you are in a long-term relationship and do not have an *enforceable* written agreement, rules of law define and govern important features of your relationship—such things as:

- How open and honest you must be with each other
- Who owns income earned by either of you during the relationship
- Who can manage the money and assets
- Who owes debts incurred by either of you before or during the relationship
- Who owns property acquired during the relationship
- Who can parent children or adopt
- Who can be covered by health insurance
- Who can get family care leave
- Who can authorize medical or mental health treatment
- Who can visit in a hospital or jail
- Who can order care, apply for benefits after disability
- Who inherits if there is no will
- Who is included in the retirement plan
- Who sees to the partner's wishes after death

You have a choice: accept the rules imposed by law, or tailor the terms of your relationship in a written agreement to better suit your needs and preferences.

B. When the rules matter —events that force the issue

You might go for years without encountering an event that forces your legal relationships to your attention, or something might happen tomorrow, or you might wander into a situation and not realize the consequences until it's too late.

If you don't know the rules (and who amongst us knows them all?), you can at least be aware that there *are* rules, where to find them, and—most important—when you need to know them. If you read this book, you'll satisfy all three, because:

1. You now know that there are rules (laws) that govern your relationship
2. Part Three is where you can look to get an overview summary of the rules that relate to married couples, domestic partners, unmarried couples living together, parents, and couples dealing with domestic abuse.

3. Below are some examples of events that can bring the rules of law into play and when you might want to know about them:

Filing income tax returns	Applying for financial aid for a child
Large debts or risky business	Moving to another state
Seeking health insurance	Saving for retirement
Purchasing on credit	Retirement
Borrowing money	Loss of job or income
Refinancing your home	Applying for benefits
Immigration issues	Accident
Buying or renting a place to live	Chronic illness
Transfer of real estate to the other	Death or disability
Making gifts to your mate or others	Bankruptcy
Naming someone else as insurance or pension beneficiary	Getting sued
	Acts of discrimination
Going for Social Security benefits	Splitting up
Deciding to have or adopt a child	

C. How the rules are applied

If an event comes up that puts the rules into play, a judge would look first to see if you have an *enforceable* agreement that applies. A marital agreement is not enforceable unless it meets an array of legal requirements, but don't worry—if you follow the steps in this book, your relationship agreement will be enforceable.

If you have an enforceable agreement, its terms will be followed. If not, the matter will be decided according to the rules of law for people in your form of relationship: marriage, registered domestic partnership, or unmarried and living together. These are the rules discussed in Part Three. But remember: if you have a relationship agreement like ours, you are unlikely to ever come before a judge.

D. Volatility —when rules change

Laws can and do change. Check www.nolocouples.com to see if important changes have occurred since January 2005, when this book was printed.

Marriage has been an established institution for many centuries, yet lawmakers continue to tinker with the rights and duties of married people. Significant changes might take place only from time to time, but you never know when this can happen and no one sends you a notice, like credit card companies must do, telling you that your contract has just been changed by forces beyond your control. This is one good reason for making written agreements, so your legal relationship stays put.

Domestic partnership was created in California only in 2002, but was vastly expanded in 2003 by a law that took effect January 1, 2005. Because it is so new and controversial, it will probably get a great deal of attention from lawmakers, so you can anticipate frequent changes for years to come.

Same-sex marriage is the Wild, Wild West of relationship law. Not quite yet arrived, this form of relationship is battling mightily to emerge. At this writing, gay marriages have taken place in Massachusetts; Portland, OR; San Francisco, CA; Sandoval County, NM; Asbury Park, NJ; and New Paltz, NY; but their validity is in question as lawsuits and legislative actions intended to invalidate them are ongoing. The California Supreme court voided marriages that have already taken place[2] but did not decide whether the law preventing them is constitutional, so that lawsuit is still alive and well. In July 2003, the high court in British Columbia legalized same-sex marriage, so we now have U.S. gay couples in possession of valid Canadian marriage licenses, calling into question the obligation of U.S. states under international treaties. The rules concerning this form of relationship will be fought over and continue to be unstable for years to come. If this is your area of interest, you should watch special-interest Web sites, such as www.lambdalegal.org.

E. Couples on the move

The laws of the state where you reside are what define your legal relationships, and this almost guarantees that significant changes will occur when you move from one state to another. For example, in California, the earnings of either spouse is community property that belongs to both and both have the right to spend it or sell property

---

[2] Lockyer vs. City and County of San Francisco, CA Supreme Court S122923 (2004)

purchased with it. However, in many states, income belongs to the spouse who earned it as does anything purchased with that income. This is quite a big difference, determined solely by where you reside.

With a Couples Contract, you are free from this concern. You create a degree of stability by agreeing that the laws of California will govern the agreement and all matters in your relationship, no matter where you move. This will go a long way toward preventing surprises.

If you are moving to another state, or have recently arrived here, you need to review the relationship laws of your new state before you make the move, or as soon as possible afterward. Some of your rights and obligations as a couple will probably have changed in significant ways that you should know about. If you have a written agreement, you also want to know how your new state interprets agreements the couple made in another state.

Domestic partners get a little more predictability than married couples when it comes to breaking up. No matter where you move or for how long, you can always come back to California courts to get separated or divorced. However, when you move to another state, most of the rights you secured when you registered in California will probably not be recognized in most other states. If you move, be sure to see a family law attorney in the new state and ask about your rights in the new state.

If you are in a domestic partnership (or equivalent) that was created in another state and is "substantially equivalent" to a California domestic partnership, it will be recognized in California and treated under domestic partnership rules here. If you want to be sure you have a domestic partnership here, you should register your partnership after you arrive. This area of law will be fought over for years to come. Take a close look before you move.

*   *   *

Now you know a little about how the law affects couples. It's time to find out about the vital advantages that every couple can gain from having at least the basic Couples Contract.

CHAPTER 2

How a written agreement can enhance and possibly save your relationship

A. Clearing up the bad reputation of marital agreements

This book marks the introduction of a new approach to marital agreements, which have had a bad reputation for being legalistic, money-grubbing things, negatively preoccupied with all that might go wrong in the future, and too often used to strip a woman marrying a wealthy man of her rights to property, support, and inheritance.

It doesn't have to be that way—and it won't be that way for you. Marital contracts have an honorable history going back thousands of years, but they have not been put to good use for modern couples because no one thought to do it. So, we have now morphed traditional marital contracts into a new relationship agreement, the Couples Contract, that is going to do well by doing good. It is a different animal entirely—affirming and forward-looking—whose purpose is to do constructive things for loving couples and add features to their relationship that can only help.

Positive, clear language. When we gave the Couples Contract its positive purpose and new role, the first thing that had to go was the terrible legalistic, sphincter-tightening language that lawyers tend to use, often as an awkward substitute for clear thinking and competent writing. It has no place here. The Couples Contract is written as much as possible in loving and affirming language and at all times in simple terms that everyone can understand.

Commitments. The Couples Contract affirms your intention to enter into a lasting relationship based upon mutual affection, respect and friendship. In it, you also commit to a high degree of openness, honesty and good faith in all dealings with one another. In fact, this high standard of care is imposed on every married couple by California law, so why have we never seen it stated in a traditional marital contract? Never mind; it gets pride of position in our Couples Contract.

B. What you can accomplish with a Couples Contract

The advantages of the Couples Contract can be had by any couple at any time. It doesn't matter if you are married, soon-to-be married, or simply living together. If you are a committed couple, you should have a Couples Contract. In fact, you can't afford to be without one. Here's why:

The basic Couples Contract

In the basic agreement, you get very important advantages without having to go into discussions of finances or other details of your relationship. Just do it and you get these essential benefits:

- Make a loving commitment to a lasting relationship
- Introduce concepts that can help solve relationship problems if any arise
- Make sure your relationship never ends up in court
- Keep the terms of your relationship stable, no matter where you move

A sample basic agreement is at the end of this chapter so you can see what one looks like. How to build your own is discussed in detail, clause by clause, in chapter 5.

Beyond the basics

You don't have to, but if you want, you can add some variations to your basic agreement that *will* take some thought and discussion, such as:

- Tailor your financial relationships to make them more suitable to your family's needs, which for some couples will be a must (chapter 6).
- Introduce faith-related principles into your family life (chapter 7)

You can start with the simpler basic agreement first, then tailor it later or never, or you can tailor your agreement at the outset. In either case, your agreement can be modified at any time by following the steps described in chapter 10G.

C. Introduce constructive principles into your relationship

One of the most important features you can add to any relationship—a gift that you can give yourselves—is planning in advance, while everything is smooth and lovely, to deal with issues that might threaten your relationship in the future. If you want a lasting relationship, there are specific things you can do to increase your chances.

The purpose of this section in your basic Couples Contract is to plant some seeds (or lay a foundation) that will help you unravel predicaments that come up for most couples sooner or later. Most couples have no plan or idea for how to deal with such situations if they ever do occur, but not you—your Couples Contract is there to remind you that there are things you can do and resources you can turn to. You needn't do anything at this time (although reading a bit about it wouldn't hurt), because just having these ideas in the back of your mind will help you recognize signs that your relationship needs some attention, and you'll have some ideas for how to respond if that happens. Look at this as a form of free health insurance.

What keeps couples together

The Couples Contract states directly and clearly that your intention is to preserve your mutual affection, respect and friendship, because this is the first principle of a lasting relationship. We didn't make it up: this is the conclusion of Dr. John Gottman, a towering figure in couples counseling, who achieved this insight after more than thirty years in the research and study of couples. In his bestselling book, *The Seven Principles for Making Marriage Work*, he discusses why most marriage therapy fails, concluding that resolving conflicts and improving communication is important but not, of itself, what keeps couples together. Rather, he finds that "friendship fuels the flames of romance."

> "... happy marriages are based on a deep friendship. By this I mean a mutual respect for and enjoyment of each other's company. [Such] couples tend to know each other intimately. ... They have an abiding regard for each other and express this fondness not just in the big ways, but in little ways day in and day out." [1]

However intense or frequent their battles, the couples that last have never lost their fondness and respect for one another. After describing the kinds of behavior that undermine mutual regard, Gottman describes seven things that happy marriages have in common, then he shows you how to introduce those seven principles into your own relationship. If ever you feel that the ties that bind are weakening, this

---

[1] John Gottman, *The Seven Principles for Making Marriage Work*. Three Rivers Press (2000), page 19.

would be a good place to start looking for things you can do to rekindle affection. If you would rather look at a video or listen to a tape, the material is also available in audio or video form at www.gottman.com, where you can also learn about workshops conducted by the Gottman Institute.

Other factors that contribute to relationship success include learning to express your feelings, both positive and negative; learning to disagree in ways that are not destructive; and learning to accept things you can't change.

Beyond self-help

Beyond information in books, tapes and videos, there are couples workshops. Some might find it more effective to go directly to a good couples counselor. If one of you is allergic to the idea of counseling or therapy, look for a couples *coach*, which might be more acceptable. Enter "couples coach" into Google and see what comes up, or ask a recommended therapist to serve as a coach. Many religious organizations have trained conciliators who work with couples and many clergy are trained in couples counseling. In any case, you should only work with someone who is trained, experienced and certified to do the job. The important thing is that you not sit on your hands if one of you begins to feel that your mutual regard is fading. If you are committed to your relationship, you need to make it a priority, meaning there will be times when you have to put extra effort into it—get information, go to a workshop, get help. Above all, try to discuss things you can do to increase mutual regard and affection and decide together what steps to take.

Relationship Resources

Our companion CD has a fine article, *How to Get the Most From Couples Therapy*. Appendix B lists relationship resources that professionals have told us they recommend to their own clients. One we like is *The Five Love Languages*, by Gary Chapman, who points out that people have different ways of expressing and receiving love, so that one person might be expressing it in a way that the other does not get, as where a man works hard to earn material things for his loved one and buys her gifts, but she craves touching and nice words. It's a matter of getting your signals staight.

Other resources include the highly regarded Couple Communication workshops, which have to date trained over 600,000 people and are conducted across the U.S. by thousands of certified instructors. To find an instructor near you, visit www.couplecommunication.com.

Then there's the respected Marriage Encounter with nation-wide programs for troubled couples that are "based on Judeo-Christian concepts," though you need not be religious or belong to a religious organization in order to participate. You can find more information about them at www.marriage-encounter.org.

But wait! There's more! There's a mountain of good books, tapes, videos and workshops out there that you can substitute for our examples. Go out and browse or ask your clergy, counselors or other resource people. Time spent on this subject will be richly rewarded. That's the whole point—to make the effort.

Stay tuned. This is the most innovative part of the Couples Contract, so we look forward to feedback from readers and counselors, telling of their experiences and favorite resources, which we'll share with you on our Web site and in future editions.

D. Make sure your relationship never ends up in court

This section of your agreement just by itself makes it worth having a basic Couples Contract as it gets you a giant advantage for next to no effort.

When you buy health insurance, you don't intend to be sick, but you still get health insurance "just in case." It's exactly the same here. You don't intend or expect to ever have a disagreement you can't resolve—and you've already planted seeds for problem-solving to help make sure you don't—but if it ever *did* happen, what would you do? Without this part of your agreement, if faced with a disagreement that can't be resolved, you'd have no guidance and no alternative other than to give up or get a lawyer and go to court. Neither is acceptable.

The adversarial legal system is the worst possible place to take a family dispute, a forum where it is almost certain to get stirred up into something ugly and expensive. But, now you can make sure your relationship and family matters are unlikely to ever end up in court. Instead, your Couples Contract says that if anything comes up that you can't resolve, you will go to mediation first (which has a high success rate), but if that doesn't solve the problem or if one of you doesn't want to do it, you'll take the problem to binding and final arbitration. Believe us when we tell you that, based upon our combined experience and that of every attorney at Couples Helpline, this is a thousand times better than the alternative. You want this clause!

Mediation and arbitration are often referred to together as *alternative dispute resolution* (ADR), which has long been known to have many advantages over going to court. Courts are slow, complicated, expensive, and impersonal. If you were ever to end up there, the judge won't know you or your family and won't have much time or patience to learn about you or your problems. In our careers, we have almost never heard of a judge doing anything to try to save a relationship. By contrast, when you select your mediator, you can pick someone with a talent for conciliation who can explore that possibility and take some time to explore solutions for your problems. In arbitration, you can use a three-arbitrator panel in which two of the arbitrators can be anyone you choose, perhaps someone who knows your family and your values.

Another plus for ADR is that mediators and arbitrators can give attention to parts of your agreement that a court could not. A conciliator or mediator might help you settle lifestyle conflicts like housework or money handling, which a judge would not touch. Or, if a couple agreed to raise their children according to a certain religious faith, a judge would probably ignore that provision because the constitution requires separation of church and state; but arbitrators don't work for the state, so they can include religious or lifestyle portions of your agreement in their decision making.

E. Stability if you move

The rules that govern your relationship are determined by whatever state you live in and, as we discussed in chapter 1E, the rules can change drastically when you move from one state to another. However, your Couples Contract frees you from this threat by declaring that California law will always govern your relationship, no matter where you live. This is one way to avoid surprises. If you move to another state and find out you like some of their rules better, you can always modify your agreement (chapter 10G). It is very important to have your agreement reviewed by a family law attorney in your new state just before or right after you actually move there.

F. Tailoring financial relationships

First of all, finances aren't something you have to deal with right away or at all, but you should at least be aware that if you don't add tailoring to the basic Couples Contract, your financial and parenting affairs will be governed by California laws—one size fits all—which might not be the best fit for you.

Is off-the-shelf OK? The laws that govern relationships are discussed in Part Three, but here in a nutshell is how things work in California for married people or domestic partners if there is no tailoring:

- Income and gains made through efforts of either spouse belong to both
- Property acquired during the union is community property (excepting inheritances or gifts to one spouse or purchases made with separate funds)

- Spouses have equal rights to manage and control income and property
- The community earns an interest in the separate property, business or professional practice of a spouse whose efforts during marriage increase the value of his/her separate property or business
- One spouse might have to pay for debts incurred by the other, even those incurred before marriage
- You'll end up in court if you separate and can't agree on terms
- The duty to support children ends at age 18, or 19 if still in high school
- There's no duty to support stepchildren

Is that what you want? Because, if you don't tailor your financial relationships in a written agreement, that's what you'll get. Most couples live their lives under these rules, but California law is not ideally suited to everyone and you don't have to be rich to get some advantage from tailoring. Even couples of modest means can have sound reasons for tailoring their financial relationships; for example, to arrange for:

- The treatment of separate property
- Children of a prior relationship
- Marriage after retirement
- A spouse who is in debt, a spendthrift, or in a risky business
- Professional practice or separate business
- Staying home to care for a child, parent or disabled family member
- Anticipation of a significant inheritance
- Honoring personal preferences over California law in order to keep finances separate and/or clarify the division of responsibility

Solutions for the above situations are presented in chapter 6D, but these are just some common examples from the lives of typical families. With over 6 million couples in California, there are undoubtedly lots of other situations that deserve special tailoring, but reading through chapter 6 will help you figure out if your own situation might benefit from some tailoring and give you at least an idea of what to do about it. If you're not sure, give us a call at Couples Helpline and we'll help you decide if you can benefit from tailoring and how to do it.

Now or later. You might decide that tailoring your financial relationships would be a good idea for your family, but unless there's some pressing reason, you don't have to do it immediately. You can enter into the basic agreement first (chapter 5), and later modify it (chapter 10G) to add the tailoring. This puts your agreement in place early, gets you all the major advantages, and lets you take more time to work out the financial matters later.

Relationship Affirmations and Agreement
of Chris Brown and Jamie Jones

In loving anticipation of a lasting relationship, this agreement is made between Chris Brown and Jamie Jones, called by our first names in this agreement.

1. **Purpose.** *The purpose of our agreement is:*

   A. *To affirm our commitment to one another and to a lasting relationship based upon trust, mutual respect, affection and friendship*

   B. *To establish principles that will help us overcome personal issues that might threaten to undermine our relationship, should any ever arise*

   C. *To entirely and forever remove our relationship from the adversarial court system by committing to resolve disagreements of any nature that might arise between us, that we cannot resolve privately, by mediation or arbitration*

   D. *To govern our relationship rights and obligations according to California law, except as modified by this agreement*

   E. *To create stability and predictability by governing our relationship rights and obligations according to the terms of this agreement no matter where we might reside in the future*

2. **Commitments**

We commit ourselves to mutual respect, openness, honesty, and the highest standard of good faith and fair dealing in all matters, putting each other's best interests foremost.

3. **Current situation and plans**

We plan to marry on December 25, 2005. There are no children of our relationship

Chris. I am 38 years old, residing at 123 4th Street, Santa Theresa, CA. I am in good health. I had three years of college and am employed as a computer programmer. I am a citizen of Canada, residing here on a green card and expecting to become a naturalized citizen in about three years. I have one child, Nora Brown, a U.S. citizen, age 6, of a previous relationship. I believe I will inherit my uncle's house in Victoria, BC in the near future.

Jamie. I am 40 years old, residing at 456 7th Street, Santa Theresa, CA. I am in good health. I have an MA in education and am employed as a high school teacher. I have no children. I plan to enter graduate school in the next year or so, to undertake a three-to-five-year PhD program, which will require me to take out student loans.

4. Effective date and duration of agreement

Our agreement will become effective when we marry. If we do not marry, it will be of no effect. Once it takes effect, our agreement will remain in effect indefinitely, or until we sign a written agreement to modify or revoke it.

5. Principles for a lasting relationship

We believe that a lasting relationship is based upon mutual respect, affection and friendship. It is our goal to preserve and reinforce these features in our union.

We believe that a lasting relationship sometimes requires an intentional effort, that reinforcing positive features is essential, and that practices learned from couples counseling have an excellent record of success.

If ever circumstances arise that threaten to undermine our mutual regard, we agree to make an effort to reinforce positive qualities in our relationship and resolve issues that weaken them.

We agree that if one of us requests it, we will set aside some quiet time to discuss our relationship together and seek ways to reinforce the positive features that are vital to our well-being as a couple. We will look for information in books, tapes or videos, starting with Dr. John Gottman's material on The Seven Principles for Making Marriages Work, and we will look at Dr. Gary Chapman's material about The Five Love Languages. We will also consider going to conciliation, or to a couples workshop, or to a couples coach or counselor.

6. Parenting

We agree that, except as modified by this agreement, our rights and duties as parents of any children born to or legally adopted by us will be governed by California law.

7. Money, property and financial matters

Except as modified by this agreement, we agree that all of our mutual rights and obligations with respect to our marital and financial affairs, including our income, debts, and property, will be governed by California law no matter where we might live in the future.

8. Disclosures

Our agreement does not alter financial rights and duties under California law, therefore:

I, Chris, am sufficiently aware of Jamie's financial circumstances and freely and voluntarily give up the right to formal written disclosure or any other information about Jamie's finances.

I, Jamie, am sufficiently aware of Chris's financial circumstances and I freely and voluntarily give up the right to formal written disclosure or any other information about Chris's finances.

9. Representation and drafting

Chris and Jamie drafted this agreement together, jointly.

I, Chris, understand that I have the right to be represented by an independent lawyer in the negotiation and preparation of this agreement and I had sufficient funds to retain a lawyer for this purpose if I wanted to. Nonetheless, I choose not to be represented. I understand the terms of this agreement and have had ample opportunity to seek the advice of legal counsel or any other kind of advisor. I have read this agreement carefully and have received as much advice as I wish to receive. I freely and voluntarily choose to sign it without being represented by an attorney at this time.

I, Jamie, understand that I have the right to be represented by an independent lawyer in the negotiation and preparation of this agreement and I had sufficient funds to retain a lawyer for this purpose if I wanted to. Nonetheless, I choose not to be represented. I understand the terms of this agreement and have had ample opportunity to seek the advice of legal counsel or any other kind of advisor. I have read this agreement carefully and have received as much advice as I wish to receive. I freely and voluntarily choose to sign it without being represented by an attorney at this time.

10. Resolution of disputes

It is our desire to remove our relationship entirely and forever from the adversarial court system and to resolve any dispute that might arise between us or under this agreement by mediation and arbitration.

A. Mediation

1. If we are unable to resolve any dispute ourselves or with counseling, then on the written request of either party we will within thirty days submit our dispute to mediation with a mediator agreed upon by both of us. Unless we agree otherwise, our mediator must be a California family law attorney who specializes in family law mediation. If we are unable to agree on a mediator, we will each choose one person to make a choice on our behalf, and our two advisors together will appoint our mediator. We will

participate in mediation in good faith and pay the cost of mediation from community funds, if available, and if community funds are not available, we will each be responsible for half the cost of such mediation.

2. We are each entitled to representation in mediation by an attorney of our choice. Attorney fees will be paid from community funds, if available, and if community funds are not available, each party will be responsible for his or her own attorney's fees.

B. Arbitration

1. In the event that one of us is not willing to do mediation, or if mediation does not resolve all issues within a reasonable number of sessions, then on the written request of either of us, we will submit the matter to binding arbitration within ninety days. The arbitrator will be agreed upon by both of us, but must be a California family law attorney who specializes in mediation or arbitration, or a retired California family court judge. If we are unable to agree on an arbitrator, the matter will be decided by a panel of three arbitrators. We will each choose one arbitrator, who need not have any particular professional background, and our two arbitrators together will appoint the third arbitrator who must be a California family law attorney or retired family court judge.

2. If we use a single arbitrator, we will pay the cost of arbitration from community funds, if available, and if community funds are not available, we will each be responsible for half the cost of the arbitration. If we use a panel of three arbitrators, each of us will pay the fees of the arbitrator we appoint. The fees of the third arbitrator will be paid from community funds, if available, and if community funds are not available, we will each be responsible for half the fees of the third arbitrator and other costs of arbitration.

3. We are each entitled to representation in arbitration by an attorney of our choice. Attorney fees will be paid from community funds, if available, and if community funds are not available, each party will be responsible for his or her own attorney's fees.

4. The arbitrator(s) will have the power to interpret the terms of this agreement, decide questions of their own jurisdiction, and settle disputes arising between the parties regarding the arbitrability of claims and the interpretation of the agreement. The arbitrator(s) will not have the power to alter, modify or terminate any provision of this agreement. The arbitration will be conducted under the rules of California Code of Civil Procedure sections 1280 to 1294.2, as modified by the Nolo Supplementary Family Arbitration Rules, a copy of which is attached to this agreement as Exhibit A.

5. **Arbitration is binding and final.** The decision of the arbitrator(s) will be binding and final, not subject to review in any court. We each understand that by agreeing to binding arbitration, we are

choosing arbitration as the sole remedy for any dispute between us arising from our marriage or this agreement, and we each expressly give up our right to file a lawsuit in any civil court against one another, or to request a court to resolve any dispute between us as an ancillary matter in a family court proceeding, except to enforce arbitration or the decision of an arbitrator, and thus we also give up the right to trial by a court or by a jury. To whatever extent the law does not allow any issue between us to be decided by binding arbitration, we agree to submit such matters to non-binding arbitration before submitting the issue to any court.

11. Severability, governing law, interpretation, modification

A. Severability

Each clause of this agreement is separate and divisible from the others. Should any adjudicating authority refuse to enforce one or more clauses, in whole or in part, the remainder of such clauses, and the remainder of the entire agreement, are to remain valid and in full force.

B. Entire agreement and consideration

This agreement represents our entire agreement. It supersedes any and all other agreements, either oral or in writing, between us regarding our mutual rights and obligations arising from our relationship. The promises of each of us are consideration for the promises of the other.

C. Binding effect

Once this agreement takes effect, as described in paragraph 4, it will become binding on us and on our respective heirs and estate representatives.

D. Governing law and interpretation

This agreement has been drafted and signed by both of us in the State of California. The validity and interpretation of this agreement will be governed in accordance with the laws of the State of California. It will be interpreted fairly, simply, and not strictly for or against either party. Copies of this signed agreement may be submitted and accepted into evidence in place of the original in any proceeding to enforce or interpret the terms of this agreement.

We do not wish to have our mutual rights and obligations changed by the fact that we may choose to reside outside California some day, so we agree that the previous paragraph will apply no matter where we might live at any time during our marriage.

E. Modification

This agreement may be modified or revoked only by written agreement, signed by both of us.

Signatures

We have each read this agreement carefully and are signing it freely, voluntarily, and with full understanding of its meaning after having obtained all the advice we each, individually, feel is appropriate.

This agreement was delivered to Chris Brown by Jamie Jones on (date)

Dated: _____   _____

                                                Chris Brown

This agreement was delivered to Jamie Jones by Chris Brown on (date)

Dated: _____   _____

                                                Jamie Jones

Attachments

     Exhibit A   *Nolo Supplementary Family Arbitration Rules*

Things every couple should do

A. Be aware of the rules and when they matter

You should be aware that a vast body of California cases and statutes govern your marital, financial, and parenting relationships, as well as your relationships with third parties, like creditors, government agencies, retirement plans, and so on. You should browse through Part Three, a summary of these rules, to get an idea of subjects covered there so you'll know where to look whenever an event comes up that might make you want to know more. And remember, laws change, so check our Web site at www.nolocouples.com from time to time to see if we've posted updates.

B. Make a Couples Contract

You should definitely do the basic Couples Contract described in chapter 5. Every couple should. Are you

- **Married?**
- **Soon-to-be married?**
- **Unmarried?**

It doesn't matter: if you're a committed couple, you want this agreement. For very little effort, you can make a loving commitment to a long and lasting future together, plant the seeds for solutions to whatever issues might come up between you in the future, prevent the rules that govern your relationship from changing dramatically if you ever move to another state, and make sure that your relationship will never end up in court. You can go beyond the basic agreement either now or later to add financial tailoring to make the rules more suitable to your particular situation.

C. Think, discuss and plan together

The Couples Contract is something you will want to do together. This doesn't mean that one of you can't spend a few hours to prepare the paperwork, but both of you should take some time to discuss the ideas and options in the basic agreement (chapter 5) and consider whether you want to do financial tailoring or add faith-based features at this time, later or never. The next chapter gives you a checklist for how to proceed and some advice about how to work together on your agreement.

D. Who can help?

The basic Couples Contract is relatively simple and uncomplicated, so it will be no surprise if you do yours without any help at all beyond this book. There are a few places in chapters on financial and faith-based tailoring where we suggest that some people might want to get some information and advice from an accountant, financial planner, estate planner, clergy or family law attorney, depending on the subject being discussed. If you add financial tailoring or otherwise depart from our template, it could be useful to have your agreement reviewed by a family law attorney before you make the final draft.

Couples Helpline. Because the Couples Contract is so new and different, and because a traditional attorney's first instinct is to say "No" to things that are different, we created Couples Helpline, with our own staff of family law attorneys and document specialists, specifically to provide advice and services to couples who are working on a relationship agreement or who want to resolve family disagreements through mediation or arbitration. If ever you feel you'd like some assistance from a family law attorney, mediator or arbitrator who is completely supportive of the Couples Contract concept, call Couples Helpline and let us explain how we can help you, or go to www.CouplesHelpline.com.

CHAPTER 4

How to build your agreement
—checklist and advice

A. Give yourselves plenty of time

Don't put yourselves in a situation where you have to rush. Making a Couples Contract might take some thought and discussion with your partner before you draft and sign it. This is an important document, so you should give it the time it deserves. In cases where courts have invalidated a prenuptial agreement, it was often a factor that the agreement was signed in a hurry or under pressure.

- If you just do the basic agreement (chapter 5), allow a few weeks.
- If you tailor financial relationships or add other variations, you should allow a few months or more.

Giving yourselves plenty of time will take the pressure off, keep you relaxed, and help make it better and more meaningful.

If you feel you could use a little help or a sounding board for your ideas, don't hesitate to call Couples Helpline to discuss your situation with expert family law attorneys who understand the goals of this innovative agreement. Also consider discussing your ideas with a financial planner or personal advisors such as mentors, family members and close friends for their input and suggestions.

B. Working together

A major goal of your agreement is to safeguard mutual respect and affection in your relationship, so we know you'll keep that in mind when you work together on it.

There's not much to disagree about in the basic agreement (chapter 5), which has only positive and constructive things in it. In that case, your discussions should be relatively easy and you probably won't need much advice about how to work together.

If you tailor your financial relationships, or one of you wants faith-based clauses, you might run into things that can be a challenge to discuss. So what? You don't have to agree about everything to be in love or stay together forever, but you do have to find ways to accommodate different points of view. Loving partners sometimes have issues that are difficult to resolve, or even discuss. This doesn't mean they don't love each other, but it might mean they should work with someone skilled to help them find a successful conclusion that satisfies both of them. You are two different people, so from time to time you're going to run into things you don't agree on. Here are some suggestions, in case this turns out to be one of those times.

Back to basics. If you get stuck discussing any of the variations, just do the ones you agree on or drop variations all together and just do the basic agreement. That gets you most of the advantages of the Couples Contract and you can always modify it later (chapter 10G) whenever you reach agreement on other terms. So there's no pressure—you don't have to agree on everything, or anything beyond the basics.

Time and place. Arrange to meet at a convenient time and place specifically to discuss your agreement—a time when you can both be rested, relaxed and free of interruption and a place good for quiet but concentrated conversation. Don't make it a marathon, but set a reasonable amount of time aside and plan to meet again, as often as it takes, until you get through to the end. No rush, no pressure.

Reflection. Before you meet, and especially between meetings, take time to dig into your own thoughts and feelings and what you understand to be the thoughts and feelings of your partner. You are particularly trying to understand the interests of both parties, starting with yourself.

Discuss interests rather than what you want. An interest is not the same as what you want—it is *why* you want what you want, which you might not be aware of at first. For example, putting funds into a joint account might be what you *want*, and you know you want it, but your *interests* might be to build something together, to feel safe and secure, and to be treated fairly. When you just say what you want, you either get it or you don't, which makes it seem like your partner is trying to deny you something if he/she has different ideas. Interests are easier to discuss and can often be addressed in a variety of ways that might or might not include exactly what you want.

Speak clearly. Don't expect your partner to read your mind or guess your feelings. It's up to you to understand what you think and feel and then communicate this clearly. Speak kindly from the place where you feel affection. Don't be pushy or keep repeating yourself, but do make sure you are being understood by asking your partner to say back to you what he/she understands you to mean.

Listen attentively. Pay attention and look like you're paying attention. Listen to understand what is meant and what your partner is feeling. Don't interrupt; wait until your partner is through saying his/her piece. Don't get distracted by your own thoughts or fidget or look around. Confirm what was said by saying in your own words what you understand the other person to be saying and feeling, then ask, "Is that right?" "Do you mean . . . ?"

Take notes. Keep a journal with notes of each meeting. Write down the things you agree about and keep expanding the list. Write down things you don't agree about and see if you can break it down to see if you can agree on parts of those subjects.

Resolving differences. Once you are both satisfied that you understand each other on a certain point, try to go behind the point to your interests—why you want what you want. Take time off from your discussion and return to it after you've both thought about what was said and had a chance to think about your interests. Look for new ideas that might address your mutual interests in a different way.

Never forget your first priority. Your relationship is your first priority. The whole point of the Couples Contract is to protect your mutual affection and regard, so it would be sad and ironic (not to mention revealing) if discussing it undermined that goal. Don't let frustration make disagreement sound like anger or lack of respect. Avoid sarcasm. It's okay to disagree, but not okay to undermine your relationship along the way. Stay calm, stay loving, and at all times be kind.

If you get stuck. If you both understand each other and your mutual interests and haven't found a solution, three things are possible: (1) you haven't correctly identified your *real* interests; (2) there's an option you haven't thought of that will satisfy both of your interests, or (3) there are no viable options and you have a genuine difference of opinion that can't be resolved. It happens, but not as often as people think it happens. If you can eliminate the first two possibilities, you either compromise or get some help or drop all or part of your tailoring and just do the basic agreement. Help resources are discussed in the next section.

C.   Decide if you want help

If you are just doing the basic Couples Contract (chapter 5), there are only positive and useful things in there—not much to challenge you. But if you're digging deeper and thinking about financial or faith-based tailoring, you might come to a point where it would be good to find someone to talk to who can act as a sounding board, help you organize your facts and thoughts, give feedback, another point of view, suggest options you might not have thought of. Read through this book first, discuss it together, and write down any areas that you think need clarification or where you'd like some outside advice.

Who can help. For some kinds of questions, you could talk things over with a mentor, wise friend, clergyman, or couples counselor. An accountant could help you clarify your financial picture, as could a financial planner. However, for overall review and help with suggestions and finding options to achieve your goals, nothing beats a good family law attorney with training and experience in making agreements designed to last. Unfortunately, most lawyers don't have these skills, which is why we recommend family law attorneys who specialize in mediation as their primary form of practice. The mediator's attitude is less adversarial and more oriented toward looking for solutions that satisfy both sides to any discussion.

Representation, advice, review. Most attorneys want to represent you, which means negotiating and drafting your agreement. But this can be very expensive, especially as they will want you to each have a separate attorney, and you really don't want to be represented anyway, unless absolutely necessary for reasons we explain below. But just getting some advice is much more affordable and a family law attorney who specializes in mediation would be an ideal person to go to for information, advice and options when it comes to tailoring financial relationships.

If you want to make sure your agreement is in good form, it would be ideal if you could have an attorney review it before you sign. However, finding the right attorney to help you can be its own kind of problem.

The problem. An attorney is typically concerned with two things: (1) planning for everything that might go wrong, and (2) how to get the greatest advantage for the one person he/she represents. The Couples Contract represents the common good of the relationship, whereas an attorney is legally obligated to pursue the best interests of one party. We believe that most couples would rather avoid negative thinking and arm's-length dealing and put their energy into a more constructive vision of their future. The agreement you are trying to create is a new and different thing. It is intensely personal and comes primarily from your heart at a time when you are looking forward to a long life together, which is why you might not want an attorney's heavy hand on it. Most attorneys won't ever have seen one and, if you do show it to them, some might want to tear it to pieces—not because there's anything actually wrong, but because it's not the way they're used to doing things or because this is one way of proving that you need their services.

Many professionals distrust things that are different, and the Couples Contract is *very* different. It proceeds from positive and constructive principles; it has ideals and goals that are foreign to traditional marital agreements; it uses non-legalistic loving language; it includes clauses designed to help you solve relationship issues that are not enforceable in court; and, we instruct you to go through steps and procedures that attorneys have never used because they make your agreement enforceable without anyone being represented by an attorney.

Possible solutions. If you want to talk to a family law attorney, call for an appointment but first verify that the attorney specializes in family law mediation and does little or no litigation. When you show up for your appointment, tell the attorney you are thinking about making an agreement about your financial affairs with someone and you want some suggestions and advice but do not want to be represented in the process. Next, ask if they are familiar with Nolo's Couples Contract and have read this book or if they are willing to read it on their own time to become familiar with it. If not, or if you don't want to have this discussion, you could simply work on the financial features and not distract the attorney with the rest of your agreement. Shop around before you settle on one and verify the charge before you go in.

Couples Helpline. In response to problems noted above, we created a team of talented family law attorneys who are completely familiar with and supportive of the Couples Contract. In fact, they helped design it. Our attorneys do not represent anyone, but rather remain neutral to focus on the common good of the couple. They will support you with advice, suggest options, help you draft your agreement, or review one that you drafted yourselves. Couples Helpline is available throughout California by telephone or at our offices in San Jose, Sacramento, Santa Cruz and Walnut Creek. We can sit down with both of you and help you work through your issues to find an acceptable solution, or do mediation or arbitration if ever the need arises. Call toll-free to find out more about how Couples Helpline can help you, or to make an appointment with one of our consulting attorneys.

D. How to assemble your agreement

Notice that we said *assemble* rather than *draft* or *write*. We've already done most of the drafting for you, so most couples will be able to put an agreement together from clauses found in this book, which are also on the companion CD. So first we'll tell you how to assemble your agreement, then we'll explain how to modify clauses or draft new clauses that are different from the ones we prepared for you.

1. Assembling your agreement

To assemble your agreement, simply get the clauses you want to use from the companion CD. If you don't have a computer and can't borrow or rent one, you can type the clauses directly from the book. While not common, handwritten documents are just as legal as typed ones if they are neat and legible.

a. Do the basic. Start with the basic agreement (chapter 5) and use the clauses we give you. Be sure to change the names in the sample documents to your own names. Use Find or Replace commands to make sure you have found and changed

Checklist

☐   1.   Read this book and discuss ideas in it together

☐   2.   Decide if you want to do the basic agreement (chapter 5)

         Note. Unmarried couples who don't plan to marry or register as domestic partners should read chapter 8 after chapter 5, then continue.

☐   3.   Decide if you want to tailor your financial relationships (chapter 6)

         ☐ If yes, do financial disclosure (chapter 6F)

☐   4.   Decide if you want faith-based clauses (chapter 7)

☐   5.   Consider getting advice or independent counsel (chapter 4C)

☐   6.   Assemble your agreement (chapter 4D)

☐   7.   Prepare two additional documents (chapter 9)

☐   8.   Present each other with final agreement and explanation (10B)

☐   9.   Wait at least seven days. Sign agreement and waiver of counsel (10C)

☐   10. Notarize the signatures of you two and your witness (chapter 10C)

☐   11. Follow through (chapter 10E)

every instance of our example names. Use your names one way throughout the agreement and any other documents or attachments that go with it—for example, do not use Jamie Jones, Jamie J. Jones, and J. J. Jones in various places; pick one and stick with it. And, while this is not a legal requirement, it would be good form to name the parties in the same order from start to finish—first Chris, then Jamie—to help keep things straight in everyone's mind.

There are options in some places, so choose which of those you will use. Delete unused clauses and options and delete checkboxes—just keep the text you want to use. We have indicated a few places where you can add your own language, which is purely optional. Be sure to change the names in the sample documents to your own names. Use Find or Replace commands to make sure you have found and changed every instance of our example names. If you are only doing the basic agreement, skip to chapter 9 (checklist step 7).

b. Add variations, if any. The basic agreement is the structure for your entire agreement. If you add any of the variations described in chapters 6–8, simply insert the clauses you choose to use, or others that you have decided to write yourselves, into the basic agreement, as instructed in those chapters. Be sure to keep the section and paragraph numbers in order if you change or add clauses or data.

If you are tailoring financial relationships, also prepare the disclosure statements as described in chapter 6F and attach them to your agreement as Schedules 1 and 2.

Decide if you want advice or help with adding variations (section C above)

c. Make drafts until final. Make a draft of your agreement and go over it with your partner. Make any agreed changes and go over it again. Repeat until you both think it is final.

d. Review? If you decide to have an attorney review your agreement before you sign, now is the time to do it (section C above).

e. Final agreement. When you have both examined the draft agreement and approved it, make two duplicate originals of your final agreement, one for each of you. Go on to step 7 in the checklist.

2. How to write clauses

Our recommended language is not cast in stone, but it has been carefully thought through by family law attorneys. In the text that runs alongside the template, we point out clauses where you can feel more free to write your own language, otherwise we suggest you be cautious. If you *do* decide to write your own clauses or modify ours, you must be precise and clear with your wording and also make sure you've covered all aspects of your subject. For example, if you state that certain property is to be kept separate, you also have to say what happens to income from it, or appreciation, or what happens if community funds are used to pay for or improve it, and what happens to debts that are incurred for the benefit of the separate property. If it's not complete, you'll end up with holes in your understanding that haven't been defined.

Use simple, plain language that cannot possibly be interpreted to mean more than one thing. Be careful with punctuation, as that can sometimes change meaning. Whatever you put in your agreement must be so clear that anyone can understand exactly what you mean. One way to check on this is to show your clauses to a friend and see if he/she can understand it from reading it (*not* by you explaining it verbally). Don't just say, "Do you understand it?" Have your friend repeat back to you in their own words what they think you are saying. If it is not exactly right, change your wording and try it on a different friend. If you write your own clauses, or modify ours, even if your friends get it perfectly, it would be a very good idea to have an attorney review your agreement. See section 4C above. Call Couples Helpline.

3. Make it nice

Give some thought to making your Couples Contract look special. After all, this is a momentous special occasion. Use high-quality paper, parchment or vellum, and consider using a nice font. If you don't find a font you like on your computer, search the Internet for "free fonts." It is generally best to use just one nice font for the entire document, and you should avoid fonts that are hard to read. Put your agreement in a handsome folder or binder along with the related documents and maybe some photos of the signing and you'll have something worthy of your relationship.

4. How to use the CD

How to open the CD

- **Windows.** If the CD does not open automatically, navigate to your CD drive to view files listed on it. Click on "Start CD" to start the interface.
- **Mac.** When the CD mounts on your desktop, double-click to open it and view the folders and files on it.

Finding files

- All clauses and documents are organized according to the chapter in which they are mentioned, except the Advance Health Care Directive and Nolo Arbitration Rules, which are mentioned in several chapters, so they are located in their own folders.
- Additional files of interest are found in the folder Resources & Extras.
- Ignore the folder "Auto_G." It contains files that operate the CD interface.

Using the files

- Copy files you want to work with to a convenient folder on your computer.
- All contract clauses and documents are in RTF format, which can be opened from any word processor. Edit the basic Couples Contract and any variations you add to create your own agreement.

- The Disclosure Worksheet, Checklist and Health Care Directive are in PDF format, which you can view and print with the free program Adobe Reader. Version 5.1 or later is required, but version 6.0 or later is recommended. If you don't have the latest Adobe Reader on your computer, go to www.adobe.com and get the latest version for your particular operating system.
- The free Reader program does not allow you to save data you have entered. If you want to save data you enter in a PDF document, you can download Cute PDF Form Filler for $30 from www.cutepdf.com.
- **Open the file.** If you double-click the file, it might bring up your favorite word processor automatically. If not, open your word processor and under the File menu, select Open and navigate to the file you want to work with, then either double-click the file you want or select the file and click the Open or OK button.
- Edit the files as described in section 4D above.

Be safe!

- Save your work frequently.
- Make a backup copy of your file by saving it onto a floppy disk or CD and keep the backup copy somewhere safe.

CHAPTER 5

The basic Couples Contract

This chapter shows you how to personalize your basic Couples Contract. It isn't very difficult and is well worth the little effort it will take. When you make this agreement, you gain these vital advantages:

- Loving commitment to a lasting relationship
- Introduce concepts that will help solve relationship problems if any arise
- Make sure your relationship never ends up in court
- Keep the terms of your relationship stable, no matter where you move

In addition, you have the opportunity to tailor your financial relationships either now or in the future (chapter 6) or to add faith-based elements (chapter 7).

The basic agreement does no tailoring of legal relationships, apart from agreeing to use mediation and arbitration to resolve disagreements instead of going to court. For everything else, it simply adopts California law to govern your rights and duties, just as if you married without an agreement. This allows you to get all the positive advantages of a Couples Contract without having to discuss money and property matters—unless, that is, your situation makes it important that you do so right away (see chapter 6), or you believe as we do that the ability to discuss money and be clear about financial matters will help build a foundation for a lasting relationship.

This agreement is for couples who are either married or soon will be, and can be used whether your agreement is made before or after marriage.

Unmarried couples who will be living together should start in chapter 8 and return here as directed.

So you can see what a completed basic agreement looks like, we printed a sample at the end of chapter 2 using a decorative font. The CD files use a common font more likely to be found on every computer, but you can make yours look any way you like, depending on what fonts you have available. We also suggest you print your agreement on high-quality paper or parchment—something suitable to the importance of this document in your lives.

Domestic partners

Wherever the discussion or the agreement refer to marriage, simply make these substitutions:

marry	=	register as domestic partners
married	=	registered as domestic partners
marriage	=	domestic partnership

A. How to use the template

Be sure to read chapter 4 before you build your agreement.

The pages below are a template or pattern that you should follow closely to make your own basic agreement. It offers just a few options that you will choose to make it fit your own situation. Each clause has discussion to the left that explains what is being done and how to choose the options. If you want to change our language or add some language of your own, pay special attention to chapter 4D(2).

The following two chapters describe clauses you can add to the basic agreement if you want to, although if you prefer you can add them later or never:

- Chapter 6—Variations to tailor your financial relationships
- Chapter 7—Variations for a faith-based agreement

Chapter 9 describes two additional documents that you must use to make sure your agreement is enforceable, then, in chapter 10, we discuss the steps you should take after your agreement and the additional documents have been prepared.

After you both go over the template and discuss options in this chapter and the variations in the following chapters, you will be ready to assemble a draft of your agreement. The mechanics for doing this are described in chapter 4D.

All clauses in this book can be found on the companion CD in the RTF format that can be used with any word processor, or you can type out your agreement directly from the sample clauses in the book.

B. The basic Couples Contract

The basic agreement template is on the right side, comments are on the left. In the template, we put check boxes next to clauses that are optional and depend either on your particular situation or preference.

Heading, introduction and parties

Title. For a heading, we used "Relationship Affirmations and Agreement," but you can call it anything you like that isn't misleading. You could just put the names of the parties at the top, or Lasting Relationship Agreement, Relationship Agreement, Our Vows, or It's a Deal! This is more a matter of taste and tone, as your agreement's legal meaning will be found in the text.

Parties. We name the parties with pleasant language that gives your agreement a loving, personal feeling. The nice tone is continued by using first names of the parties from this point forward. In our sample agreement, we use the names Chris Brown and Jamie Jones to represent any couple. You, of course, will substitute your own names throughout.

1. Purpose. This section states in general terms what you intend to accomplish in your agreement. Items A through E describe very constructive features, so should be used in every agreement. If you tailor your agreement as described in chapters 6, 7 or 8, you should use any of the optional clauses that are relevant to the variations you add to your agreement. You can also add your own purpose clauses, but don't get too specific: details are handled in the main body of the agreement.

2. Commitments. Writing down your commitment to high standards of trust and openness creates a strongly positive tone for your agreement. For the most part, this clause restates existing California law for married people and domestic partners, so we can't understand why lawyers rarely feature it in traditional marital contracts.

Relationship Affirmations and Agreement
of Chris Brown and Jamie Jones

In loving anticipation of a lasting relationship, this agreement is made between Chris Brown and Jamie Jones, called by our first names in this agreement.

I. **Purpose.** The purpose of our agreement is:

    A. To affirm our commitment to one another and to a lasting relationship based upon trust, mutual respect, affection and friendship

    B. To establish principles that will help us overcome personal issues that might threaten to undermine our relationship, should any ever arise

    C. To entirely and forever remove our relationship from the adversarial court system by committing to resolve disagreements of any nature that might arise between us, that we cannot resolve privately, by mediation or arbitration

    D. To govern our relationship rights and obligations according to California law, except as modified by this agreement

    E. To create stability and predictability by governing our relationship rights and obligations according to the terms of this agreement no matter where we might reside in the future

[optional clauses to use if you add variations from chapters 6–8]

    ☐ To define and clarify our assets and debts

    ☐ To define our mutual rights and obligations with respect to financial matters

    ☐ To provide for children of a prior relationship

    ☐ To set forth our rights and obligations should we separate or divorce

2. Commitments

We commit ourselves to mutual respect, openness, honesty, and the highest standard of good faith and fair dealing in all matters, putting each other's best interests foremost.

3. Current situation and plans

State whether you are currently married, or plan to marry, and give the date in either case. State whether or not there are children of your relationship and, if so, state their names and ages. Then, for each person, state his or her age, residence, state of health, education, occupation, children of other relationships. Mention any significant future plans or anticipated events that might be relevant to this agreement.

From the sample facts, you can see that Chris should read chapter 6 carefully and consider possible options to protect income and separate assets while Jamie is in graduate school piling up student loans, and how to protect Nora, a child by a previous relationship. Such arrangements can be attended to in this agreement in section 7, or they can be taken care of later in a written modification.

4. Effective date and duration

Pre-union. If you are not married yet but intend to marry in the near future, state that your agreement becomes effective when you marry.

Post-union. If you are making this agreement after you have already married, it should become effective when signed by both parties.

Duration. Your agreement is going to stay in effect indefinitely because you want the positive and constructive features to last a lifetime. As you will discover in chapter 6, there are some situations where you might want a specific financial arrangement to terminate on a specific date or condition (i.e., when certain debts are paid).

5. Principles for a lasting relationship

Be sure to read chapter 2C, which discusses the purpose and possibilities for this section—in short, to introduce ideas and information that might someday help you reinforce the positive elements of your relationship and get more smoothly through the kinds of problems most couples face, sooner or later.

This is a new concept in both contracts and couples counseling, so there's plenty of room for variation here. This section is not meant to be a binding legal agreement, so we are not as concerned about precision of language as in other parts of the agreement. You are free to add other ideas you think might someday be useful, and you can substitute other resources for the books and tapes we used in our example. There's a lot of material out there; start with our list in Appendix B, then go out and browse or ask counselors and others who are in a position to know.

It might look like there's not much to this section (which is good because it won't get in anyone's way), but don't underestimate the value of planting the idea that a

3. Current situation and plans

☐ We plan to marry on (date).   ☐ We were married on (date).

☐ There are no children of our relationship.

☐ We have the following children of our relationship: (names, ages).

Chris: I am 38 years old, residing at 123 4th Street, Santa Teresa, CA. I am in good health. I had three years of college and am employed as a computer programmer. I am a citizen of Canada, residing here on a green card and expecting to become a naturalized citizen in about three years. I have one child, Nora Brown, a U.S. citizen, age 6, of a previous relationship. I believe I will inherit my uncle's house in Victoria, BC in the near future.

Jamie: I am 40 years old, residing at 456 7th Street, Santa Teresa, CA. I am in good health. I have an MA in education and am employed as a high school teacher. I have no children. I plan to enter graduate school next year to undertake a three-to-five-year PhD program, which will require me to take out student loans.

4. Effective date and duration of agreement

☐ Our agreement will become effective when we marry. If we do not marry, it will be of no effect.

☐ Our agreement will become effective once it has been signed by both parties.

Once it takes effect, our agreement will remain in effect indefinitely, or until we sign a written agreement to modify or revoke it.

5. Principles for a lasting relationship

We believe that a lasting relationship is based upon mutual respect, affection and friendship. It is our goal to preserve and reinforce these features in our union.

We know that a lasting relationship sometimes requires an intentional effort, that reinforcing positive features is essential, and that practices learned from couples counseling have an excellent record of success.

If ever circumstances arise that threaten to undermine our mutual regard, we agree to make an effort to reinforce positive qualities in our relationship and resolve issues that weaken them.

relationship takes some effort, that there are things you can do to promote friendship and affection, and some specific ideas for where to start. Someday you might be glad you remembered it.

6. Parenting

State whether either of you has children born to or adopted into other relationships, and whether there are children born to or legally adopted by the two of you. If so, give their names and ages. Clauses related to the religious upbringing of children are discussed in chapter 7. Support and provisions for stepchildren are in chapter 6D.

7. Money, property and financial matters

In this basic agreement, you are adopting California law to govern all marital affairs apart from your agreement to use mediation and arbitration rather than courts to resolve disagreements, if any arise. However, in certain situations, California law is not ideal and tailoring of financial relationships would be much more to your advantage. Be sure to review chapter 6 to see if you are one of those couples who would be better off tailoring financial relationships. If so, you will add some clauses after the first clause below.

This clause is intended to keep your agreement from being changed just because you move to another state. However, if you ever do plan to move, be sure to have a family law attorney in the new state review your agreement. Ideally, you'll do this before you actually pack up and move, but certainly as soon as possible after you get there.

8. Disclosures

Because this basic agreement does not tailor financial rights and responsibilities, you can get by without making financial disclosures to one another. However, if you decide to do financial tailoring along the lines discussed in chapter 6, you *must* make full financial disclosure.

Taking the high road. Sharing financial information and having discussions about your finances and spending habits is a good thing to do as it helps build a solid foundation for your future, so you might want to do financial disclosure anyway. Many couples counselors and financial planners recommend that you do.

So, whether you do disclosure because you want to or because you have to, you will do it as described in chapter 6F and replace this entire section 8 with language that is provided there.

We agree that if one of us requests it, we will set aside some quiet time to discuss our relationship together and seek ways to reinforce the positive features that are vital to our well-being as a couple. We will look for information in books, tapes or videos, starting with Dr. John Gottman's material on *The Seven Principles for Making Marriages Work*, and we will look at Dr. Gary Chapman's material about *The Five Love Languages*. We will also consider going to conciliation, or to a couples workshop, or to a couples coach or counselor.

6. Parenting

We agree that, except as modified by this agreement, our rights and duties as parents of any children born to or legally adopted by us will be governed by California law.

7. Money, property and financial matters

Except as modified by this agreement, we agree that all of our mutual rights and obligations with respect to our marital and financial affairs, including our income, debts, and property, will be governed by California law no matter where we might live in the future.

8. Disclosures

Our agreement does not alter financial rights and duties under California law, therefore:

I, Chris, am sufficiently aware of Jamie's financial circumstances and I freely and voluntarily give up the right to formal written disclosure or any other information about Jamie's finances.

I, Jamie, am sufficiently aware of Chris's financial circumstances and I freely and voluntarily give up the right to formal written disclosure or any other information about Chris's finances.

9. Representation and drafting

Indicate who prepared the agreement: one or the other of you, or both working together. While not necessary, it is better if you work on it together. The agreement is all about being a couple so it only makes sense to do it together and, besides, doing it together strengthens your agreement by making it more clear that you both signed it voluntarily and with full knowledge of its contents.

Being represented by independent counsel can be waived (given up), as we have you do here, so long as you have not touched the subject of spousal support—if you do that, you *must* be represented. Giving up your right to be represented does *not* mean you can't get advice from an attorney or anyone else. In fact, we think that, depending on the nature of your questions, it can be useful to get information and advice from a family law attorney like those at Couples Helpline or, depending on the subject and your questions, other professionals such as financial planners, tax accountants, couples counselors or clergy.

10. Resolution of disputes —mediation and arbitration

Read chapter 2D. This section alone is worth the small effort it takes to make this agreement. It replaces the conflict-oriented court system with something much more suitable for the resolution of family disputes—mediation and arbitration. You need to go into some detail about how things should be done and who pays for it, so this section is longer than others in the basic agreement. Mediation and arbitration are known as *alternative dispute resolution*, or ADR. California law encourages ADR so a judge will almost certainly send you packing out of her courtroom if anyone tries to head there to avoid arbitration.

You can use ADR methods informally and at any time, even for relatively minor disagreements. In real life, people do it all the time: they may go to a friend, relative, clergy or other advisor and say, "We have this problem; please help us figure out what to do." This is a form of ADR. People even arbitrate minor disputes using a coin toss instead of a human being as arbitrator. Any form of ADR beats going to court.

Mediation

Mediator qualifications. Using a family law professional for a mediator is important because such a person will know the law and can advise you *during mediation* how the laws apply to your situation or when someone's expectations are outside the bounds. Most family mediations will benefit from this kind of expertise. However, if the primary focus of mediation is possible reconciliation or parenting issues, a profes-

9. Representation and drafting

☐ Chris and Jamie drafted this agreement together, jointly.

☐ This agreement was primarily drafted by ☐ Chris. ☐ Jamie.

I, Chris, understand that I have the right to be represented by an independent lawyer in the negotiation and preparation of this agreement and I had sufficient funds to retain a lawyer for this purpose if I wanted to. Nonetheless, I choose not to be represented. I understand the terms of this agreement and have had ample opportunity to seek the advice of legal counsel or any other kind of advisor. I have read this agreement carefully and have received as much advice as I wish to receive. I freely and voluntarily choose to sign it without being represented by an attorney at this time.

I, Jamie, understand that I have the right to be represented by an independent lawyer in the negotiation and preparation of this agreement and I had sufficient funds to retain a lawyer for this purpose if I wanted to. Nonetheless, I choose not to be represented. I understand the terms of this agreement and have had ample opportunity to seek the advice of legal counsel or any other kind of advisor. I have read this agreement carefully and have received as much advice as I wish to receive. I freely and voluntarily choose to sign it without being represented by an attorney at this time.

10. Resolution of disputes

It is our desire to remove our relationship entirely and forever from the adversarial court system and to resolve any dispute that might arise between us or under this agreement by mediation and arbitration.

A. Mediation

1. If we are unable to resolve any dispute ourselves or with counseling, then on the written request of either party, we will within thirty days submit our dispute to mediation with a mediator agreed upon by both of us. Unless we agree otherwise, our mediator must be a California family law attorney who specializes in family law mediation. If we are unable to agree on a mediator, we will each choose one person to make a choice on our behalf, and our two advisors together will appoint our mediator. We will participate in mediation in good faith and pay the cost of mediation from community funds, if available, and if community funds are not available, we will each be responsible for half the cost of such mediation.

2. We are each entitled to representation in mediation by an attorney of our choice. Attorney fees will be ☐ borne by each party separately ☐ paid from community funds, if available, and if community funds are not available, each party will be responsible for his or her own attorney's fees.

sional conciliator or marriage therapist could be more effective than a famil law attorney. In that case, when it comes time to mediate, you can (perhaps should) agree to use a different kind of mediator. However, if legal issues come up during mediation, you might wish you had gone with the attorney-mediator in the first place.

Arbitration

The Nolo Supplementary Family Arbitration Rules. Arbitration is always con-ducted under a specified set of rules, and while many are excellent, we could not find a set that was completely suitable for family arbitration, so we created our own supplemental rules. The Couples Contract has you use California's statutory rules as modified by the Nolo Supplementary Family Arbitration Rules, which adds two essential features: (1) procedures to cover emergencies in the period before arbitra-tors have been appointed, and (2) procedures to cover events that might arise after arbitration has been concluded. These features are discussed in more detail in the Appendix, where the Nolo Rules are printed.

Must be attached. A copy of the Nolo Rules must be attached to your agreement as Exhibit A, so if you ever need arbitration in the future, the arbitrators will know exactly how to proceed. A copy of these rules can be found on the companion CD so you can print it out. If you don't have a computer, simply make a copy of the rules from the Appendix and attach that as Exhibit A.

The three-arbitrator panel, described in clause 10B(1), is a tried-and-true method with a long history. One of the advantages, depending upon whom you choose, is that the dispute doesn't necessarily have to be decided by a total stranger.

How to choose wisely

Not just any mediator or arbitrator will do—you need someone with knowledge, experience and a good record at their job. Naturally, we think you couldn't do better than to call on Couples Helpline for your mediation or arbitration needs, but we are not the only fish in your sea. Make sure that mediation or arbitration is the primary focus of the family attorney's practice and litigation is either minimal or not done. Ask how many mediations they have successfully concluded. If you move to a distant state, your problem will be to find a professional who knows California law, the basis of your agreement. You'll want to look for someone who promises to brush up on California law, or you might travel to California for the time it takes, or import a mediator or arbitrator from California rather than go there yourselves.

B. Arbitration

1. In the event that one of us is not willing to do mediation, or if mediation does not resolve all issues within a reasonable number of sessions, then on the written request of either of us, we will submit the matter to binding arbitration within ninety days. The arbitrator will be agreed upon by both of us, but must be a California family law attorney who specializes in mediation or arbitration, or a retired California family court judge. If we are unable to agree on an arbitrator, the matter will be decided by a panel of three arbitrators. We will each choose one arbitrator, who need not have any particular professional background, and our two arbitrators together will appoint the third arbitrator who must be a California family law attorney or retired family court judge.

2. If we use a single arbitrator, we will pay the cost of arbitration from community funds, if available, and if community funds are not available, we will each be responsible for half the cost of the arbitration. If we use a panel of three arbitrators, each of us will pay the fees of the arbitrator we appoint. The fees of the third arbitrator will be paid from community funds, if available, and if community funds are not available, we will each be responsible for half the fees of the third arbitrator and other costs of arbitration.

3. We are each entitled to representation in arbitration by an attorney of our choice. Attorney fees will be ☐ borne by each party separately. ☐ paid from community funds, if available, and if community funds are not available, each party will be responsible for his or her own attorney's fees.

4. The arbitrator(s) will have the power to interpret the terms of this agreement, decide questions of their own jurisdiction, and settle disputes arising between the parties regarding the arbitrability of claims and the interpretation of the agreement. The arbitrator(s) will not have the power to alter, modify or terminate any provision of this agreement. The arbitration will be conducted under the rules of California Code of Civil Procedure sections 1280 to 1294.2, as modified by the Nolo Supplementary Family Arbitration Rules, a copy of which is attached to this agreement as Exhibit A.

5. **Arbitration is binding and final.** The decision of the arbitrator(s) will be binding and final, not subject to review in any court. We each understand that by agreeing to binding arbitration, we are choosing arbitration as the sole remedy for any dispute between us arising from our marriage or this agreement, and we each expressly give up our right to file a lawsuit in any civil court against one another, or to request a court to resolve any dispute between us as an ancillary matter in a family court proceeding, except to enforce arbitration or the decision of an arbitrator, and

11. Severability, governing law, interpretation, modification

A. As mentioned before, your agreement includes some clauses, like paragraph 5 in particular, that are probably not enforceable in court and might not be enforced by an arbitrator. Therefore, it is very important to make clear that each part of your agreement is separate, so that enforceable clauses will stay in force even if some parts are found to be not enforceable. Don't leave this one out.

B. This clause says that this is now the only agreement between you, replacing all others and any oral understandings you might have had.

Caution! If you have other agreements between you, written or oral, either write them into this agreement or forget about them, because anything you leave out will not be enforceable. Likewise, be careful in the future that you don't overlook a clause like this in the fine print of some other agreement you might make between you, as this Couples Contract will then be canceled.

C. This makes your agreement binding on your heirs and executors.

D. Among other things, the first paragraph fixes the state of California as the governing law for your contract, while the second paragraph makes it clear that you want your rights to be controlled by California law even if you move to another state.

thus we also give up the right to trial by a court or by a jury. To whatever extent the law does not allow any issue between us to be decided by binding arbitration, we agree to submit such matters to non-binding arbitration before submitting the issue to any court.

[Optional]

6.   If an action is required to enforce the use of binding arbitration required by this agreement, or the decision of an arbitrator, the costs and expenses of the prevailing party in such judicial proceeding, including, but not limited to, his or her reasonable attorney's fees, will be paid by the unsuccessful party.

11. Severability, governing law, interpretation, modification

A. Severability

Each clause of this agreement is separate and divisible from the others. Should any adjudicating authority refuse to enforce one or more clauses, in whole or in part, the remainder of such clauses, and the remainder of the entire agreement, are to remain valid and in full force.

B. Entire agreement and consideration

This agreement represents our entire agreement. It supersedes any and all other agreements, either oral or in writing, between us regarding our mutual rights and obligations arising from our relationship. The promises of each of us are consideration for the promises of the other.

C. Binding effect

Once this agreement takes effect, as described in paragraph 4, it will become binding on us and on our respective heirs and estate representatives.

D. Governing law and interpretation

This agreement has been drafted and signed by both of us in the State of California. The validity and interpretation of this agreement will be governed in accordance with the laws of the State of California. It will be interpreted fairly, simply, and not strictly for or against either party. Copies of this signed agreement may be submitted and accepted into evidence in place of the original in any proceeding to enforce or interpret the terms of this agreement.

We do not wish to have our mutual rights and obligations changed by the fact that we may choose to reside outside California some day, so we agree that the previous paragraph will apply no matter where we might live at any time during our marriage.

Optional clause. This is another novel idea and perhaps a mixed blessing. On the one hand, many couples have had their rights changed by legislation in significant ways without their knowledge or consent, perhaps to their detriment, but others have had laws change to their advantage. If you freeze the laws at a given date, this implies that you are going to review your agreement regularly, maybe every year, to see if anything has changed that you want to adopt in your agreement. The authors are divided on the wisdom of this option, but we agree that you should stay in touch with our Web site every year to see if any changes make it worth the effort to modify your agreement.

E.   The modification clause makes clear that your agreement cannot be changed or terminated except by written agreement signed by both of you.

Signatures —enter date but don't sign yet

Above each signature line, enter the date you hand each other the final draft of the agreement and the Explanation of Agreement (chapter 9), but do *not* actually sign it yet. The actual signing takes place later, as described in chapter 10C. Take some time to read the agreement very carefully, every word, and clarify any parts you don't understand or find confusing. If you want to get advice or discuss the agreement with someone, this is when you should call Couples Helpline or another family law attorney. There must be a minimum of seven days between the date you first received the final agreement and the date you actually sign it. This is to give you time to read, think, and get advice. In some cases, more time will be required (see chapter 10B).

Attachments. Indidate what documents are attached to your agreement. Every agreement will have Exhibit A, the Nolo Rules. Schedules 1 and 2 will be attached if you did financial disclosure as discussed in chapter 6F.

[Optional]

We do not want our mutual rights and obligations changed without our knowledge or consent, therefore we agree that our mutual rights and obligations under this agreement will be governed in accordance with the laws of the State of California as they existed on January 1, 2005, and no new laws enacted in the State of California after that date will apply to our property, debts, income, rights or obligations of mutual support, unless we specifically agree to it.

E. Modification

This agreement may be modified or revoked only by written agreement, signed by both of us.

Signatures

We have each read this agreement carefully and are signing it freely, voluntarily, and with full understanding of its meaning after having obtained all the advice we each, individually, feel is appropriate.

This agreement was delivered to Chris by Jamie on (date)

Dated: _____   _____

                                Chris Brown

This agreement was delivered to Jamie by Chris on (date)

Dated: _____   _____

                                Jamie Jones

Attachments

Exhibit A   Nolo Supplementary Family Arbitration Rules
Schedule 1   Chris's financial disclosure
Schedule 2   Jamie's financial disclosure

C. Lifestyle agreements

Some couples would like to agree in detail about how they plan to live together—everything from whether they'll have children to what part of their incomes they'll invest to who will do the dishes. Some even want to write down their agreements about fidelity or sexual practices. Taken as a group, these are called *lifestyle* agreements, and courts don't want anything to do with them. You can't get a court order compelling the other person to do housework or be thrifty and a court won't assess damages against a spouse or registered domestic partner who refuses. They are generally unenforceable.

Traditional lawyers regard lifestyle agreements as "trivial" and recommend leaving them out of marital contracts altogether because they are not enforceable and they fear such clauses might undermine the enforceability of the rest of the agreement if a judge decides they were a major consideration for making the agreement.

We disagree, at least in part. To the couple, such agreements are not trivial or they would not have taken the trouble to work them out, and including them in your agreement won't make other parts unenforceable because you stated in clause 11A that unenforceable portions are not intended to affect parts of your agreement that are enforceable. Another point is that the Couples Contract requires that all disputes be settled by mediation or arbitration, so questions of enforceability will be decided by an arbitrator, not a judge, and it is at least possible that an arbitrator might consider lifestyle agreements in ways that a court would not.

We think it is a good idea for couples to discuss their ideas and expectations for how they want to live together, and if it pleases you to write things down in the form of an agreement, go ahead.

Separate document is preferred. There are advantages to putting lifestyle agreements in a separate contract or letter that you both sign, which is why we recommend you do it this way rather than putting them in your Couples Contract. The first consideration is about flexibility: people and circumstances change, so you will probably want to adjust your lifestyle agreements from time to time; but, if they are part of a formal relationship agreement, this means going through a formal modification (chapter 10G), which takes some effort and bother. If they are in a separate document, you can simply tear it up and write another one. The other consideration is a matter of tone and privacy. When you sign your agreement, you'll probably have a witness present (chapter 10C) and you might even make it into a bit of a ceremony for close friends and relatives who will want to see your agreement. If your Couples Contract involves real estate or creditors, at some point strangers might need to examine it. Does it feel entirely comfortable for you to have other people read your lifestyle agreements? If not, you'd be better off putting them in a separate letter or contract which is kept entirely private between the two of you. On the other hand, if these are things you want your arbitrator to consider and decide, you might favor putting them in your agreement.

How to do it. If you decide you must have lifestyle clauses in your Couples Contract, you would insert a new section 6 into your basic agreement, like this:

6. Lifestyle agreements

We understand that lifestyle agreements might not be enforceable in a court of law, but we wish to include them here in order to remind ourselves of our plans for how we want to live together. This section is not the consideration for our consent to any other portion of our agreement.

A. [insert your agreements . . .]

Of course, parenting (the old number 6), and all other sections that follow, must be renumbered.

Don't mention sex. Do not include expectations about your sex life or refer to a party as "lover" in your Couples Contract because courts are hypersensitive to sex and can't be trusted to react reasonably to it in a legal setting. Yes, your agreement requires arbitration, not court; but if the validity of the agreement as a whole were attacked in court, a judge could possibly interpret your agreement as inherently and basically a contract for sex, which is a crime, so the whole thing could be thrown out, arbitration clause and all. Not very likely, but why take the chance?

CHAPTER 6

Variations to tailor your financial relationships

This chapter is primarily for people who are married, or who plan to marry.[1] Unmarried couples who do not plan to marry should skip to chapter 9, then return here to browse for ideas that might be relevant, then on through the checklist.

A. Who should do it

First, let's find out if you are one of those couples who should do financial tailoring. Remember, you can always do the basic Couples Contract first and do your financial tailoring later.

Is off-the-shelf OK? If you don't add tailoring to your basic agreement, your financial and parenting affairs are governed by California law, one size fits all. These laws are discussed in some detail in Part Three, but here, in a nutshell, is how financial affairs are governed if there is no tailoring:

- Income from the efforts of either spouse belong to both as community property
- Property acquired during the union is community property (excepting inheritances or gifts to one spouse or purchases made with separate funds)
- Spouses share the management and control of marital income and property
- the community can acquire an interest in the separate property, business or professional practice of a spouse
- One spouse might have to pay for debts incurred by the other, even those incurred before marriage
- You'll end up in court if you separate and can't agree on terms
- Duty to support children ends at age 18, or 19 if still in high school
- There's no duty to support stepchildren

Is this what you want? Most couples live under these rules, but California law is not equally suitable for everyone. A lot of couples, across the economic spectrum, have very good reasons for wanting to tailor their financial relationships—you don't have to be rich to get some advantage from it. Tailoring can, for example, make special arrangements for such things as:

---

[1] **Domestic partners.** References in this book to marriage and spouses also refer to registered domestic partners unless clearly stated otherwise.

- A spouse who is heavily in debt, a spendthrift, or in a risky business
- A spouse who gives up a career to stay home and care for an in-law
- Children of a prior relationship
- A separate business or professional practice
- A couple getting married near or during retirement
- Personal preferences that are different from California law

Review, consider, discuss. Review sections C and D below to see if any of the examples remind you of circumstances in your life that might benefit from financial tailoring. Discuss financial tailoring with your partner, what you might like to accomplish, and decide if you want to proceed. If you want to see how things work without financial tailoring, read chapters 11–13.

B. The romantic side of money discussions

If you think you might benefit from tailoring your financial relationships, you will have to have some detailed discussions with your significant other about money and property. For those who are still in the throes of romance and love, this might seem like a burden on your bliss: a dash of cold water when all you desire is to keep those fires burning. Even if you've been living together for years, discussing financial affairs can seem as appealing as having your teeth drilled.

If you can't discuss money . . . well, don't you have to wonder how strong your relationship is? You're not alone if just thinking about it makes you edgy—perhaps a majority of couples don't handle money discussions very well. In fact, failure to come to terms with money is a leading cause of breakups, even ahead of infidelity. Many experts believe that marital agreements can actually strengthen relationships, because by dealing with money matters you can either expose a problem area that needs attention or eliminate it as a possible threat to your future. Financial discussions will give you the valuable experience of working together on a demanding task and help build a sound foundation for your future.

Disclosure. If you're going to do financial tailoring, you *must* exchange financial information in writing so that you both have the opportunity to make decisions based on full awareness of the facts. This is called *disclosure*. How to do it is described in detail in section F below.

Advice. Be sure to read chapter 4B, which has tips that will help you work together more smoothly. Go over each other's financial information together, as described in section F below. Consider going to a certified financial planner or family law attorney for advice. Discuss your goals, our sample agreement clauses, and ideas for what could go in your own agreement. Agree on specific clauses to use.

C. What an agreement can (and can't) do

Tailoring can define your relationship as a couple to premarital assets and debts and to your marital finances: assets, income, expenses, debts, child support and estate matters. In each category, you have options for how your relationship to them can be modified, as outlined below. The next section shows how these options can be applied to tailor representative situations commonly faced by couples. It doesn't matter whether you read section C or D first, as you'll probably end up going back and forth once you begin to see how tailoring can apply (or not) to your own situation.

The things you can do

Here is the range of financial tailoring that can be accomplished in your Couples Contract:

1. Define premarital assets and debts

Clarify how you will treat assets and debts that were owned and owed prior to union— real estate, a business or professional practice, retirement plans, savings or invest-ment accounts, and specific special possessions. Even if you are making your agree-ment after marriage, it is still possible to declare the status and treatment of separate assets and debts that were owned before marriage. These are the issues:

- Will separate assets and debts continue to be separate after marriage?
- What happens if you use community funds to pay off a separate debt, pay the mortgage on separate real estate, or improve a separate property?
- What happens if a separate asset appreciates or is sold?

a. Assets
Your agreement can treat all items the same, or various items differently, by agreeing that on marriage, one or all or your existing assets:
- Will become community property.
- Will be apportioned between community and separate property according to a formula.

- Will remain separate and
  * All traceable profits or increases remain separate (state law).
  * Community acquires an interest to extent it pays down the mortgage or makes improvements that increase value (state law).
  * Community acquires no interest under any circumstances.
  * Community acquires no interest, but
    - Community contributions to be reimbursed (with interest?).
    - Profits or increases in value will be community property.

b. Debts

Your agreement can't prevent creditors from reaching community assets to pay the premarital debts of either party, but spouses can arrange to have no community assets and they can agree between themselves who will be responsible for certain debts and what will happen between them if community assets are used to pay them.

- Each to be responsible for his/her own premarital and/or marital debts.
- If community assets are used or taken to pay separate debts, the community is entitled to reimbursement (plus x% interest).
- The community will pay off all debts with no reimbursement.

2. Marital finances

Clarify how you will handle income, expenses, debts, and assets acquired during marriage, including such things as real estate, businesses or professional practices, inheritances, gifts, retirement benefits, and so on. Your agreement can treat all items the same, or various items differently, by agreeing how to treat one or more items in each category:

a. Income
- Earned income will be community property (state law).
- Earned income will be the separate property of the recipient.
- Earned income will be apportioned according to a formula.

b. Community expenses
- Owed by the community (state law).
- Shared according to some plan or formula.
- To be paid by one person.

c. Debts incurred during marriage

Your agreement can't change the rights of creditors created by the law or by contracts you make with them, but spouses can agree between themselves who will be responsible for certain debts and what will happen between them if community or separate assets are used to pay them.

- The community will be responsible for certain debts, and if separate funds are used, the community will reimburse the spouse who pays them.
- Each responsible for own debts incurred during marriage and community funds will be reimbursed (plus x% interest) if community funds used to pay such debts.
- Treat differently debts incurred for mutual benefit vs. debts incurred by a spouse in operation of a separate business.

d. Assets acquired during marriage

- Community property if acquired with community funds (state law).
- Gifts or inheritances to just one spouse will be separate property (state law).
- Assets to be kept entirely separate, no CP rights accrue.
- Determined according to how title is held.
- Owned proportionately according to a formula.

3. Children

Your agreement can provide for the care of children of a previous relationship (stepchildren). Religious upbringing is discussed in chapter 7. We don't recommend making commitments to support children through advanced education because there are so many variables that making a specific agreement far in advance is unwise. For example, the child could sue if you declined to fund her halfhearted attendance in a program that you did not care to support. This matter is best dealt with when the time comes.

4. Future plans

This includes such things as treatment of anticipated inheritances, saving for children's college education, buying a house, and so on.

5. In case of separation

You can define what will happen in case one or both of you want to separate or divorce. We feel this is handled well enough for most couples by the mediation/arbitration provision and the financial tailoring clauses, but if you have a family business or particular assets you want to protect, you'll probably want to see an attorney or call Couples Helpline for more options.

6. Estate matters

We do not cover the extensive subject of estate planning in this book, nor do we believe that such plans should normally be included in relationship agreements. However, in certain situations, as where retired people, each with their own estates, decide to marry but want to leave their entire estates to their own heirs, it might be appropriate for each to waive all inheritance rights and claims against the estate of the other, or variations on that theme. If you want estate planning terms in your agreement, we suggest you call a certified estate planner, a certified financial planner, an attorney who specializes in estate planning, or Couples Helpline for advice and assistance.

Limitations —things you can't do

Most limitations on relationship agreements are understandable, like not being allowed to agree to a criminal act or make an agreement that would defraud creditors—say, by putting all community property in one spouse's name just before the other is about to be sued. A bit less clear is the rule that you can't make an agreement that goes against public policy—for example, rewarding someone for getting a divorce or trying to limit the courts' authority to protect the best interests of children. If you stay close to our model, you'll stay clear of legal limitations.

1. Creditors

Sometimes one spouse needs protection from the debts, or potential future debts, of the other. In California, the community is liable for the debts of either spouse incurred before or during marriage, but separate property of one spouse cannot be taken except to pay for necessities of life for the other spouse or children (food, medicine, etc.). Likewise, the earnings of one spouse cannot be taken to pay the other's premarital debts, so long as they are kept in a separate account.

To some extent, the rules can be redefined by agreement. No matter what you agree between you about how debts will be paid, creditors who already have a right against your separate or community assets will not be affected. Your agreement can only affect new creditors who know, or had the opportunity to know, that you keep your income separate and have disavowed responsibility for each other's debts. To protect your income and separate assets, you must take practical steps:

- Make a Couples Contract that defines all income, assets and debts as separate (section D below)
- Keep your earnings in an account in your own name that your spouse cannot access
- Cancel all joint accounts and credit cards; get new ones in your name only
- Never co-sign with your spouse on any accounts or credit applications that you don't want to be liable for

2. Out-of-state property

California arbitrators and judges can make decisions about out-of-state property, but cannot directly change title to property outside California. If you own property in some other state or country, you have to inquire there to find out how they go about enforcing an arbitrator's award on a contract in California. It'll probably work out fine, but you won't know for sure until you do the research or get expert legal advice in the jurisdiction where the property is located.

3. Child and spousal support

Don't touch spousal support. Here's a rule that should make you wonder: an agreement relating to spousal support that is made before marriage won't be enforced unless the person against whom enforcement is sought was represented by independent counsel. Counsel can't be waived—no attorney, not enforceable. Not only do we feel this is an unconstitutional infringement on the right of a sound-minded adult to make a valid contract, we also think it is useless to everyone but lawyers. It isn't that hard to find a lawyer who will sign off on almost anything, so this impediment only adds cost without really protecting anyone. But this is the rule for premarital agreements—if you're already married, you can't limit spousal support at all, with or without counsel.

On the other hand, we can't think of very many good reasons for tampering with spousal support, but if this is something you feel a strong need to do, you'll have to hire at least one attorney, maybe two, or face an uncertain future for that clause in your agreement. If you aren't married or partnered yet, and don't want to be obligated to support each other financially, you might consider living together instead. Take a look at chapters 8 and 14 to see if that might suit you better.

Don't touch child support. The right to support belongs to the child and is zealously guarded by courts who will not give up their authority, so don't attempt to limit child support without advice from a family law attorney as to what can be done.

D. Example situations with sample clauses

Our goal here is to illustrate some reasonable solutions for situations common to couples across the economic spectrum. For a broader range of possibilities, take a look at Nolo's excellent book, *Prenuptial Agreements*, by Stoner and Irving. In law libraries, you can find many large volumes full of variations and possibilities for marital contracts, but we can't cover it all here.

After wrangling with ourselves over these examples, we came to realize that a slight change in circumstances might require different terms and most examples could become quite complicated if we kept asking, "What If?" We've come to believe that unless your situation is clear and the financial clauses obvious, you would be better served to do your homework here then talk it over with an experienced family law specialist attorney (see chapter 4C). If you find yourself in a situation you want to deal with but you aren't confident how to go about it, call Couples Helpline and talk to one of our consulting attorneys to get some ideas and options or a review of your Couples Contract.

Common situations. The situations illustrated below are common to many couples, organized according to their primary factual concern, as follows:

For each example situation, we show sample clauses that could be used to tailor the couple's financial relationships by adding them to existing sections of the basic agreement, mostly section 7, which starts out like this:

7.   Money, property and financial matters

A.   Except as modified by this agreement, we agree that all of our mutual rights and obligations with respect to our marital and financial affairs, including our income, debts, and property, will be governed by California law no matter where we might live in the future.

Label the first basic clause "A," as shown. Example clauses shown below are then inserted under this opening clause and labeled B, C, D, etc., in order. More discussion about how to add clauses to your basic agreement is found in section E below.

Explanations. Following the sample clauses is a sample explanation that you will use in the Explanation of Agreement document, which is described in chapter 9A.

Read them all. Many of the sample solutions use a variety of options, so you should read the agreements used in every example, as some clause used for a seemingly unrelated situation might trigger a thought about your own life.

Get help. These examples and solutions are relatively simple. Unless your situation and tailoring efforts are also straightforward, we urge you to have a family

law attorney review financial and parenting terms of your agreement (see chapter 4C). Couples Helpline attorneys are available to help you with this.

1. Clarifying the treatment of separate property

Lots of people have separate property when they get married that is either of special meaning or value or both. Not everyone wants to mix their separate property into the community, but the community can get an interest in it over time, even without anyone intending it—unless there's an agreement, that is. In situations like these three examples below, it is much better if you write down what you intend to have happen to your separate property. If you're already married, you can still clarify what is separate and what is not.

a. Situation

K was in a marriage that ended badly. She struggled for years and was finally able to buy her own home. K and L, a gardener who might go back to school, live in her house. For her own sense of security, she wants to keep the house separate and does not want the community to acquire any interest in it.

Comment

Under California law, the community acquires an interest in separate property to the extent that the mortgage is reduced by payments from community funds, or the value is increased either by the effort of either spouse or by improvements paid for with community funds. For a different outcome, you have to specify exactly how you want things to work.

b. Situation

B owns a condo and D owns a few acres in the country, about equal in value. They plan to sell the condo some day, buy a nice house they'll own together and eventually build a cottage on the country property. They agree that both separate properties will become community property.

Agreement for situation 1(a)

B.   K's house located at (address) was and will remain K's separate property, as will all rents and appreciation. Under no circumstances will the community gain an interest in K's house.

So long as we occupy K's house, the community will not be reimbursed for community funds used to pay the mortgage principal or interest, property taxes, insurance, maintenance, or repairs.

If we do not occupy K's house, the community will be reimbursed for community funds used to pay the mortgage, property taxes, insurance, maintenance, or repairs.

If community funds are used at any time to pay for capital improvements to K's house, those funds will be reimbursed (plus __% interest?) in the event that K dies, the house is sold, or we separate.

Explanation (for use in chapter 9A)

By signing this agreement, we agree that K's house at (address) is and will remain her separate property and that all rents and appreciation from it will also be her separate property. L is giving up the right to claim any interest in K's house under any circumstances. While we live in K's house, we may use community funds to pay the mortgage, taxes, insurance, maintenance and repairs. L gives up the right to claim that these make the house partly community property or to claim any reimbursement for these community funds. If we don't live there, K will be completely responsible for all expenses connected with the house, and if community funds are used in connection with the house while we don't live there, K will reimburse the community. If the house is sold or if we separate or if K dies, the community will also be reimbursed (with __% interest) for any community funds spent on capital improvements, whether made while we live there or not.

Agreement for situation 1(b)

B.   We agree that upon the effective date of this agreement, B's condominium at (address) and D's property at (address or other description) will both become community property. All other property owned by either of us on the date of our marriage will remain the separate property of the person who owns it. We agree to sign new deeds on or after this agreement becomes effective changing title to these properties to community property (optional: with right of survivorship).

Or

B.   We agree that all property of every kind owned at this time by either of us will become our community property on the date this agreement takes effect. To the degree that either of us might now have any separate right or interest in any property, we transmute that interest to community property. This does not apply to the ownership of property that either of us might acquire in the future. We agree to sign new deeds on or after this agreement becomes effective changing title to these properties to community property (optional: with right of survivorship).

c. Situation

A and M each have rental properties that they want to keep separate, but because they will work together to manage their properties, they feel that profits from their properties should be marital property.

2. Children of a prior relationship

Situation

T and A both have children by prior relationships who will often be in their home. Rather than keep detailed accounting records, they decide it makes more sense to share all household expenses equally, including reasonable expenses for their children, by depositing all community earnings, plus separate earnings if necessary and on an equal basis, into a community account. Any child support payments received will also be deposited to the community account.

Comment

The duty to support a child of another relationship is a separate obligation. Community funds used to pay for a spouse's separate child support obligation are entitled to reimbursement, but only to the extent that separate income was available but not used. For a different outcome, you need to specify how community and separate funds will be used to benefit stepchildren and to what extent there will be reimbursement. Here is just one possible arrangement; you'll want to detail your own solution in your agreement.

Explanation (for use in chapter 9A)

We each now own separate property (listed on Schedule 3). We understand that we each have the right to keep all our separate property separate. We wish for

☐ (describe specific property to become community property)

☐ all of our respective separate real properties (listed in Schedule 3)

to become community property from the date this agreement takes effect, and understand that this agreement will accomplish this, whether or not we actually sign and record the deeds we have promised to sign. We are each freely and voluntarily giving up the right to keep separate these separate properties.

Agreement for situation 1(c)

B. The separate property assets belonging to A, listed on Schedule 3, and the separate property assets of M, listed on Schedule 4, were and will remain their own separate properties, but all net profits flowing from those properties will be their community property from the effective date of this agreement.

A will be responsible for all debts incurred in the operation of or for the benefit of A's separate properties and will indemnify, defend and hold M harmless from any action to collect such debts from community assets or M's separate property, including paying any costs and attorney fees in connection with such an action.

M will be responsible for all debts incurred in the operation of or for the benefit of M's separate properties and will indemnify, defend and hold A harmless from any action to collect such debts from community assets or A's separate property, including paying any costs and attorney fees in connection with such an action.

Explanation

We understand that our respective separate real properties, listed in Schedules 3 and 4, will remain separate, but that we are each giving up the right to keep separate ownership of net profits from our separate properties, choosing instead to make it community property. We are agreeing to each be responsible for all debts incurred for the benefit of or in the operation of our separate properties.

Agreement for situation 2

B   T has children of a prior relationship: Terry, age 10 and Tommy, age 7. A has children of a prior relationship: Annie, age 6 and Andrew, age 3. We love and welcome these children into our home as we would our own natural or adopted children. We agree that community resources can be used for their benefit for all ordinary costs of living, health insurance, education, court-ordered child support and medical care, without need for reimbursement. All stepchildren will be named as beneficiaries of health insurance policies, to the extent they are eligible, and will be named as beneficiaries in any life insurance policies on an equal basis with our own natural or adopted

3. Marriage after retirement

Situation

L, age 67 and J, age 70, both have grown children from earlier relationships, adequate nest eggs, and small monthly incomes from consulting and freelance activities. They want to register a California domestic partnership, but feel it doesn't suit them to embrace the California community property system and they want all their assets to descend to their own heirs.

Comment

Seniors who are married or marrying sometimes have fears from past divorce trauma or they might be faced with their adult children's fears of loss of inheritance or affection or concern that financial or emotional advantage is being taken. The children of senior couples would not want a family feud after their parents pass on, so they might be more comfortable if both parties were represented by separate attorneys to make their agreement as bulletproof as possible. The more value in the estate, the stronger our recommendation that you secure independent counsel for both parties, if for no other reason than to reassure the children. With counsel, you will not need the Explanation document and the attorneys will assist in the negotiating, drafting and signing of your agreement. Show them this book and tell them that you want the positive and constructive features of it in your agreement, in addition to the financial ones that they will construct for you.

children, if any. Any child support or other funds received for any child will be deposited into our community accounts. If community income is not sufficient to pay all community expenses, we will make deposits from our separate funds on an equal basis into our community account in amounts necessary to cover all expenses.

Explanation

We agree to use community resources for the benefit of our respective children by other relationships, and to include them as beneficiaries under any health or life-insurance policies to the extent they are eligible. We understand that under some circumstances the community can have a right to reimbursement of money paid as child support for children of other relationships, and that some payments for their education or life insurance for their benefit could be considered a gift, voidable by the other spouse or reimbursable to the community. By this agreement, we are waiving all rights to claim reimbursement for such expenses or to treat money spent on the children as a gift made without the consent of the other spouse. We give up any and all claims to reimbursement of such funds. We also agree to treat any child support that either of us may receive during our marriage as community property and give up any right we may have to claim it as separate property.

Agreement for situation 3

B.   Separate assets. J's assets and debts, listed on Schedule 1, were and will continue to be J's separate property, along with all rents and appreciation, including profits resulting from the efforts of either of us. L's assets and debts, listed on Schedule 2, were and continue to be L's separate property, along with all rents and appreciation, including profits resulting from the efforts of either of us. The community will under no circumstances acquire any interest in J's or L's separate property.

We each consent to the other person naming whoever they wish as death beneficiary in their will, trust, retirement plan, account, insurance policy, or anything else that allows a person to designate a death beneficiary. We will each sign any document that is required in order to carry out our intent.

C.   Domestic partnership assets and income to be separate. All property (real or personal) acquired during our domestic partnership, including but not limited to income from personal services, pensions and retirement plans, and unearned income, shall remain separate property of the partner receiving it. J and L will maintain separate bank and credit accounts.

D.   Debts. J and L will be responsible for their own debts, whether incurred before or during the domestic partnership, and each will indemnify, defend and hold harmless the other from any action to collect the one's debts from the other's property, including paying any costs and attorney fees in connection with such an action.

E.   Expenses. J and L will, as necessary, make equal deposits into a joint bank account to pay for their joint living expenses, which they will share equally.

F.   Joint purchases. If J and L jointly purchase a home or other real estate, ownership will be according to the manner in which the title is held. Personal property will belong to the person who pays for it unless we make a separate writing to cover such property.

Variation for clause G

A variation for bequests, clause G, would be to agree to leave the surviving partner a life estate in the home, or a lease for a period of years at no rent.

4. A party who is in debt, a spendthrift, or in a risky business

Situation

H owns a risky contracting business, likes to gamble, and is frequently in debt. S owns a separate home and has a steady, decent income that she wants to protect. They agree that it's safest for her if they keep everything separate.

Comments

The only way you can prevent creditors of one spouse from reaching the community property is to arrange not to have community property. This couple must follow through by carefully keeping everything truly separate because careless mixing of assets could undermine their plan. They won't open any joint accounts except the household checking account for routine expenses, and won't sign any loan or credit applications together or use the other's assets or income on any application, or make available to the other any credit card associated with their separate accounts without getting legal advice first. They can call Couples Helpline if this ever comes up. Married couples attempting to keep separate property separate sometimes run into problems with lenders or title companies if they try to refinance separate real estate (see chapter 12F(3)).

If the house were in both names, they would not want to transfer it to S's separate property at a time when there were any large debts outstanding or expected, as the change in title could be seen as a transfer to defraud creditors.

There are tax advantages to community property at the time one spouse dies. For most couples, these and other advantages outweigh the risks. If you are trying to protect yourselves against specific risks by making this kind of agreement, we recommend you get some tax advice about such matters as "stepped-up basis" on community property on death, and weigh the risks and benefits for yourselves. Like the other financial tailoring examples, this one might sound like a good idea for many people, but it definitely isn't for everyone.

G. Bequests. We each want our separate property to descend to our own heirs, therefore we each waive and forever give up any and all right or claim we might acquire in the separate property of the other due to our domestic partnership and we each agree not to assert any right we might have in the estate of the other. Neither of us has made any promises to make the other a death beneficiary of anything. However, we do not waive the right to receive any bequest or gift the other may elect to make by will, trust, or other express designation as beneficiary.

Explanation

1. The terms and basic effect of the agreement we drafted are intended to keep the property and income of each of us separate, rather than acquiring any community property. We each want to keep our property separate, and in the event of our death, to leave our property to our respective heirs and not to each other. If we decide to buy property together, it will be owned according to the way we hold title or agree by another written agreement, and there will be no right of reimbursement unless we specifically agree to it in a later written agreement. Neither of us has promised the other anything upon our death. Neither of us will claim we are entitled to anything because of our status as domestic partners upon the other's death. The only rights either of us will claim after the other's death will be those, if any, specifically given in writing by the deceased partner. For example, if we open a joint checking account to pay our household expenses and designate it as a joint tenancy account, owned by the survivor upon the death of either of us, we are not waiving our rights to claim such an account after the other's death, since that claim would be based on a specific written agreement, and not on our status as domestic partners.

2. By signing this agreement, we are each giving up our right to claim, under any circumstances and at whatever time, that the income, earnings or property of the other partner is community property. We are each giving up the right to have our children or legal representatives make this kind of claim on our behalf in the event of our death or disability.

Agreement for situation 4

B. S's house, located at (address), was and will remain her separate property. All property acquired during the marriage, including property held in joint title, will be separate property and not community property. All income of any nature whatever will be the separate property of the person who earns or receives it and will be kept in separate bank accounts to which the other has no access. Neither party will be responsible for the debts of the other, whether incurred before or during marriage, and each will indemnify, defend and hold harmless the other from any action to collect the one's debts from the other's property, including paying any costs and attorney fees in connection with such an action. We agree to deposit funds from our separate accounts, on an equal basis, in amounts sufficient to pay our joint expenses, into a joint account that will be used only to pay joint expenses.

Explanation

We agree that S's house will remain her separate property, and H's contracting business, (name of business), will remain H's separate property. No community interest will be created in S's separate property or H's separate property by reason of any work or earnings invested in them during the

5. Professional practice or separate business

a. Situation

J operated an accounting practice for ten years prior to his marriage to G. They decide that the practice will remain J's separate property, but that this clause of their agreement will terminate after ten years, retroactively, so that things will be treated afterward as if the agreement had never been made.

b. Situation

Z is one of numerous officers in a business that his great-grandfather started. He owns a share of the business, as do siblings, uncles, and cousins who also own shares and work in the business, and some who just collect dividends. Since grandfather's time, only direct heirs have been allowed to own shares, with nothing passing to widows, widowers, or divorced spouses. Z is under great pressure to make a premarital agreement to protect the family business and might lose his position and shares without one. Z's fiancée, Y, will be a homemaker. They agree to make things fair by putting 10% of Z's income into Y's separate account.

Comment

Ordinarily, the community could acquire an interest in a separate business to the extent that a spouse's efforts increase its value. Since that possibility is being given up, the parties here want to do something to make their agreement fair. Premarital agreements have often been made with no effort to balance the equities, which is how they got their bad reputation. There are many ways to make things fair if you want to, depending on the situation of the parties. For example, Z could make Y the beneficiary of a life insurance policy that will be increased a certain amount each year they are married, promising to maintain the policy and keep her or her estate as beneficiary until the day he dies, no matter what. Or, if Y had her own income, retirement and stock options, they could agree to make that entirely her own separate property. In situations like this, we strongly urge you to use independent counsel for both parties to negotiate and draft the financial part of your agreement.

marriage. Everything we acquire during our marriage will be separate property. If we acquire anything in joint title, each of us will own our share of it as separate property, and not as community property. All income of any nature will also be separate property of the person who earns or receives it. We agree to each be responsible for our own debts and protect the other party from any action to collect the debts of one from the other. By making this agreement, we are each giving up the right to claim a community property interest in income of the other party. We are each giving up the right to a community property interest in any assets that might be acquired by the other party or that might have work or earnings invested in them during our marriage, and we are each undertaking an obligation to protect and defend the other party's income and assets from any debts that we might incur. We are both obligated to share equally any joint expenses.

Agreement for situation 5(a)

B. The community will acquire no ownership or interest in J's accounting practice or in any increase in value it might enjoy, no matter how much time or effort either of us might devote to it. If J sells his practice or exchanges it for another asset, the proceeds or acquired asset will also be J's separate property. The agreement in this paragraph will automatically terminate ten years from the date it becomes effective and our rights and obligations will be governed by other provisions of this agreement as if this paragraph had never existed.

Explanation

By this agreement, G is giving up any right to claim that the community has acquired an interest in J's accounting practice or in proceeds if J sells it or exchanges it for some other asset, no matter how much effort either party puts into it. However, if we are still together in ten years, this paragraph will terminate and the community will have the same rights as if this part of our agreement had never existed.

Agreement for situation 5(b)

B. We agree that the community will not for any reason or under any circumstances acquire an interest in Z's shares in his family business, ZeeCorp, which shall remain Z's own separate property. In exchange, at the end of each calendar year, starting December 31, 2007, Z will deposit 10% of his net annual after-tax income into Y's separate account, to be her own separate property, and neither Z nor the community will have the right to reimbursement for such sums.

Explanation

By signing this agreement, we agree that the community cannot acquire any interest in Z's shares in ZeeCorp, his family business, and that Z will make annual deposits of 10% of his net after-tax income into Y's separate account, starting December 31, 2007. Y is giving up the right to claim a community property interest in Z's shares in ZeeCorp, and Z is giving up the right to reimbursement to himself or the community for sums converted to Y's separate property by operation of this clause.

6. Staying home to care for child, parent or disabled family member

Situation

Z is quitting a solid career to stay home and care for Y's injured child, Z's stepchild, C. This means giving up seniority, retirement benefits, earnings and opportunities for promotion for what might take a couple of years. The couple feel something should be done to balance the equities and compensate Z for the sacrifice.

Comment

After marriage, you can't agree to compensate one spouse for caring for the other spouse or a parent's own child as the obligation of care is inherent in the relationship. However, it is okay to agree *before* marriage to compensation for the care of a spouse because no obligation exists at that time. In this case, the care is for a stepchild to whom no inherent duty of care is owed, so compensation is permitted and Y has separate funds to pay it. Depending on your situation, you could make a gift to the caregiver of some community property without right to reimbursement. There could be tax consequences here (if the IRS ever found out about it), so check first with a tax accountant.

7. Anticipation of a significant inheritance

Situation

F and J have cared for F's aged mother, M, for several years with most of the burden falling on J, but saving the family the expense of long-term care. They agree that J's efforts are worth at least $2,000 per month, so whenever M dies, J can choose either to have any gifts or inheritance F gets from M be treated as community rather than separate property or to have an amount equal to $2,000 for each month she cared for M be paid into her separate account.

8. Honoring personal preferences over California law

Situation

H and S are fiercely competitive executives. They want all their assets and earnings to be separate property and kept separately, but they will contribute equally (or in proportion to their previous years' net income) into a joint account to cover expenses. However, they plan to buy a house and make some joint investments together, and if they ever have a child together, they understand that keeping

Agreement for situation 6

B.   In recognition of the fact that Z has quit a stable career in order to stay home and care for C, Y's child and Z's stepchild, and thus giving up seniority, retirement contributions, earnings, and opportunities for promotion and advancement, we agree that (1) Y will transfer $5,000 of Y's separate funds into Z's separate account, and (2) Y will transfer $2,500 from Y's separate account into Z's separate account on the last day of each month, or portion of a month, that Z continues to care for C.

Explanation

Because Z is abandoning a successful career to care for Y's child, C, we agree that Y will deposit funds from Y's separate account into Z's separate account and make monthly deposits as long as Z continues to care for C. Y understands that by this agreement he is giving up the right to keep the agreed amount as his own separate property.

Agreement for situation 7

B.   Since May 2002, most of the burden of caring for F's mother, M, during her declining years has fallen on J. We agree therefore that when M dies, J can choose either (1) to have any gift or inheritance F receives from M treated as our community property no matter when it is received, or (2) to have an amount equal to $2,000 for each month between May 2002 and M's demise paid into J's separate account as her own separate property from F's separate funds.

Explanation

I, F, understand that I am, at J's choice, either (1) giving up the right to keep any inheritance from my mother as my own separate property, or (2) promising to pay J an agreed sum from my separate funds. I feel this is fair because the care J has given my mother is worth more than the agreed amount and has saved my mother and us the considerable expense of nursing home care. My mother's estate would be much less if not for J's help.

Agreement for situation 8

B.   Except as otherwise specified in this agreement, we agree that:

1.   During our marriage all gifts, inheritances, earned and unearned income will be the separate property of the person who earns or receives it, even if it is received at a later time.

2.   We intend to own all property acquired during our marriage as separate property, so long as it is kept in separate accounts or separate title. All income and appreciation flowing from separate property shall remain separate. Property without title will belong to the person who paid for it.

3.   Any property or accounts that we intend to own jointly will be owned according to how the title or account is held.

everything separate won't be appropriate. Married couples attempting to keep separate property separate sometimes run into problems with lenders or title companies if they try to refinance separate property (see chapter 12F(3)).

E.   How to add clauses to your basic agreement

To tailor financial relationships, you just add clauses under existing sections of the basic agreement, mostly section 7, which starts out like this:

7.   Money, property and financial matters

A.   Except as modified by this agreement, we agree that all of our mutual rights and obligations with respect to our marital and financial affairs, including our income, debts, and property, will be governed by California law no matter where we might live in the future.

Label the first basic clause "A," as shown. Each clause you add will then be labeled B, C, D, etc., in order, depending on how many you use.

Married? If you're not yet married, you should define your premarital assets and debts and what will become of them after marriage. If you're already married, you can still clarify the ownership of assets and debts by defining which are separate and which are community and what's to become of the profits and proceeds.

Schedules and exhibits. Whenever you are dealing with more than a few items of property in any clause, rather than list them all in your agreement, you can attach lists at the back of the agreement and label them Schedules 1 or 2, or Exhibit A or B. The particular number or letter will depend on whatever has come before it in your agreement. In our example, Exhibit A is always the Nolo Supplementary Family Arbitration Rules, which are always attached. Schedules 1 and 2 are the financial disclosures of the two parties, which are used if you do disclosure.

Termination. Don't forget that any clause can be made to terminate on a specific date or condition—say, when debts are paid off or if a child is born or adopted—in which case you must decide if the termination is (a) retroactive to the beginning, so things become as if the clause never existed, or (b) not retroactive, leaving everything as it was on the day the clause terminated. See situation 8 in section D above.

Get help. These examples and solutions are relatively simple. Unless your situation and tailoring efforts are fairly straightforward and similarly simple, we urge you to have a family law attorney review financial and parenting terms of your agreement (see chapter 4C).

4.   We agree to deposit funds from our separate accounts, on an equal basis, in amounts sufficient to pay our joint expenses, into a joint account that will be used only to pay joint expenses.

5.   Nothing in the above paragraphs should be construed to restrict anyone's right to make a gift or to voluntarily spend additional separate funds on joint expenses, and there will be no right to an accounting to equalize contributions from past months.

6.   In the event that we adopt or have a child born to us, clauses B1, B2 and B3 will automatically terminate and have no further effect. From that time forward our rights and duties will be governed by the other clauses of this agreement. The termination will not be retroactive, so that all property and debts defined as separate by this agreement will remain separate. Upon the birth or adoption of our first child, we will each deposit or transfer into community ownership funds or assets equal to 25% of our respective net worth.

C.   We will each be responsible for our separate debts, whether incurred before or during our marriage, and debts incurred in connection with our separate affairs. We will each indemnify, defend and hold harmless the other from any action to collect the one's debts from the other's property, including paying any costs and attorney fees in connection with such an action.

Explanation

By making this agreement, we are each giving up our right to have earnings during our marriage become community property. If we want anything we own to become community property, we will specifically designate it as such by taking title that way. We will each contribute equal amounts to family living expenses, but anything either of us earns beyond that amount will belong to the person who earned it, to do with as he or she pleases.

We each have the right to decide to spend extra separate funds on joint expenses without any right to demand later that it be made equal. For example, if one of us wishes to pay the entire cost of a vacation or buy something extra for both of us out of our own funds, the other will not have to contribute an equal amount. We are both able to earn a good income, and we think it is fair for each of us to have complete ownership and control over whatever each of us earns beyond paying our half of our monthly living expenses, so long as we don't have children together.

We do not know whether we will have children in the future. If we do, we are agreeing that we will then each keep 75% of our separate property and contribute 25% of our net worth to the community, and after that, whatever each of us earns will be community property as it would be under California law if we married on that date without an agreement. We think this is fair because if we become parents we want the flexibility to curtail either of our careers for the sake of the family and share everything either of us earns equally. We also understand that we would not be obligated to give any of our separate property to the community, so if we have a child together, we are giving up the right to keep our separate property separate to the extent of 25% of our net worth on that date.

F. How to do financial disclosure

If you decide to do any tailoring of financial relationships in your agreement, then well before your agreement is signed you must—repeat, *must*—make a full and fair disclosure to each other of your finances, which means to exchange a written list of all your assets and their values, amounts owed, and your annual income. The purpose for doing this is (1) to make sure both parties have the opportunity to understand both the agreement and the financial affairs of both parties sufficiently well to make a sound decision; (2) to allow you or your executor to sort out separate from community assets and debts in the future; and (3) to withstand scrutiny if one party later claims they were misled or not given accurate or sufficient information.

So, no fewer than seven days before you sign your agreement, you must each receive a copy of the final agreement and a written explanation of the agreement (chapter 9) and, at the same time or earlier, you must each present the other with a list of your financial information—the disclosure. The waiting period is to show that you both had time to consider the final agreement and the background financial information before deciding to sign. How to do disclosure is explained in this section.

Disclosure worksheets. To do disclosure, you must each prepare a written list of all your assets and their values, amounts owed, and your annual income. To help you organize this information, and as a checklist to make sure you haven't overlooked anything, we've prepared a disclosure worksheet that you'll find on the companion CD. There is also a Simplified Schedule that you can use if you prefer.

The disclosure statement. For the actual written disclosure, you can use either a completed Disclosure Worksheet or the Simplified Schedule, one for each of you. Both are on the companion CD. The Simplified Schedule is illustrated on the next page. However you do it, the information you present to each other must be attached to your agreement as Schedules 1 and 2 to show what was disclosed.

Detail. Valuable assets like real estate, businesses, savings accounts, retirement funds, vehicles, and the like should be listed and valued separately, as should anything of special significance to you, no matter how much it costs. Likewise, obligations like mortgages, bank loans and large credit card debts should be listed separately. However, for all the stuff in between, you can lump things together in categories, like household furnishings, tools, jewelry, computers and electronics, etc.

Values. Valuations in modest estates can cost little or nothing: get values from similar properties for sale in newspaper, penny-saver classifieds, or on eBay, and so on. Cars can be valued for free on the Kelley Bluebook Web site at www.kbb.com. If

Schedule 1
Financial Information of Chris Brown

ASSETS

Description	Approximate value
Residence at 123 4th Street, Santa Theresa, CA	$325,000
Savings account at Wells Fargo, Santa Theresa, CA	8,325
1998 Toyota Corolla, CA lic. no. 3XYZ123	2,500
Household furniture and personal possessions	6,000
Computer and other electronics	1,200

DEBTS

Owed to	Approximate balance due
First mortgage on residence at 123 4th Street, Santa Theresa, CA	$180,000
Line of credit on residence at 123 4th Street, Santa Theresa, CA	21,000
Master Card	2,200
Hi-Tech Emporium	450

Approximate annual income:	$42,575
Approximate annual expenses:	$38,250

Date: November 18, 2005

_____
Chris Brown

Schedule 1   Page 1 of 1

you have but little equity in a home, ask a Realtor for current values. However, as an asset's worth increases, the need to be more accurate also increases. If you have a lot of equity in a home, a real estate appraisal would be worth getting for a few hundred dollars. Businesses are famously difficult to value and appraisals are not only very expensive, they are not particularly reliable. So, instead of valuing a business, make a statement that says what kind of business it is, the value of its assets (such as equipment and accounts receivable), how long it has been operating and how much money it earns per year. Also say how it is organized—partnership, a corporation, sole proprietorship, or some other kind of organization. If it's a partnership or corporation, state your share of ownership. This is enough information for your partner to get advice about its potential value. If your partner asks for more information, give it to them. If you are already married when you sign an agreement, you *have* to let your spouse see all the books if they ask.

Valuing retirement funds that are similar to savings accounts, like a 401k plan, just requires a look at the latest statement to know how much is in the fund. However, defined benefit plans, where you don't get anything until you retire, are a can of worms and must be valued by a qualified pension plan evaluator. If you haven't many years invested in the plan, just use the plan statement with a note that says you're not sure of the true value but have *x* years contributing to it. However, if you have quite a few years, you might have to get an appraisal. Call Couples Helpline for a referral to a qualified pension plan actuary.

Credit history. If your credit is pretty good, no need to go into it, but you should to make a statement revealing bad credit, unpaid debts, lawsuits, judgments, bankruptcies, or the like. It is relatively easy to order a copy of your own credit report either on the Internet or from any credit reporting agency, which you could attach to your disclosure. If one of you is in a large-size business, you might also include a report from Dun and Bradstreet.

Attach to agreement. To show what disclosure has been given, you will attach copies of each party's disclosure documents to your agreement as Schedules 1 and 2.

Replace section 8 in the basic agreement. Because you are doing disclosure, you need to replace section 8 of the basic agreement (waiver of disclosure) with language confirming that each of you fully disclosed financial information to the other. Here below is the language you will now be using instead of that shown in chapter 5:

8. Disclosures

Each of us has made a full, fair and reasonable disclosure to the other of annual income, all assets owned and all obligations owed on the date such information was presented.

A list of income, assets owned and obligations owed by Chris is set forth in Schedule 1, which is attached to and made part of this agreement. **[Optional:** Attached to Schedule 1 is/are the following additional document(s:) ☐ Chris's federal and/or state tax return for years (years) ☐ the following appraisals: (name them) ☐ other (specify).**]**

A list of income, assets owned and obligations owed by Jamie is set forth in Schedule 2, which is attached to and made part of this agreement. **[Optional:** Attached to Schedule 2 is/are the following additional document(s:) ☐ Jamie's federal and/or state tax return for years (years) ☐ the following appraisals: (name them) ☐ other (specify).**]**

We each understand that values set forth in Schedules 1 and 2 are approximate values on the date presented, estimated to the best of our ability, but not necessarily exact.

I, Chris, received a copy of Schedule 2 [and attached documents named above] on (date), and reviewed that information before signing this agreement. I consider this information to be sufficient and am satisfied with the information I have received.

I, Jamie, received a copy of Schedule 1 [and attached documents named above] on (date), and reviewed that information before signing this agreement. I consider this information to be sufficient and am satisfied with the information I have received.

G. Estate matters

The Couples Contract is forward-thinking; planning for a lasting future. So is estate planning. Estate planning is about providing for the future with things like durable powers of attorney for health care and finances, wills, living trusts and other ways to avoid probate and taxes. This is not only beyond the scope of this book, but we think estate planning is generally best done outside your relationship agreement. We think it best not to include estate planning terms in your Couples Contract unless recommended by a certified financial planner or an estate planning professional, who would supply recommended language. Nolo has several excellent estate planning books and some articles to help you get pointed in the right direction at www.nolo.com.

Health care planning. Because it is so important and so easy to do, we included an Advance Health Care Directive form on the CD. Everyone should have this. It comes in two parts: the first lets you name one or more individuals to make medical decisions for you if you are unable to do so, and the seond part lets you declare in advance how you would like to be treated medically in case you are unable to speak for yourself.

Variations for a faith-based agreement

In recent years, perhaps no issues in America have been so controversial and divisive as those related to "family values." While partisans of every stripe launch law suits and publicity campaigns, many religious leaders have come to believe it is better for each faith to govern its own families rather than struggle for legislation to make state laws match their beliefs and values. They wonder if the ancient tradition of marriage contracts can be resurrected to achieve this goal. We think they can.

A. Religious contracts and the faith-based agreement

Covenant, Ketubah, or Aqd. Some religions make signing a marriage contract part of the marriage ritual. These contracts might be just between the couple or they might also involve their families and other members of the community. In a wedding "after the manner of Friends" (Quaker), the bride and groom recite vows to each other, sign their marriage certificate, then the guests sign as witnesses. In traditional Jewish weddings, the bride and groom sign a *Ketubah*, which is often written in elaborate calligraphy, framed and hung in the couple's home. An Islamic *Aqd* is signed by the groom and an adult male member of the bride's family as her agent, or by the bride herself. Other faiths also have their own versions of the religious marriage contract.

Unenforceable in court. While these may be referred to as contracts, and may even contain contract language, it is important to understand that California courts probably won't treat them that way. The couple might think of them as legally binding, as might courts in other countries, but our state and federal constitutions require separation of church and state, so judges will typically regard religious marriage contracts as inherently religious in nature and not something they have the power to enforce (see section E below).

The faith-based agreement. If you really want your marriage to be governed by the laws of your faith rather than state law, you will need to sign a separate agreement that looks like a contract to lawyers and judges. This is what we mean by a faith-based agreement. By adding clauses like those described below to our Couples Contract, a couple can pledge to maintain their family according to the beliefs of their faith, to raise their children in the faith, and to submit any family problems or disputes to conciliation, mediation, and arbitration within the faith community.

B. Pros and cons

Not many subjects these days are without controversy, and this is no exception. Many religious organizations are eager to keep the problems of their families within the bosom of the faith community. More, they would like to conciliate, mediate and, if all else fails, arbitrate according to the beliefs of their faith rather than the laws of California. This is certainly understandable and even laudable, but not without risk and not without some dissenting opinion. For example, this news story from The West Australian printed January 5, 2004:

> Father Joe Parkinson, head of the Catholic Church's L. J. Goody Bioethics Centre, said a legal contract that took effect when a marriage ended was contrary to the Christian understanding of marriage. "An unconditional commitment is at the very heart of the Christian understanding of marriage," he said.

And, referring to prenuptial contracts as "prenups," Rabbi Shmuley Boteach, wrote in his Internet "Kosher Coupling" column at www.beliefnet.com:

> Those who insist on prenups are more interested in money than in love. They think that since what motivates them is financial, the same must be true for everybody else. We do not ask a spouse to sign an agreement that they will look after us in our old age, or that they will stay with us if we fall sick or lose our looks. A commitment that transcends such superficiality is implied in the vows we take when we marry. We trust these things will come to pass based on the character of the mate we have chosen and not by a document they have signed.

Of course, these good clergymen were thinking of the traditional prenuptial contract and didn't know about our kinder-gentler Couples Contract, which does not include provisions that are specifically in anticipation of separation. On the other hand, our clause that refers all disputes to mediation and arbitration would certainly be called into play if one party wants to end the relationship.

Our concern goes to who, exactly, in your faith community will undertake mediation and who will be the arbitrator, empowered to make final decisions regarding property, support, custody and parenting. Not just anyone can do these demanding jobs: they require training, knowledge, experience and skill. Will your conciliator be trained in couple counseling? Will your mediator have the training and experience it takes to do a good job? Will your arbitrator be familiar with California family law? Will that person be intolerant and decide punitively toward a spouse who wants to separate or leave the fold? Is the faith community large enough and does it contain a talent pool of qualified leaders who could be fair to parties who have developed divergent views?

Agreeing to have marital matters decided by a member of a faith community can expose parties to decisions by a person not familiar or sympathetic with California family law, or not skilled at dealing with couples in opposition, and there is no provision in these agreements to protect a spouse who, years later, becomes disillusioned and wants to leave the fold, or who converts to another faith.

Many faith communities recognize these problems, too, and are taking steps toward developing recognized bodies of talented people trained to work with these kinds of issues, even developing model agreements for their members to sign, but most are just getting started. Unless your faith community has an established organization with recognized procedures for resolving family disputes, you take a risk putting the decision-making power that goes along with a binding arbitration agreement in their hands. On the other hand, families who are deeply religious may still trust their faith community more than they trust the civil courts to make decisions, if necessary, on a basis that is consistent with their values.

Our personal preference and strong recommendation to you at this time would be to have your faith agreement provide for religious conciliation and mediation only—but do not refer arbitration to your faith community unless your faith group is affiliated with a large organization that provides well-established religious court or arbitration services by people who are trained and certified for the job. As more and more religious organizations develop these resources, you can modify your agreement later to add faith-based binding arbitration to your agreement. Another option we provide says you will use a panel of three arbitrators, one of whom is appointed by your faith community. This allows matters of faith to be an important part of the decision-making process, but eliminates most of the risks that concern us, described above.

As faith-based groups begin to consider these issues and look for better ways to resolve family problems within their communities, several of them have developed model agreements tailored to their faith. However, laws that deal with relationship agreements vary greatly from one state to another, and the model agreements we have seen might be difficult to enforce in California. At the end of this chapter, we reproduce two model agreements that have been endorsed by religious organizations and discuss the problems we see with trying to enforce them in California. If your faith community endorses a model agreement, we recommend you read the sections where we talk about these, and compare the model you are given with the basic agreement in this book. You will need both legal and religious advice to modify another organization's relationship agreement to make it enforceable in California. Talk to your religious advisor, then discuss your proposed agreement with a California family law attorney, or call Couples Helpline.

Resources. Take a look at the Peacemaker Ministries and Institute for Christian Conciliation at www.hispeace.org and see their Rules for Christian Conciliation. For another flavor, see the Beth Din organization at www.bethdin.org, where arbitrators are available to render decisions according to Jewish principles, or search the Internet under "Beit Din" or "Bet Din" for some others. Then there's the highly-regarded Marriage Encounter, which offers nation-wide programs for troubled marriages that are "based on Judeo-Christian concepts. You can get more information about them at www.marriage-encounter.org.

We searched but were unable to find similar resources for other faith organizations. If you know of any, please let us know. We encourage the creation of resources for marriage contracts and conciliation, mediation and arbitration services in all faith communities and would be pleased to consult with any who wish to do so.

Caution! Please, before you decide to make a faith-based agreement, take this book to the leadership of your religious community and discuss the ideas in it. Ask if they have leaders in your community with couples-communication training, or mediators and arbitrators who are also family law attorneys or otherwise qualified to decide a couple's rights under such an agreement. Perhaps they have already developed some contract language of their own, in which case you should call Couples Helpline to get a neutral opinion about their language from family law attorneys who understand the goals and risks of a faith-based Couples Contract.

C. Enforcement

Because state and federal constitutions require separation of church and state, courts have to ignore agreements about religious matters most of the time. However, arbitrators might enforce portions of your agreement that a court could not or would not; so, if your agreement says all marital disputes will be submitted to arbitration, a court can order you to arbitrate without getting tangled up in religious questions, and the arbitrators don't work for the state, so they can decide the religious questions along with everything else. Courts will never surrender ultimate authority over support or the best interests of children, so faith arbitrators must keep California laws in mind when they make decisions. For example, if an arbitrator were to forbid a child to ever see an otherwise fit parent who left the faith, a court would likely invalidate that part of the decision. This is one reason why the agreement requires your arbitrator, or at least one of them, to have a background in California family law.

D. Sample clauses

In this example, the couple belongs to a faith community and would like, as much as legally possible, to keep their relationship, parenting, and other family issues that might arise, within the fold of that community rather than going to courts or outsiders. By referring their conciliation, mediation, and arbitration clauses back into their faith community, they maximize the chances that problems in their relationship will be solved according to the principles of their chosen religion. They understand that California courts will never surrender final jurisdiction over support issues or what is in the best interest of any child, but they hope that things will never go that far if the parties accept the decisions of their chosen arbitrator.

Financial matters. Financial matters are discussed in chapter 6, but there is also one faith-related variation below. Please remember, if you tailor financial rights in your agreement, you will have to do full disclosure as described in chapter 6F.

Faith-based variations for the basic Couples Contract

Paragraph numbers below refer to paragraphs in the basic agreement in chapter 5 that you can modify as shown here.

Title. While you can title your agreement almost anything you want, it would be best to avoid a title that makes it appear that the agreement is fundamentally religious.

5. Principles for a lasting marriage. You are free to treat this section of the basic agreement any way you like: keep it as it is, add to it, modify it, or do it the way we suggest in this example.

Variations for the basic Couples Contract

2. Commitments

(after first paragraph, add the following:)

We agree that our religious faith and relationships in our faith community are fundamental and that we will establish a household and a family that will live in accord with the beliefs of the (name) faith. We agree to maintain our membership in (name) or another similar faith community, should we move or mutually decide to change our religious affiliation. We agree to attend religious services regularly together. We agree that any children that may be born to us or adopted by us will be raised in the (name) faith and that we will observe the practices of that faith in our home.

5. Principles for a lasting marriage

It is our intention to create a lasting marriage based upon mutual respect, affection and friendship, and the principles of marriage taught by our faith. Should issues ever arise between us that threaten to undermine our closeness and mutual regard, we agree to take steps together to improve our relationship with the help and guidance of our faith community, including, if available, counseling and conciliation programs.

[Continue with any other clauses from the basic agreement that you want to keep or adapt.]

6. Parenting

[add this paragraph at the end of the paragraphs in the basic agreement]

We agree that any children that may be born to us or adopted by us will be raised in the (name) faith and that we will observe the practices of that faith in our home for their benefit as well as our own.

7. Money, property and financial matters

Except as modified by this agreement, we agree that all of our mutual rights and obligations with respect to our financial affairs, including our income, debts, and property, will be governed by California law no matter where we might live in the future.

10. Resolution of disputes

A. Mediation.

If we are unable to resolve any dispute privately, then on the written request of either party, within thirty days we will submit our dispute to mediation with a mediator agreed upon by both of us. Unless we agree otherwise, our mediator must be a member of (faith community) and preferably a California family law attorney who specializes in family law mediation or, if such is not available, someone who has experience with family mediation. If we are unable to agree on a mediator, we agree that

☐ we will each choose one person within our faith community and our two advisors together will appoint our mediator.

☐ the (rabbi/pastor/elders/other appropriate title) of (name of faith community), or of the faith community we both belong to at the time of the dispute, may appoint a mediator to help us resolve our dispute. If we are not at that time members of the same faith community, the mediator will be appointed by the rabbi/pastor/elders of the last faith community we both belonged to.

We will participate in mediation in good faith and pay the cost of mediation from community funds, if available, and if community funds are not available, we will each be responsible for half the cost of such mediation.

B. Arbitration

1. In the event that one of us is not willing to do mediation, or if mediation does not resolve the issue within a reasonable number of sessions, then upon the written request of either party, we will submit the matter to binding arbitration within thirty days. Our arbitrator must be an experienced California family law attorney who specializes in mediation and arbitration, or a retired family court judge, with preference given to one who is a member of our faith community. The arbitrator will be agreed upon by both of us. If we are unable to agree on an arbitrator,

☐ we will each choose one person within our faith community and our two advisors together will appoint an arbitrator who meets our agreed qualifications.

☐ the (rabbi/pastor/elders/other appropriate title) of (name of your faith community), or of the faith community we both belong to at the time of the dispute, may appoint an arbitrator who meets our agreed qualifications. If we are not at that time members of the same faith community, the arbitrator will be appointed by the (rabbi/pastor/elders) of the last faith community we both belonged to.

☐ the matter will be arbitrated by a panel of three arbitrators. We will each choose one arbitrator without regard to professional qualification, and our two arbitrators together will appoint the third arbitrator, who must be an experienced family law attorney who specializes in mediation and arbitration, or a retired family court judge.

2. If we use a single arbitrator, we will pay the cost of arbitration from community funds, if available, and if community funds are not available, we will each be responsible for half the cost of the arbitration. If we use a panel of three arbitrators, each of us will pay the fees of the arbitrator we appoint. The fees of the third arbitrator will be paid from community funds, if available, and if community funds are not available, we will each be responsible for half the fees of the third arbitrator and other costs of arbitration.

3. We are each entitled to representation in arbitration by an attorney of our choice. Attorney fees will be ☐ borne by each party separately. ☐ paid from community funds, if available, and if community funds are not available, each party will be responsible for his or her own attorney's fees.

4.   The arbitrator(s) will have the power to interpret the terms of this agreement, decide questions of their own jurisdiction, and settle disputes arising between the parties regarding the arbitrability of claims and the interpretation of the agreement. The arbitrator(s) will not have the power to alter, modify or terminate any provision of this agreement. The arbitration will be conducted under

☐ the rules of California Code of Civil Procedure sections 1280 to 1294.2,

☐ the arbitration rules of (faith-based organization),

as modified by the Nolo Supplementary Family Arbitration Rules, a copy of which is attached to this Agreement as Exhibit A.

5.   **Arbitration is binding and final.** The decision of the arbitrator(s) will be binding and final, not subject to review in any court. We each understand that by agreeing to binding arbitration, we are choosing arbitration as the sole remedy for any dispute between us arising from our marriage or this agreement, and we each expressly give up our right to file a lawsuit in any civil court against one another, or to request a court to resolve any dispute between us as an ancillary matter in a family court proceeding, except to enforce arbitration or the decision of an arbitrator, and thus we also give up the right to trial by court or jury. To whatever extent the law does not allow any issue between us to be decided by binding arbitration, we agree to submit such matters to non-binding arbitration before submitting the issue to any court.

[Optional]

6.   If an action is required to enforce the use of binding arbitration required by this agreement, or the decision of an arbitrator, the costs and expenses of the prevailing party in such judicial proceeding, including, but not limited to, his or her reasonable attorney's fees, will be paid by the unsuccessful party.

Optional provision for children

6.   We agree that if we should ever separate, the arbitrator(s) may decide custody, visitation and support issues for any children we may have together and, in making such decisions, the arbitrator(s) may consider the reasons for our separation, along with any other factors that may be just and fair, keeping the best interests of the children uppermost. The arbitrator(s) may consider, among all other factors affecting the children's welfare, each parent's willingness and ability to continue to raise the children according to our agreement about their religious upbringing. Nothing in this agreement shall be construed to adversely affect the right to support of any child.

Optional provision for faith-based division of property

6.   We agree that if we separate or it appears necessary to the arbitrator(s) for us to separate, the arbitrator(s) may divide our community property equitably between us. In making such division, the arbitrator(s) may consider the reasons for our separation, along with any other factors that may be just and fair according to the laws and principles of the (name) faith. We each specifically waive our right under California law to an equal division of community property.

Variation for faith-based division of property

Comment on the last optional clause on the previous page. Some religions have their own well-defined rules about property rights upon divorce and a religious court capable of dividing their property. If a couple wants this system to be used to divide their property, rather than California law, which requires an equal division of community property, they would have to be careful what they say because California's public policy favoring no-fault divorce means California courts won't enforce an agreement that explicitly penalizes a spouse for marital misconduct. If you add this clause at the end of section 10, it gives the arbitrator authority to divide property according to the rules of your religion.

Caution! This kind of financial agreement requires a high degree of trust in the rules, systems and arbitrators in your religious community. California's insistence on strict equality in the division of property creates a high degree of predictability, which is a good thing. Still, equal division sometimes seems unfair to the spouse who doesn't want the divorce. Few religious organizations have enough of a track record to allow you to predict what would happen in case you ever needed to rely on them to apply this clause. Even fewer have rules and procedures that allow a bad decision to be appealed. It makes divorce or separation a much more risky prospect, which might be what your religious leaders want, but is it really what you want?

A variation would be to say that the arbitrators "must divide our community property in a fair and substantially equal manner." This is similar to the current laws of many other states where precise mathematical equality is not required, as in the California courts, but the decision makers are not given a blank check to do anything they think is right.

Alternative dispute resolution clauses from Peacemaker Ministries

Frankly, we are partial to our own language, but here for comparison are clauses that bring the agreement under the Rules of Procedure for Christian Conciliation. Do **not** sign either of these clauses without carefully studying the Rules referred to, which you will find on the companion CD that comes with this book.

It would be used in place of both 10A and 10B in the basic Couples Contract.

10. Resolution of disputes

Any claim or dispute arising from or related to this agreement shall be settled by mediation and, if necessary, legally binding arbitration in accordance with the *Rules of Procedure for Christian Conciliation* of the Institute for Christian Conciliation, a division of Peacemaker® Ministries (complete text of the Rules is available at www.HisPeace.org). Judgment upon an arbitration decision may be entered in any court otherwise having jurisdiction. The parties understand that these methods shall be the sole remedy for any controversy or claim arising out of this agreement and expressly waive their right to file a lawsuit in any civil court against one another for such disputes, except to enforce an arbitration decision.

They also offer this clause:

10. Resolution of disputes

The parties to this agreement are Christians and believe that the Bible commands them to make every effort to live at peace and to resolve disputes with each other in private or within the Christian church (see Matthew 18:15-20; 1 Corinthians 6:1-8). Therefore, the parties agree that any claim or dispute arising from or related to this agreement shall be settled by biblically based mediation and, if necessary, legally binding arbitration in accordance with the *Rules of Procedure for Christian Conciliation* of the Institute for Christian Conciliation, a division of Peacemaker® Ministries (complete text of the Rules is available at www.HisPeace.org). Judgment upon an arbitration decision may be entered in any court otherwise having jurisdiction. The parties understand that these methods shall be the sole remedy for any controversy or claim arising out of this agreement and expressly waive their right to file a lawsuit in any civil court against one another for such disputes, except to enforce an arbitration decision.

Caution! If you decide to use one of these clauses, or a similar one from another organization, be sure to find out whether the rules are designed for family disputes that might require emergency orders for such things as child custody and support while waiting for the arbitrator to be chosen and other issues decided, or modification of child custody and support after arbitration if circumstances change. Unless the organization has a set of rules specifically designed to handle these matters in family disputes, we recommend you add this language immediately after naming the rules of your organization: "as modified by Nolo Supplementary Family Arbitration Rules, a copy of which is attached to this Agreement."

E. Other religious marriage contracts

Two large faith-based dispute resolution organizations, the Peacemaker Ministries and Beth Din of America, have pioneered the concept of faith-based marriage agreements for Christian and Jewish couples, respectively. We include their model agreements here, and describe the problems we see with enforcing them in California.

As other religious organizations follow suit and publish recommended relationship agreements, we will post links to them on our Web site at www.nolocouples.com. If your faith community has experience with marriage contracts, please let us know so we can post your information there, too.

1. Peacemaker Ministries

Many Christians are strongly opposed to divorce on moral grounds. As the divorce rate has climbed over the last 50 years, many Christian organizations have looked for ways to reverse the trend and help keep Christian couples together. Some have advocated elimination of no-fault divorce, at least for some couples. The states of Louisiana, Arizona and Arkansas have enacted covenant marriage laws. These laws generally require couples to have a certain amount of premarital counseling and to sign an agreement to have their marriage governed by a different set of laws, similar to the old fault-based divorce laws, making it more difficult for them to get a divorce. It is doubtful, however, that any California court would recognize a covenant marriage from one of these states as creating any different rights than normally exist under California's marriage and divorce laws.

Peacemaker Ministries has published this model *Marriage Covenant*, which is intended to allow couples to elect a covenant marriage, even in states like California that do not have a covenant marriage law. The purpose is to prevent one spouse from demanding a divorce against the wishes of the other spouse and without a good reason. A second purpose is to require both spouses to go to their church for marital help before going to court for a divorce. Our comments about the enforceability of this agreement in California follow.

Our Marriage Covenant

Believing that God, in His wisdom and providence, has ordained and establishes human marriage as a covenant relationship intended to reflect the eternal marriage covenant established through the death, burial and resurrection of His Son with His Church, and therefore believing that human marriage is a sacred and lifelong promise, reflecting our unconditional love for one another, and believing that God intends for the human marriage covenant to reflect His promise never to leave us or forsake us because of what He has done for us through His Son, Jesus Christ, we, the undersigned husband and wife, male and female, as image of God, do hereby affirm and reaffirm our solemn pledge to fulfill our marriage vows, so help us God; we furthermore pledge to exalt the sacred nature, glory and permanence of God's eternal marriage covenant in His Son with the Church through our marriage, by calling others to honor and fulfill their marriage vows; and we, upon full and informed consent and with full knowledge and understanding of this covenant and with the intent to enter into and be bound by the terms of this covenant, hereby irrevocably covenant and consent to submit any marital dispute we may have that we cannot resolve and any question concerning whether our marriage should be dissolved to the peacemaking process, including nonbinding Christian mediation and, if neces-sary, binding arbitration, in accordance with the Rules of Procedure of the Institute for Christian Conciliation, a division of Peacemaker® Ministries (www.HisPeace.org), and under the jurisdiction of our local church of which we are members, or if not members of a local church then under the jurisdiction of any church to which we can agree, but in any event if we cannot reach agreement as to a church for such purposes, then we consent and agree to submit to the peacemaking process as provided in the Rules of Procedure of the Institute for Christian Conciliation, a division of Peacemaker® Ministries, to and including binding arbitration of all matters pertaining to our marriage and family, believing that any and all marital and family disputes and issues involve deeply important religious questions that should be resolved by Christians according to the standards set forth in the Holy Bible, and therefore we do both hereby agree to be bound by any arbitration decision as to any such dispute or issues concerning our marriage and family, which is made in accordance with the Rules of Procedure of the Institute for Christian Conciliation, a division of Peace-maker® Ministries.

In the presence of God and these In the presence of God and these witnesses, and by a holy covenant, I, witnesses, and by a holy covenant, I,

_____	_____

Husband's Name

joyfully receive you as God's perfect gift for me, to have and to hold from this day forward, for better, for worse, for richer, for poorer, in sickness and in health, to love you, to honor you, to cherish you and protect you, forsaking all others as long as we both shall live.

Wife's Name

joyfully receive you as God's perfect gift for me, to have and to hold from this day forward, for better, for worse, for richer, for poorer, in sickness and in health, to love you, to honor you, to respect you, forsaking all others as long as we both shall live.

Husband's Signature

Wife's Signature

Witnessed this __ day of _____, by

Witness

Witness

Unless the Lord builds the house, the builders labor in vain. **Psalm 127:1**

Comments for California

The Covenant is simple and its main points are very similar to our basic Couples Contract after you add the clauses described in this chapter. The first part of the Covenant is a suitable variation to our section 5—Principles for a lasting marriage. The second part is similar to our section 10—Resolution of disputes. However, there are several potential problems with enforcing the Covenant in California.

Unenforceable? It is intended to be signed on the couple's wedding day, during or at the conclusion of the ceremony. Its purpose, according to Peacemaker Ministries, is to make it harder for a Christian marriage to be dissolved at the request of one spouse without "biblical grounds for divorce." Although it contains language about dispute resolution, it makes no mention at all of the usual subjects of a prenuptial agreement—that is, financial or property matters. These characteristics may cause a court to decide it is a religious marriage certificate, not a legally binding prenuptial agreement.

Procedural flaws. California has built a tall fence around prenuptial and marital agreements in reaction to many abuses. If you were to sign the Covenant without following all the procedural safeguards recommended for our Couples Contract (financial disclosure plus checklist steps 8 through 11), it is unlikely that it could be enforced.

In one California case,[1] a couple signed an Islamic marriage contract quite similar to this one, in that it said their marriage would be governed "in accordance with his Almighty God's Holy Book and the Rules of his Prophet." It specified the dowry, which is an Islamic marriage custom, but otherwise contained no financial agreements. The court decided it was not a prenuptial agreement, but a marriage certificate, and therefore ignored the part of the agreement that referred to Islamic Law and to the financial dowry. It is possible that had the agreement said all disputes would be resolved by a particular Islamic court, the judge would have viewed it differently, but this is not certain. The absence of any financial terms was a major reason the court decided to ignore it.

Paragraph 11D of our basic agreement is intended to avoid this problem as simply as possible. It says that no matter where the couple may live, they intend for their property to be community or separate, according to California law.

---

[1] *In re Marriage of Shaban* (2001) 88 Cal. App. 4th 398

The third problem with the Covenant is that it says the church will decide "any question concerning whether our marriage should be dissolved." In the material published by Peacemaker Ministries to explain the Covenant, they say that if one spouse files for divorce, the court would stop the divorce case until the church decided this question. We do not believe California courts would enforce the Covenant in this way. We think California courts would interpret the Covenant to say the church can decide whether the couple is entitled to a *religious* divorce, but it would have no effect on their *legal* divorce. A California court could be persuaded not to decide the financial part of the divorce case when there is a valid arbitration agreement, but will not give up the power to grant a no-fault legal divorce. A couple of California cases have held that no-fault divorce is a matter of public policy in California. This Covenant does not have a severability clause like paragraph 11A of our Basic Agreement, so it is also possible a California court would hold the whole Covenant unenforceable because of this clause.

What's the solution if you belong to a church that is promoting this Covenant? We think you could sign this Covenant at your wedding as a marriage certificate, but sign a separate Couples Contract before the wedding, modeled on our basic agreement with clauses added from this chapter. You can use language copied from the Covenant in paragraphs 5 and 10, and leave out of your Agreement the phrase, "whether the marriage should be dissolved."

2. Beth Din of America

Jewish Law, called *Halakha*, gives the husband the right to divorce his wife, but does not give the wife the same right. If the wife obtains a legal divorce, but not a religious divorce, she and her children by a later marriage can be severely penalized within the Jewish faith. A Jewish woman who is legally, but not religiously, divorced is known as an *agunah*, or "chained woman."

In recent years, Jewish communities have seen an increase in the number of women in this situation, and have given considerable attention to finding ways to deal with this problem. One of the leading Orthodox Jewish religious courts, the Beth Din of America, has developed a prenuptial agreement as a possible solution that can be enforced under both American civil law and Jewish law. The purpose of this agreement is to require a separated or divorced Jewish husband and wife to take care of the Jewish religious divorce. This is done by requiring the husband to pay the wife $150 per day from the day they separate until the Jewish divorce is completed. If the wife refuses to cooperate, the husband can have her summoned before the Beth Din and ask them to end his obligation. Our comments about the enforceability of this agreement in California follow the agreement.

In spite of misgivings like those expressed by Rabbi Boteach earlier in this chapter, many rabbis recommend or require couples to make this kind of agreement. In counseling them, they explain to couples that the purpose of the agreement is not so much to plan ahead for their own divorce, but to take a stand against allowing any former husband to make his former wife a "chained woman." In other words, a couple who signs this agreement is making a statement that no Jewish couple should ever treat each other that way, and proving it by their own promises.

THE BETH DIN OF AMERICA
BINDING ARBITRATION AGREEMENT

THIS AGREEMENT MADE ON THE _____ DAY OF THE MONTH OF _____ IN THE YEAR 20 __, IN THE CITY/TOWN/VILLAGE OF _____STATE OF _____.

between:

HUSBAND-TO-BE: _____

RESIDING AT:_____

WIFE-TO-BE: _____

RESIDING AT: _____

The parties, who intend to be married in the near future, hereby agree as follows:

I. Should a dispute arise between the parties after they are married, so that they do not live together as husband and wife, they agree to refer their marital dispute to an arbitration panel, namely, The Beth Din of the United States of America, Inc. (currently located at 305 Seventh Ave., New York, NY 10001, tel. 212 807-9042, www.bethdin.org) for a binding decision.

II. The decision of the Beth Din of America shall be fully enforceable in any court of competent jurisdiction.

III. The parties agree that the Beth Din of America is authorized to decide all issues relating to a *get* (Jewish divorce) as well as any issues arising from this Agreement or the *ketubah* and *tena'im* (Jewish premarital agreements) entered into by the Husband-to-Be and the Wife-to-Be. Each of the parties agrees to appear in person before the Beth Din of America at the demand of the other party.

(Sections IV:A and IV:B are optional. Unless one of these options is chosen, the Beth Din of America will be without jurisdiction to address matters of general financial and parenting disputes between the parties.)

☐ IV:A(1). The parties agree that the Beth Din of America is authorized to decide all monetary disputes (including division of property and maintenance) that may arise between them.

☐ IV:A(2). The parties agree that the Beth Din of America is authorized to decide any monetary disputes (including division of property and maintenance) that may arise between them based on principles of equitable distribution law customarily employed in the United States as found in the Uniform Marriage and Divorce Act.

☐ IV:A(3). The parties agree that the Beth Din of America is authorized to decide any monetary disputes (including division of property and maintenance) that may arise between them based on the principles of community property law customarily employed in the United States as found in the Uniform Marriage and Divorce Act.

☐ IV:B. The parties agree that the Beth Din of America is authorized to decide all disputes, including child custody, child support, and visitation matters, as well as any other disputes that may arise between them.

IV:C. The Beth Din of America may consider the respective responsibilities of either or both of the parties for the end of the marriage, as an additional, but not exclusive, factor in determining the distribution of marital property and maintenance, should such a determination be authorized by Section IV:A or Section IV:B.

V. Failure of either party to perform his or her obligations under this Agreement shall make that party liable for all costs awarded by either the Beth Din of America or a court of competent jurisdiction, including reasonable attorney's fees, incurred by one side in order to obtain the other party's performance of the terms of this Agreement.

VI. The decision of the Beth Din of America shall be made in accordance with Jewish law (*halakha*) or Beth Din ordered settlement in accordance with the principles of Jewish law (*peshara krova la-din*), except as specifically provided otherwise in this Agreement. The parties waive their right to contest the jurisdiction or procedures of the Beth Din of America or the validity of this Agreement in any other rabbinical court or arbitration forum other than the Beth Din of America. The parties agree to abide by the published Rules and Procedures of the Beth Din of America (which are available at www.bethdin.org, or by calling the Beth Din of America) which are in effect at the time of the arbitration. The Beth Din of America shall follow its rules and procedures, which shall govern this arbitration to the fullest extent permitted by law. Both parties obligate themselves to pay for the services of the Beth Din of America as directed by the Beth Din of America.

VII. The parties agree to appear in person before the Beth Din of America at the demand of the other party, and to cooperate with the adjudication of the Beth Din of America in every way and manner. In the event of the failure of either party to appear before the Beth Din of America upon reasonable notice, the Beth Din of America may issue its decision despite the defaulting party's failure to appear, and may impose costs and other penalties as legally permitted. Furthermore, Husband-to-Be acknowledges that he recites and accepts the following:

I hereby now (me'achshav), *obligate myself to support my Wife-to-Be from the date that our domestic residence together shall cease for whatever reasons, at the rate of $150 per day (calculated as of the date of our marriage, adjusted annually by the Consumer Price Index–All Urban Consumers, as published by the US Department of Labor, Bureau of Labor Statistics) in lieu of my Jewish law obligation of support so long as the two of us remain married according to Jewish law, even if she has another source of income or earnings. Furthermore, I waive my* halakhic *rights to my wife's earnings for the period that she is entitled to the above stipulated sum, and I acknowledge that I shall be deemed to have repeated this waiver at the time of our wedding. I acknowledge that I have effected the above obligation by means of a* kinyan *(formal Jewish transaction) in an esteemed* (chashuv) *Beth Din as prescribed by Jewish law.*

However, this support obligation shall terminate if Wife-to-Be refuses to appear upon due notice before the Beth Din of America or in the event that Wife-to-Be fails to abide by the decision or recommendation of the Beth Din of America.

VIII. This Agreement may be signed in one or more duplicates, each one of which shall be considered an original.

IX. This Agreement constitutes a fully enforceable arbitration agreement. Should any provision of this Agreement be deemed unenforceable, all other surviving provisions shall still be deemed fully enforceable; each and every provision of this Agreement shall be severable from the other. As a matter of Jewish law, the parties agree that to effectuate this agreement in full form and purpose, they accept now (through the Jewish law mechanism of *kim li*) whatever minority views determined by the Beth Din of America are needed to effectuate the obligations contained in Section VII and the procedures and jurisdictional mandates found in Sections I, II, III and VI of this Agreement.

X. Each of the parties acknowledges that he or she has been given the opportunity prior to signing this Agreement to consult with his or her own rabbinic advisor and legal advisor. The obligations and conditions contained herein are executed according to all legal and *halachic* requirements.

In witness of all the above, the Husband-to-Be and Wife-to-Be have entered into this Agreement.

SIGNATURE OF HUSBAND-TO-BE: _____

SIGNATURE OF WIFE-TO-BE: _____

WITNESS: _____

WITNESS: _____

Comments for California

The Beth Din of America agreement is intended to motivate a separated Jewish couple to take care of their religious divorce as quickly as possible. Rabbis and lawyers spent years trying to find a way to do this without violating either state laws or Jewish religious law. The best solution they could find was to require the husband (the one who holds most of the religious rights) to pay the wife $150 per day from the time they separate until they go to the Beth Din for the religious divorce. But this raises a problem in California, because it requires a form of spousal support in certain circumstances, so it would not be enforceable in California unless at least the husband, and preferably also the wife, is represented by an independent attorney.

In addition to Beth Din's provisions for the religious divorce, you could also include other matters from our basic and faith-based agreement. Be sure to get advice from your rabbi about whether anything you want to add will violate Jewish law.

The Beth Din can decide on all marital disputes, including property and financial matters, and matters relating to children if you agree, although you must remember that the state court is always the ultimate arbiter of child support and deciding what is in the best interest of a child. The Beth Din of America can decide financial questions according to state law, rather than Jewish law if the couple agrees. They recommend you state specifically whether financial questions are to be decided according to Jewish law or according to state law. Since California's community property system is quite different from the Jewish marital property system, it is very important that you get specific advice comparing the two systems to help you make the kind of agreement you want. In section D above, we presented a replacement for clause 10 of the basic Couples Contract, to allow arbitrator(s) to divide community property according to religious law rather than state law.

While the Beth Din attempts to offer services nationally, you need to find out if they are conveniently accessible where you live, so we suggest you consult your rabbi or the Beth Din on this before naming the Beth Din as your arbitrators in California. Be sure to also inquire about their ability to arbitrate nonreligious issues of a separation or divorce.

California law does not require this kind of agreement to be witnessed, but since this agreement is intended to be binding under both state law and Jewish law, you should not skip any of the procedures we prescribe for our Couples Contract (financial disclosure plus checklist steps 8–11), or any recommended by your rabbi.

CHAPTER 8

Variations for unmarried couples

A. Becoming aware

Unmarried people living together without a written agreement remind us of those old movies where you see a couple tied up on train tracks with a train barreling along in the distance and everyone is riveted by the imminent disaster. The main difference is that in the movies the couple is *aware* of the threat and they *always* get saved.

For unmarried couples, awareness is the most important thing. Are you aware that without a written agreement you are living in a state of financial ambiguity that is full of risk but has no up side? Do you know that you and your partner are exposed and vulnerable, so that if you don't actually get run over by that train it won't be because of anything you did to avoid it? Do you know that you can protect each other far better if you write some stuff down? Making agreements is not just about avoiding train wrecks—writing some things down is about positive advantages for both of you and for your relationship.

Are you aware of how the law treats unmarried couples who have no written agreement? If not, no problem—just be sure to read chapter 14, and pay special attention to things that you can't affect in a contract, like child support, federal tax returns, Social Security, appointing beneficiaries under some kinds of retirement accounts and investment funds, and so on.

Are you aware of the positive advantages for writing some things down in an agreement?

B. You two and the others

There are two good reasons for unmarried couples to write some things down: one is to make matters clear between you two, and the other is to make things clear for others. In many situations, making your wishes known to others can be essential to protecting you and your loved one.

1. Writing it down for others

a. Medical emergencies. In case of accident, illness or advanced age, who do you want to step in and take care of you? What happens if you are incapacitated and can't speak for yourself? Without a written document, an unmarried partner has no right to order medical treatment and cannot take charge. He/she might even have trouble getting into a hospital to visit, because, as far as the law is concerned, you two are strangers. However, if you and your partner each sign a simple document called a Health Care Directive, this will solve the problem. It comes in two parts: the first is addressed to any treating physician, spelling out your wishes if you are incapacitated; and the second part gives the person of your choice the power to order and supervise your health care, including to hire and fire medical personnel, visit you in the hospital, have access to your medical records, and get court authorization to enforce your written health care wishes. You'll find a Health Care Directive on the companion CD.

b. Financial power of attorney. Similarly, if one of you becomes incapacitated, who will manage your financial affairs? Without written instructions, a family member or your partner will have to go to court for authority. If you each prepare a Durable Power of Attorney for Finances, problem solved. You can give your partner (or other person) authority to do such things as: use your assets to pay bills and ongoing expenses; buy, sell, maintain and pay expenses for real estate; collect Social Security benefits, Medicare, insurance, or the like; invest your assets; buy insurance, file and pay taxes, operate your business, claim inheritances, hire an attorney, and so on. Go to www.nolo.com to find books and software for making such a document.

c. Creditors. Here's just one example. Let's say your partner holds title to property or an account that you both think belongs in some degree to both of you, but the named owner later goes into debt or runs over someone who sues. Creditors could take the whole asset unless it is clear that you had a prior claim or ownership. Trying to change title after the event looks suspiciously like a transfer to defraud creditors and could land you in a nasty legal squabble. It's best to make everything clear *before* anything happens.

d. Relatives, friends, business associates. In case anything happens to one of you, a contract is a good way to let everyone else know who owns what and keep the other partner out of unnecessary squabbles.

e. Wills. If an unmarried partner dies without a will, the other partner gets nothing unless there is a contract or some property is held under joint title or in a joint account. It might be possible for the surviving partner to get something anyway, but it would likely involve a long delay and possible struggle in probate court with relatives of the deceased. To protect the surviving partner, you must either make a will, a contract or both. You can make a contract of the type described in this book, or in Nolo's *Living Together*, which has a wider range of contract clauses and a simple form will as well. Nolo has some excellent books and software for making wills, which you can find at www.nolo.com.

      f.   Estate planning. Beyond simple wills, you might want to find out how to avoid the delay, trouble and expense of probate by doing some estate planning. This would include setting up revocable living trusts, joint accounts with right of survivorship, payable-on-death bank accounts, gifts, joint tenancy in real estate, and the naming of beneficiaries in retirement accounts, securities, investment accounts, and life insurance. Nolo has several excellent books and programs to help you deal with estate planning and probate matters, which you can find at www.nolo.com.

2. Writing it down for your own benefit

If you don't expect to be together very long and don't have much in the way of assets, maybe you don't need a written agreement, but everyone else surely does. Here are a few good reasons for writing some things down for your own good:

- You make things clear between you
- You can introduce ideas that might help your relationship in the future
- You can tailor financial relationships to be more suitable to your situation
- If it ever happened, you'd have a smoother breakup
- You can keep your relationship forever out of court

      Unintended implied contracts. Agreements can later be construed from the behavior of the parties, so careless or generous behavior can later be seen as an agreement (see chapter 14B). An important reason for writing things down is to avoid a later claim that there was an agreement implied by the behavior of the parties. This kind of claim can take a lot of time and energy to prove or disprove. Far better for people who live together to spell out what they intend, no matter what that is.

      Even if you don't want to write down your understanding of your financial affairs, at the very least you'll want to incorporate the advantages of our basic agreement (see chapter 2) into your relationship.

3. Writing it down to change the rules

Okay, we lied: there's a third good reason to write things down, and that is to change the rules that determine your financial relationship. If you have no agreement, your rights and obligations are much the same as if you did not love each other and live together. Neither of you has any right or obligation to share property or income or support each other in any way. If you want something different from this, you'll have to create what you want in a Couples Contract.

C. Financial clarity

There's much to be gained from writing some things down even if you do not define your financial affairs. The advantages of the basic Couples Contract don't require financial discussions or clarity. So, you can actually accomplish a great deal without much effort or discomfort.

However, failure to define your finances can leave you vulnerable to misunderstanding and unprotected in the event of illness, accident or breakup. If things go bad between you, you can end up in a terrible conflict that could have been avoided. So what's the problem? Why do so many couples prefer having their teeth pulled to talking about money?

All couples, married or not, find money a difficult subject to discuss. But the problem is especially intense for unmarried couples who aren't clear about the depth of their commitment, because discussing money can force you to delve into your true feelings and intentions, something that many unmarried couples desperately avoid. Some people are more comfortable if they just ignore the elephant in the room and never mention it. So you're stuck between the desire to protect someone you care about and the fear of having some defining conversations.

Now, a word of hope: for those of you who really are in it for the long haul, experts tell us that working through to financial understanding and agreement can strengthen your relationship. It's one of those things that may not be fun but it's good for you, like exercise and a healthy diet.

1. What can be done

When thinking about how to tailor your financial relationships, these are the things you'll want to think about. Actual contract clauses are described in section F below.

    a. Income. If nothing is defined, all income of any kind belongs to the person who earns or receives it. If you want to pool your income, or some of it, in a more committed kind of way, you should make an agreement as to how this will be done. There are two kinds of income to consider: earned income comes from time and effort, while unearned income comes from assets that you own, interest, dividends, and even rent if you don't work much to get it. You need to define both if both are present in your life.

    b. Support. There is no legal obligation for one to support the other, but in a long-term relationship you might want to make the committment to support each other. Or, it might be reasonable for one partner to agree to support the other, either for love or practical considerations, as where one has moved a long distance or given up a good job or career to move in and devote time and energy to the house or to support the business or career of the one paying support. And, unlike married people who can't do it, you are free to agree to support in exchange for services, like housekeeping (but not sex). Similarly, you can agree to take turns supporting each other through years of education, but should say what happens if you break up midway through. If support is in your agreement, you have to decide how long the obligation will continue and what support will include. For example, married couples are expected to support each other after a breakup at a level as close as possible to their lifestyle while together, for at least a long enough time to allow the supported spouse to get back on his or her feet. An unmarried partner can agree to support the other, but in a specific or limited way. You have to define what you intend.

    c. Expenses. Many couples want to define how expenses get paid, either shared equally or in some proportion, or completely covered by one partner. Without an agreement, there is no clarity as to who is responsible for your joint expenses or how they will get paid.

    d. Debts. Debts are owed by the partner who incurs them, the one whose name is on the credit card or account. If you have joint income or assets, you need to define how debts get paid. If you pool your income or assets or both, and if one or both of you have separate estates or business, you should agree that joint funds will not be used to pay debts incurred for the benefit of a separate asset or business.

e.   Major assets. Unless you put assets into joint title or a joint account, they will belong entirely to the person whose name is on the title or account. You might want to create a joint estate by agreeing to transfer or buy assets in both your names, or simply to agree in writing that one of you owns an interest in the asset of the other. If one of you is contributing effort or value to benefit a separate asset of the other, an agreement should be made as to how this will be compensated.

f.   Income from assets or accounts. When dealing with an asset, you have to also consider how to treat any income or appreciation that flows from it. Equities can produce dividends; a house can produce rent; intellectual property can be licensed and earn royalties over a long period of time. A house might appreciate in value just by sitting there, or you might put money and effort into fixing it up to increase its value. Unless defined by agreement, all such income belongs to whoever owns the base asset.

g.   Children. The rights and duties of parents do not depend on whether they are married. See chapter 15 for a discussion of parenting. Many couples decide to get married or register their domestic partnership when they have a child or start thinking seriously about it. If marriage or domestic partnership isn't right for you, an agreement is more important than ever. You will both have obligations to support your child, as well as rights to custody. One of you might qualify for head of household tax filing status by claiming the child as a dependent, but you can't both claim the same child. You'll want to make some agreements about these sorts of things.

h.   Work on project or business. If you work together on a onetime project (like building a sailboat or restoring an antique auto) you could define your relationship to it in this agreement (see section F below), but for activities that are more like a business, you should *definitely* make a separate partnership agreement. When people live together and work on a business without a partnership agreement, it can require a court action to prove an implied contract to gain an equity interest in the business. See Nolo's *The Partnership Book*.

Combinations. Some situations require careful coordination of the options you choose. For example, where a couple owns separate estates and also want to create a joint estate, they'll need to carefully think about distinguishing between joint and separate income, earned income and income from assets, and protecting the joint estate from debts incurred to benefit a separate business or asset.

If you feel uncertain how to accomplish your goals or want to make sure your agreement is being done correctly, call Couples Helpline and make an appointment to talk to one of our family law attorneys to get some advice and options.

2. Tax issues —caution!

It's not as if financial considerations aren't already complicated enough without being made more so by tax laws, but such is the case. Do not design your financial agreement without first getting advice and input from a good tax accountant. For example: Shared earnings are taxed first to the earner, then possibly taxed again to the recipient. Support for services require full treatment as wages. Deposits in a joint account can give rise to imputations of taxable income where one puts in more than the other. Transfers of title to property can be taxed. One partner might be able to claim exemptions for the other partner or partner's children if they are members of his/her household and receive more than 50% of their support from the claimant. Ask about estate tax consequences for jointly held property. Go over your goals with the tax accountant and see if you can find a way to accomplish them that is relatively painless from a tax point of view. Shop around for a tax accountant who is not just an extension of the IRS; one who is practical and inventive about how things can be done without arousing federal attention.

From a tax point of view, the safest thing is to keep separate bank accounts, avoid commingling funds, and make an agreement stating that there is no intention to pool earnings or other income or gifts or inheritances and neither has interest in future earnings of the other from whatever source. Of course, taxes and money aren't the only consideration, but it is something to think about.

D. How committed are you?

The rest of this chapter is most suitable for couples who are interested in a long-term committed relationship because our basic Couples Contract is optimized for people who hope to be together forever.

We understand you might be taking things a day at a time and, even if those days pile up into years, you might not be comfortable with a lot of focus on commitment or long-range planning. The less committed you are, or the more short-term your view, the more we believe you should make your contracts with the help of Nolo's excellent book, *Living Together,* which takes an entire book to cover a far broader range of issues and clauses for unmarried couples than we can cover in this one chapter. But, there is one part of the basic agreement that you should definitely keep in any contract you write—section 10 is extremely important, as it guarantees that no matter what happens, you'll never end up in court. This, alone, is worth the price of admission and the effort it takes to make an agreement.

Everyone can benefit from continuing on with us, but from this point to the end of the chapter, we are primarily addressing issues we think are common to unmarried couples who expect to be together for the long haul.

Unmarried together forever. Some people like the feeling of waking up every morning and knowing they are together because they want to be, not because they signed up for life. Some just don't feel the need to make it official, or to involve the church or state in their personal lives. Some are together because they just are: never thought about it, don't want to think about it. Some are not married because they are still married to someone else and haven't gotten a divorce yet. There must be a host of other reasons, but one thing you all have in common is that you expect to be together indefinitely.

To the extent that you care about each other, you will want to protect one another with the kinds of agreements and documents we described in section B1 above: durable powers of attorney for health and financial matters, wills, and an agreement that spells out for relatives and others who owns what. Be sure to review the designated beneficiaries on any retirement plans, investment accounts or insurance policies. And, you surely will want to get the advantages of our basic Couples Contract (see chapter 2). We show you how to tailor the basic Couples Contract for your needs in the next section.

Still married to someone else. If you are living together while one of you is still married to someone else, you are in a precarious situation until the marriage is legally resolved by either a divorce or legal separation. The old relationship is a threat hanging over your heads, even if you haven't seen or heard from the old spouse for ages. If you mix your incomes and assets, the old spouse or a creditor for common necessities could show up some day and make a claim which, even if you fend it off, could involve you in an expensive and tiresome squabble.

Get advice. The reasons for staying married while living with someone else vary widely—reluctance to deal with it, reliance on marital benefits, or a spouse who is afflicted with Alzheimer's or other disability. What they all have in common is that they could conceivably involve you in a thicket of legal tangles, so if you are still married, you should definitely get some legal advice from a family law attorney on your specific situation before you enter into any sort of legal agreement to live together. Call Couples Helpline.

E.   Changes to the basic agreement

The basic Couples Contract (chapter 5) is optimized for couples who are interested in a long-term relationship. Its goal is to reinforce your commitment to each other, plant ideas that might help you resolve relationship issues in the future, and keep your relationship forever out of court. While you're at it, you can also make some financial agreements (section F below).

Being an unmarried couple, you need to make a few changes to the basic agreement and think carefully about the commitments in section 2.

Section 2. Commitments. The law imposes on married people and domestic partners the highest standard of care in dealing with one another, called a *fiduciary* duty, which is pretty much as described in section 2 in the basic agreement.

Unmarried couples are presumed to be dealing with each other at arm's length, just like any other adults doing business. However, a *confidential* relationship exists when one person has gained the confidence of the other and claims to be acting in the other's best interest, in which case a *fiduciary* duty is imposed. A *fiduciary* relationship can exist between unmarried partners where one has control of the other's property, at least as to the property being controlled.

Because our Couples Contract is about commitment to a lasting relationship, and because most committed couples are at least arguably in a confidential relationship anyway, we are going to suggest that you leave this section as written and clearly state that you are undertaking the highest duty toward each other.

Section 3. Current situation and plans. Replace the options about marriage with the following language, and continue with the statements about children and circumstances.

3.   Current situation and plans

We are two people in love who desire to live together in a long-term committed relationship. We have no plans to marry or register a domestic partnership.

Section 4. Effective date and duration. Replace section 4 of the basic agreement with the following:

4.   Effective date and duration of agreement

This agreement will become effective once it has been signed by both parties and will terminate upon the marriage or cohabitation of one party with a third person, or upon the marriage of the parties to each other, or __ days after the written notice by one party to the other that our relationship and our agreement is being ended, unless we begin conciliation during that period of time. During conciliation, this period of __ days will be suspended, and will begin again if one party gives written notice to the other and to the conciliator(s) that conciliation is terminated and the separation is final.

The termination will not be retroactive, so all property and debts defined as joint or separate by this agreement will remain joint or separate, unless specified otherwise elsewhere in this agreement. However, any provisions of this agreement that last for a specific period of time will not be terminated by this notice. Any provisions of this agreement that begin when we separate will begin then.

Section 7. Money and property. These are discussed in section F below.

Section 8. Disclosure. If you are not tailoring your financial relationships, and don't otherwise decide you want to do financial disclosure, then use the clause in the basic agreement as it is. However, if you do tailor financial relationships, you *must* do financial disclosure and use the disclosure clause shown in chapter 6F.

F. Tailoring your financial relationships

Tailoring financial relationships means thinking about how to manage your income and expenses, who pays which debts, and ownership of assets. This is done in the context of your separate personalities, your relationship, and your situation in life. Be sure to review *What can be done* in section C above.

Caution! Do not make a financial agreement without advice from a tax accountant. Almost every feature could have potential tax consequences which you should be aware of before you decide what to do. See section C2 above.

Caution! Don't mention sex. Not that you were going to, but don't. Any clause or portion of your agreement in which sex is a basis cannot be enforced and it can threaten your entire agreement if it is seen as a central feature. Nothing about sex is enforceable, so best to not mention it *directly*. An agreement to live together, share property and have children will be seen as an agreement for a committed relationship and therefore enforceable, even though we all know how babies are made.

Advice. We think that unless your situation is simple and the financial clauses obvious you should do your homework here then review your agreement with an experienced family law specialist attorney (see chapter 4C). This is especially true if you aren't sure how to go about tailoring your agreement. Call Couples Helpline to talk to one of our consulting attorneys to review your agreement or get some ideas and options for how to deal with your particular situation.

How to do it. To tailor financial relationships, you change the title of this section to "7. Money and property," then you just add clauses under existing sections of the basic agreement, which now would start like this:

7. Money, property and financial matters

A.   Except as modified by this agreement, we agree that all of our mutual rights and obligations with respect to our marital and financial affairs, including our income, debts, and property, will be governed by California law no matter where we might live in the future.

Label the first basic clause "A" and delete the reference to marital affairs. Each additional item you add is entered as B, C, D, etc., in order, depending on which ones and how many you use.

Explanations not needed. In chapters 6 and 7, you will see explanation language after each sample agreement which is used in the Explanation of Agreement document (chapter 9A). It all goes to show that each party knows what rights are being given up by signing the agreement. Unmarried couples don't have any rights that are being given up as a result of their relationship, so they have no need to use the Explanation of Agreement, thus no explanation language is given below. However, when you come to the signing ceremony, it is still a good idea to have each party discuss the agreement and show that both are familiar with the contents and know what they are doing when they sign.

Schedules and exhibits. Whenever you are dealing with more than a few items of property in any clause, rather than list them all in your agreement, you can attach lists at the back of the agreement and label them Schedules m and n, or Exhibit A or B. The particular number or letter will depend on whatever has come before it in your agreement. In our example, Schedules 1 and 2 are the financial disclosures of the two parties and Exhibit A is always the Nolo Supplementary Family Arbitration Rules.

Example clauses. Our goal in this section is to illustrate some reasonable solutions for common situations faced by committed unmarried couples. In addition to the situations and clauses below, you might also review chapter 6C and 6D as there could be some ideas there you can adapt.

1. Keeping everything separate

While it might not be emotionally satisfying for couples who see themselves as lifetime partners, this arrangement is cleanest from a tax point of view, and it is highly recommended if one partner is in debt or in a risky business, or where a partner is still married to someone else. It assumes that the parties have their own sources of income so that one is not financially dependent on the other. Financial tailoring to keep everything separate could look like this:

B. Separate assets. The separate assets and debts of Chris, listed on Schedule 1, and the separate assets and debts of Jamie, listed on Schedule 2, were and will remain their own separate assets and debts, including all profits and appreciation flowing from those assets.

C. Income and acquisitions are separate. We agree that, unless stated otherwise in this agreement, all income, from whatever source, as well as all acquisitions made with that income, and all gifts or inheritances, will be the separate property of the person who earns or receives it. Neither party will acquire any interest in the separate income or assets of the other party and the separate property of one cannot be transferred to the other unless done in writing.

D. Separate debts and accounts. We will each maintain separate accounts for all financial activities, such as banking, investments, retirement funds, credit cards, and the like.

Chris will be responsible for all debts incurred by Chris or in the operation of or for the benefit of Chris's separate assets and Chris will indemnify, defend and hold Jamie harmless from any action to collect such debts from joint assets or Jamie's separate property, including paying any costs and attorney fees in connection with such an action.

Jamie will be responsible for all debts incurred by Jamie or in the operation of or for the benefit of Jamie's separate assets and Jamie will indemnify, defend and hold Chris harmless from any action to collect such debts from joint assets or Chris's separate property, including paying any costs and attorney fees in connection with such an action.

E. Joint accounts. From time to time we might maintain a joint checking or savings account into which we will make equal deposits sufficient to cover our ordinary household expenses for accommodation, food, entertainment, services, utilities, cleaning supplies and the like. Our joint account can also be used to buy

---

property we have agreed to own jointly, in which case the details of our joint ownership will be put in writing or in the ownership document to the property.

F. Division on termination. If this agreement should terminate, as defined in section 4 above, we will each be entitled to immediate possession of our separate property. If, at that time, we possess any jointly owned personal property, it will be immediately divided by mutual agreement and, if we cannot agree on how to divide it, we will (insert here one of the ten ways to divide property from chapter 17K).

2. Keep things separate, but . . .

Here are two variations for the "keep everything separate" agreement above, that can be used if you decide to purchase a major item such as a home together, or do a significant joint project together. You can add one of these clauses to the above agreement as section 7G or use them both as 7G and H. You can also add these variations at some later time by modifying your agreement as described in chapter 10G, using the language below in the modification template.

Optional. In either of these situations, you might want to provide for life insurance as a safety net in case one of the partners dies.

a. Joint purchase of real estate

This variation is used for buying titled property, which is typically purchased on time, like a car or, in this example, a home or other real estate.

G. Joint purchase of real estate.

1. We agree to jointly purchase the real property at (address),

☐ which we will own equally and take title as (joint tenants/tenants in common)

☐ of which Chris will own __% and Jamie will own __% and take title to it as tenants in common stating those percentages of ownership.

2. We will share all costs of ownership, including the down payment, closing costs, mortgage payments, taxes, insurance, repairs and routine maintenance (equally/according to our percentage of ownership in the property). If one party pays all or part of the other party's share of the expenses, careful records must be kept as such payments will be entitled to reimbursement plus _ % interest.

3.   Capital improvements will be made only by mutual consent to the nature, extent and cost of such improvements, and costs will be shared (equally/according to our percentage of ownership in the property).

4.   Upon termination of this agreement as defined in section 4 above, one of the following will happen:

(a) The parties can agree that one of them will assume sole ownership on terms and conditions to be mutually agreed by the parties at that time;

(b) If neither party wants to assume sole ownership, or if they are unable to agree on terms for one party to purchase it from the other, the property will be listed with a licensed real estate broker within __ days. Net proceeds from sale, if any, will be divided between the parties (equally/according to their percentage of ownership in the property). "Net proceeds" means the total amount received less sales commissions, costs incident to the sale, and amounts paid to discharge outstanding mortgages, liens, encumbrances, or costs defined in G2 above.

Personal loans. If you want to own property equally, or engage in a project together, but one partner can't come up with money, the other partner can lend the money. If this happens, be sure to draw up a promissory note detailing the terms of the loan. You can find a promissory note form in stationery stores; call around.

Buying into an existing home. This can be done either with a cash payment up front or buying in a little at a time and acquiring a certain ownership interest with each payment. This all needs to be carefully defined, as well as how routine maintenance, repairs, taxes and insurance will be paid at each stage, and what happens if the agreement is ever terminated. You might need a lawyer's help to draw up this kind of agreement. Contact a lawyer who specializes in real estate transactions, or call Couples Helpline.

Buy and fix up. Sometimes one partner will buy the home and the other will contribute sweat equity to fix it up. If this happens, you need to tailor a different agreement to explain how your deal is going to work. You can adapt some ideas from the example below.

b. Joint project

This variation is used if you go into a large onetime project together, like buying and fixing up a home for resale, or building an airplane. Number this section according to where it appears in the rest of your agreement.

G. Joint project

1. We agree to join together to build an Acme Firefox XG airplane

☐ which we will own equally

☐ of which Chris will own __% and Jamie will own __%

2. ☐ We will each contribute (lump sum/amount per month)

☐ Chris will contribute (amount/amount per month) and Jamie will contribute (lump sum/amount per month)

for the purchase of necessary parts, supplies, tools, and work space overhead. These funds will be kept in one or more joint accounts that will be used solely for this project and both of our signatures will be required to withdraw funds from these accounts. If one party pays all or part of the other party's share of the expenses, careful records must be kept as such payments will be entitled to reimbursement plus _ % interest.

3. We will each work diligently on this project, which means Chris will work at least __ hours per month and Jamie will work at least __ hours per month on the project, and we will each keep a record on the site of all hours worked.

4. Should either of us die while we are still joint owners of the project, the survivor will become sole owner.

5. Should either of us wish to end his/her participation in this project, then within __ days of giving written notice of intention to withdraw, one of the following will happen:

(a) One of us will assume sole ownership on terms and conditions to be mutually agreed at that time;

(b) If neither of us wants to assume sole ownership, or if we are not able to agree on terms, the project will be liquidated and sold and net proceeds after paying all related debts and obligations will be distributed between us according to our percentage of ownership in the project.

(c) For purposes of this buy-out clause, "the project" means all money in the joint project accounts and all materials, tools, and supplies contributed to or purchased for the benefit of the project.

(d) Withdrawal from the project will not imply termination of the rest of our agreement, but if our agreement is terminated as defined in section 4 above, the project must also be terminated and divided as specified in this clause unless we make a new written agreement to continue.

3. Share income and acquired assets

In this variation, the couple acts more like a traditional family and decides to pool their energies and resources. The first clause itemizes assets and debts that are to be kept separate, if any, and the second clause protects the joint estate from debts incurred to benefit anyone's separate estate. However, you could decide to convert all assets to joint property, and do away with separate property and debts altogether. Pooling has the potential for serious tax disadvantages, so do not make this kind of agreement without the advice and input of a good tax accountant.

Caution! Support and transfers of money or property are potentially taxable events (section C2 above). You have to wonder how the IRS will hear about money used to support another person or another person's child, but it is best to be aware there is a potential problem. See a tax accountant before making this kind of agreement; preferably one who does not seem to be a spokesperson for the IRS.

a. Pooled income and assets, no support

This agreement pools income and assets but does not require that one party support the other. Following this agreement are clauses for adding support to the agreement.

B. Separate assets. The separate assets and debts of Chris, listed on Schedule 3, and the separate assets and debts of Jamie, listed on Schedule 4, were and will remain their own separate assets and debts, including all profits and appreciation flowing from those assets.

Any gifts or inheritances received by either of us will also be the separate property of the recipient. No interest in the separate property of one of us can be transferred to the other except in writing.

C. Separate debts

Chris will be responsible for all debts incurred by Chris or in the operation of or for the benefit of Chris's separate assets and Chris will indemnify, defend and hold Jamie harmless from any action to collect such debts from joint assets or Jamie's separate property, including paying any costs and attorney fees in connection with such an action.

Jamie will be responsible for all debts incurred by Jamie or in the operation of or for the benefit of Jamie's separate assets and Jamie will indemnify, defend and hold Chris harmless from any action to collect such debts from joint assets or Chris's separate property, including paying any costs and attorney fees in connection with such an action.

D. Shared earnings and assets

1. We agree to combine our efforts and earnings and share any assets accumulated through our individual or combined efforts. All earned income, that is, funds and assets acquired by the efforts of either or both of us together, will be owned as (joint tenants/tenants in common) and will be deposited to joint accounts to which we both have access and/or held in joint title.

2. We will have equal rights of management and control of joint funds, which can be used by either of us to acquire assets on behalf of both of us, for the personal expenses of either of us individually or both of us. Neither of us may use joint funds, or funds we have agreed to pool, for the benefit of one party's separate estate without written consent of the other, and any funds so used without written consent must be reimbursed to our joint account with __% interest.

3. The contribution of each of us will be deemed to be equal to the contribution of the other regardless of the actual amounts contributed.

E. Support. Other than the obligation to share our earnings, neither of us will be obligated to contribute to the support of the other during the relationship or after termination of this agreement.

F. Taxes. Each of us will report his or her own income on his or her own income tax returns. Taxes that are attributable to earned income, that this agreement requires to be pooled, will be a joint expense payable from our joint account. Taxes attributable to unearned income from separate sources will be the sole obligation of that person and payable from that person's separate income.

G. Division of property. Upon termination of this agreement, as defined in section 4 above, all liquid assets will be divided equally in kind and non-liquid assets will be divided by mutual agreement so that each receives equal value. If we cannot agree on the division of non-liquid assets, we will (insert here one of the ten ways to divide property from chapter 17K).

b. Adding support for a partner

One partner can agree to support the other, which is especially suitable where one is financially dependent on the other or has sacrificed a job or education in order to be together. Support for a child of the two of you is already defined by state law, but if one of you has a child by another relationship, you might want to provide for support of the child. In either case, you need to decide if support will continue after the agreement terminates, or after one partner dies, and for how long if at all.

To add support to the agreement above, just replace section E with the one below.

E. **Support** [Optional: Chris will use her best efforts to generate income sufficient to provide a mutually acceptable standard of living. Jamie will render services as companion, housekeeper and cook and assume responsibility for related household tasks.] Chris will provide all of Jamie's financial support at the same standard of living at which Chris supports herself, beginning on the date of this agreement and continuing until (time period after) termination of this agreement as defined in section 4 above. [Optional: If Chris dies, the support obligation will continue as an obligation of Chris's estate for (time period).] However, this support obligation will terminate absolutely and completely on the first to occur of either the death of (Chris/Jamie/Chris or Jamie) or the marriage or cohabitation of Jamie with a third person. Each party waives and disclaims any right to support from the other after the support obligation ends as defined above.

Variation to add child support

E. Support

1. Support for Jamie. [Optional: Chris will use her best efforts to generate income sufficient to provide a mutually acceptable standard of living. Jamie will render services as companion, housekeeper and cook and assume responsibility for related household tasks.] Chris will provide all of Jamie's financial support at the same standard of living as which Chris supports herself, beginning on the date of this agreement and continuing until (time period after) termination of this agreement as defined in section 4 above. [Optional: If Chris dies, the support obligation will continue as an obligation of Chris's estate for (time period).] How-

ever, this support obligation will terminate absolutely and completely on the first to occur of either the death of (Chris/Jamie/Chris or Jamie) or the marriage or cohabitation of Jamie with a third person. Each party waives and disclaims any right to support from the other after the support obligation ends as defined above.

2. Support of child of another relationship. Chris will provide for the ordinary living expenses, medical and dental care, and education for (name each child and state age), who is a/are child(ren) of Jamie and another person. This support obligation shall continue as to each child named until the child reaches the age of majority,

☐ notwithstanding the termination of this agreement for any reason.

☐ or until termination of the obligation to support Jamie as defined in section 7E(1), whichever comes first.

CHAPTER 9

Two required documents

In this chapter and the next we describe steps you *must* take to make sure your agreement is enforceable. These steps are to satisfy checks that were put in place by courts and lawmakers to help prevent abuses. The laws in this regard are intricate in some situations and vague in others. But don't worry; we've worked it all out for you and we're not even going to make you wade through a thicket of rules. Just follow our instructions and you'll be fine. It goes like this:

- ☐ Do full financial disclosure if you are tailoring your financial relationships
- ☐ Complete the two additional documents in this chapter
- ☐ Present the final agreement and Explanation to each other (chapter 10B)
- ☐ Observe the waiting period (chapter 10B)
- ☐ Have a little signing ceremony (chapter 10C)

It's all laid out for you here and in the next chapter. If you want to know why we've advised you to take these steps, read section C below.

A. Explanation of Agreement

This document should be prepared and presented to each party along with the final draft of the Couples Contract, at least seven days before it is signed.

This is a bit of bother, since you need to make sure that every significant feature of your agreement is explained in relatively simple terms and explained again in terms of what each party is giving up. Don't worry, we'll help you do it. Here's the template for your Explanation.

Title. Use the words, "Explanation of" followed by whatever title you gave your relationship agreement, then add "between (names)" if your title didn't already include those words.

Unmarried couples. In section C, you would replace "during our marriage" with "during the term of our agreement."

Explanation of Relationship Agreement
Between Chris Brown and Jamie Jones

We, Chris Brown and Jamie Jones, give this explanation to each other of the terms and basic effect of our relationship agreement and the rights and obligations that will be given up by each of us if we sign it.

A. **We hereby advise each other** to seek independent legal counsel in connection with the negotiation, drafting and signing of this relationship agreement before signing it.

B. General terms:

   1. The general terms of our relationship agreement and their basic effects are:

      a. To affirm our commitment to a lasting relationship based upon mutual respect, affection and friendship.

      b. To establish principles that will help us resolve personal issues, should any arise, that might threaten to undermine our relationship.

      c. To commit ourselves, in relations between us, to mutual openness, honesty and the highest standard of good-faith dealing in all matters, putting each other's interests foremost.

      d. To make our relationship agreement effective from (date of signing/date of our marriage) and to remain in effect indefinitely, or until we sign a written agreement to revoke or modify it.

      e. To govern our rights and obligations, wherever we might reside, according to California law, except as otherwise specified in this agreement.

      f. To waive our right to further disclosure beyond that which is attached to and described in this agreement.

      g. To each waive our right to be represented by independent counsel in the negotiation and preparation of this agreement.

      h. If ever any dispute should arise between us, or under this agreement, we will not take it to court, but instead we will go through mediation and, if one of us chooses not to mediate or if mediation fails, we will submit our dispute to binding arbitration.

2. By signing this agreement, we are each giving up the following:

a. The right to have this contract, or our mutual rights and duties, determined by the laws of any other state, in which we might someday reside.

b. The right to have further financial disclosure beyond that which was given or to claim that what was given was not sufficient.

c. The right to be represented by independent counsel in the negotiation, drafting or signing of this agreement. We both understand the wisdom of getting advice from independent counsel, and both had the funds to do so had we wished. We have both had the time and opportunity to ask for as much advice from lawyers or other professionals as we desire.

d. The right to go to court over any dispute that might arise between us or under this agreement, being required instead to resolve such disputes by mediation or binding arbitration, and the right to have a court choose a mediator for us.

e. The right to claim that consent was not given knowingly or voluntarily.

C. Financial terms, their basic effects, and rights given up:

☐ We agree that during our marriage, wherever we might reside, our financial affairs will be governed according to California law. We are each giving up the right to have our financial affairs governed by the law of some other state in which we might reside in the future.

☐ We agree that during our marriage, wherever we might reside, our financial affairs will be governed according to California law, except as follows:

A. ...

B. ...

This document was presented to Chris by Jamie , along with the final draft of our relationship agreement, on _____, 2005.

Date: _____   _____
                             Chris Brown

This document was presented to Jamie by Chris , along with the final draft of our relationship agreement, on _____, 2005.

Date: _____   _____
                             Jamie Jones

B. Waiver of counsel and receipt of Explanation

This document, illustrated on the next page, accomplishes two important purposes. It is a waiver of right to counsel and declaration that the Explanation and final draft of your agreement were received on a certain date. You'll need one of these documents for each party, to be signed at the same time you sign your Couples Contract. We illustrated only one document here, but the other party must sign one exactly like it, only with the names reversed.

C. But, why?

Some of the steps we ask you to take in this chapter and the next may seem mysterious until you dig into historical abuses and political overreaction and study the cases and statutes that resulted. Here are few words of explanation.

Premarital agreements. Because they were so often used for unprincipled purposes, legislators put up hoops that you must jump through in order to make an enforceable premarital (prenuptial) agreement. This explains the need for (1) full financial disclosure, and (2) the two additional required documents described in this chapter, where the parties must explain to each other in detail the basic effect of the agreement and what rights and benefits are being given up, and state in another document how they really, no kidding, definitely, honest, do not want to retain independent counsel for each party. Oh, well, it's just a little more paperwork.

Marital agreements. After you're married, you are supposed to look out for each other's best interests—that's the fiduciary relationship in action—so if you make an agreement where it looks like one spouse gained an advantage, a judge would presume that undue influence was exerted and refuse to enforce the agreement in that regard (though other parts can remain valid). This presumption can be rebutted, but the burden is on the spouse who gained the advantage. No problem; if you follow the same steps we use to protect the enforceability of a premarital agreement, it will be perfectly clear that the agreement was signed with full knowledge of its meaning and without undue influence.

Living together. There are few legal limits on agreements between unmarried adults, but because most such couples are in a close and trusting relationship, it is always possible for one to claim they were in a *confidential* relationship when the agreement was signed and that an unfair advantage was taken. So you, too, will take the extra steps we prescribe to make sure your agreement is not open to attack at some later date.

Protecting your agreement

No matter when you make your agreement or what's in it, here are the steps you'll take to make sure your agreement is enforceable and not open to attack. First, if there was any financial tailoring, you'll do a careful and thorough job on the financial disclosures (chapter 6F) and likewise on the Explanation of Agreement (section A above). Finally, at the time you sign your final agreement, you will also sign a waiver of counsel (section B above).

While all this is essential, it is still not enough, because nothing you can write down and sign is certain to convince a judge that there was no undue influence. This is because judges know that spouses and lovers trust each other and it is quite common for one to sign a document without reading it when asked by the other. So, you need to find some *external* way to demonstrate that a spouse or lover who gives up something understands completely what is being given up and is agreeing to do so without being influenced because he/she thinks it is fair.

Signing ceremony. The best way to protect your agreement is to have a signing ceremony where you videotape the two of you discussing the agreement in a way that shows that both of you understand the agreement, what is being given up, why it seems fair, and that you are each signing the agreement voluntarily without any influence being exerted by the other. You should have a reliable witness to this ceremony—a minister, accountant, lawyer, notary, or other professional would be good—who signs a notarized declaration as to what was said and done. How to do this, and how to make it a lovely event if you want to, is described more fully in chapter 10C.

Waiver of Right to Independent Counsel and Acknowledgment of Receipt of Explanation

I, Chris Brown, hereby declare that I am about to execute a relationship agreement with Jamie Jones. I will refer to us from now on by our first names.

A.   Our relationship agreement was prepared by ☐ Chris ☐ Jamie ☐ both of us working together.

B.   We presented each other with a final draft of our agreement on (date). At that time Jamie advised me, in writing, to seek independent counsel before negotiating, drafting or signing our agreement. On that same date, I received from Jamie a copy of the Explanation of Agreement, which I read and understood. I am fully informed of the terms and basic effect of the agreement, as well as the rights and obligations I am giving up by signing it. This was explained to me both verbally and in writing in English, and I am proficient in the English language.

C.   I have obtained as much advice, legal and otherwise, as I wish to receive regarding this agreement. I had sufficient funds available to me to retain counsel or other assistance had I wished to do so. I hereby expressly waive my right to be represented by independent legal counsel in the negotiation, drafting or signing of our relationship agreement.

D.   The agreement and this declaration were executed freely and voluntarily, without duress, fraud, or undue influence. I am over the age of 18 and have legal capacity to enter into an agreement.

I declare under penalty of perjury under the laws of the State of California that the foregoing is true

This declaration was executed on (date) at (place).

_____

Chris Brown

After you complete your agreement

A. Lawyer review?

Have you decided to have your agreement and other documents reviewed by a family law attorney? This was discussed in chapter 4C. Now that you have assembled your Couples Contract, Explanation of Agreement, and Waiver of Counsel documents, you are ready for a lawyer review if you want to do that. Take your documents and a copy of this book to your attorney, or call Couples Helpline and arrange to mail or fax us copies of your documents. Our entire staff is already supportive of this new kind of relationship agreement and completely familiar with it. Our experience has been that we can almost always make suggestions for improvements or ask about things you might not have thought of. If you want a lawyer (or any other expert) to review your agreement, we think it must be made clear to both of you that you're still looking for input and are open to making changes to get a better agreement.

If you are not having a lawyer review your documents, or if they have already been reviewed and are now in final form, it's time for the presentation.

B. Presentation and waiting period

Duplicate originals. You should make at least two copies of every document—one for each of you—and, possibly, a third set for your witness (section C below). While not necessary, you might want to print your relationship agreement on high-quality paper of heavier weight, perhaps even vellum, to give it the feel and appearance it deserves.

All copies should be crisp and clean as you will both sign them later as duplicate originals. This means that you will each end up with a signed original of each document: your relationship agreement with any attachments, the Explanation of Agreement, and the Waiver of Counsel. If you have a witness to the signing (section C below) you will also have a duplicate original of the Witness Declaration.

Presentation means only that at some convenient time and place in California, you hand each other the following documents in their final form:

- [ ] The Couples Contract in its final form
- [ ] If financial tailoring is involved, your two financial disclosures must be attached to the agreement as Schedules 1 and 2 (chapter 6F)
- [ ] Explanation of Agreement (chapter 9A)

Date and sign. At this time, you each date and sign the Explanation of Agreement. At the bottom of the relationship agreement, you should enter the date you exchange it, but do *not* sign it at this time.

Waiting period. After the presentation, you must wait *at least* seven days before you sign the agreement. This is to make it obvious that you each had time to consider the agreement in its final form, the attached financial disclosures, and the Explanation of Agreement. If either of your financial disclosures includes information that might lead a reasonable person to write away for a credit report or ask a professional to review business records or appraisals, you have to wait long enough that it will later appear obvious that a person would have had plenty of time to look into these matters it they wanted to—several weeks or more, depending on what is in the disclosures. Give yourselves plenty of time so you don't have to rush to sign documents before a wedding or any other planned event.

If one or the other of you requests changes to the agreement, prepare the modified agreement, then repeat this presentation step and start the waiting period again.

C. Signing your agreement and waiver

After the reasonable waiting period described above, you can both sit down together at a convenient time and place in California and sign duplicate originals of your Couples Contract and the Waiver of Counsel.

Signing ceremony. The best way to make sure your agreement was signed voluntarily with full knowledge of what was in it is to have a bit of a ceremony when you sign it. At a minimum, this means that you will sign in the presence of a reliable witness and make a video and/or audio recording of the two of you discussing what you're agreeing to before you each sign it. The purpose for this signing ceremony is to create *external* evidence that shows you both understood the agreement as well as any advantages that were being given up by signing it, and that signing the agreement was voluntary and without undue influence being exercised by anyone.

Make it an event? You might want to make this into a special occasion, which it truly is. You have accomplished something important together and by your signatures you are making a profound commitment to a lasting relationship. This can be a dress-up event with appetizers, champagne, flowers, candles, family and close friends, and someone to take photos for your album. Let your heart be your guide.

Privacy. To keep your financial affairs to yourselves, you might want to have a private meeting with just you two and the witness where you go over those details, then emerge and read to each other the nicer commitment parts of your agreement, then you and the witness sign documents. Good show.

Skip it? Do not skip the signing ceremony if your agreement adds variations from chapter 6 or 7, or if you are already married or registered domestic partners when you sign. If you are not already married or registered, and you are only doing the basic agreement in chapter 5, you can, if you wish, simply sign your agreement without the witness, taping or other ceremony and move on to section D below.

How to do it. Of the three ways to preserve evidence that the signers were fully aware and voluntary, the declaration of a witness has highest priority because a signed and notarized document can be kept indefinitely for future use. A video recording would be the most convincing evidence, but you might some day face the problem of finding antique equipment to view whatever you created. Imagine having to go out today to find an 8-millimeter film projector or an 8-inch floppy disk drive or an eight-track tape player. Don't let that stop you from making the video or audio tape, but be sure to get the notarized declaration of a witness above all else.

Any adult can be a witness, but you should choose a mature person who is not a relative of either party. It would be icing on the cake if your witness is someone in a profession or trade that implies reliability—a minister, attorney, accountant, etc.

What to say. At the very least, before signing documents, each of you needs to say enough out loud to show the witness—and anyone who watches your video or listens to your audio tape—that you know what the agreement means, what rights you are giving up when you sign it, that you are not being influenced by the other party or anyone else, and that you are signing the agreement voluntarily because you want to and think it is right and fair to do so. Below is a sample script for how this could go. The other party should follow the same script but would, of course, change the names. This script is only a guide: you can use your own words, no need to be formal. If you prefer, you could make a checklist of topics covered in the agreement, and each party could say something about what they understand it to mean or why they want to put it in the agreement. Above all, relax. Don't be worried you'll make a mistake in your ceremony. You are doing something new to show your commitment to each other, and you want to share this with your witness.

Signing and notarization. When you have each spoken your piece, you each sign two copies of your relationship agreement and Waiver of Counsel.

Signing Ceremony Script
for Chris Brown

Today, with a full heart and open mind, I am entering into a relationship agreement with Jamie Jones.

[Optional]

I am making this agreement in order to commit myself to a long and lasting relationship based on mutual respect, affection and friendship.

I am committing myself to the highest standard of good faith, openness and honesty in all matters between Jamie and me.

In this agreement, we establish principles and guidelines that can help us resolve personal issues, if any should ever arise, that might threaten to undermine our mutual regard.

[Add any other language you feel suitable to the agreement or the occasion]

I understand that by signing this agreement, I am giving up certain rights.

A.   I am giving up the right to be represented by independent counsel in the negotiation and drafting of our agreement. I am aware that I have the right to have independent counsel represent me, and I had enough time, opportunity and funds available to get as much advice or assistance as I wanted, but, nonetheless, I have chosen not to be represented.

B.   We do not believe that any serious disagreement will ever come between us that we won't be able to resolve, but we also want to make sure our relationship never ends up in court, so we are agreeing that if we ever do have a disagreement that we can't resolve even with help, we are both giving up the right to take our family problem to court. Instead we will use mediation and, if that fails, we will get a final decision through binding arbitration.

[Faith-based option] We have agreed that any conciliator, mediator or arbitrator we use will be a member of (state organization or faith), which means we are giving up the right to choose otherwise qualified professionals who are not members of (organization or faith).

C. I am completely satisfied with the financial disclosure that Jamie gave me and feel that I know all that I want or need to know about our present financial facts. I am giving up the right to ask for any more disclosure before I sign, or to claim that the disclosure I received was not sufficient. We'll continue to be open with each other about our finances in the future, but at this moment I'm satisfied that I know enough to sign this agreement intelligently.

D. Except as modified by our agreement, we are agreeing to have the rights and duties of our relationship governed according to the laws of California, no matter where we might live in the future, which means I am giving up the right to have my rights governed by the laws of another state we might move to.

    1.   [Financial or faith-based explanations added to the basic agreement, taken from the Explanation language given in each chapter]

    2. ...

E. I understand the terms of this agreement and what I am giving up by signing it. I am not being influenced to sign it by anyone or by any factor other than my own good judgment. I am signing because I think it is fair and in my own best interest to do so and I am giving up the right to claim otherwise in the future. In short, I am signing this agreement freely and voluntarily because I want to.

Initial each page. While not required, it is good practice for each party to initial the lower left corner or lower right margin of each page of the agreement and attachments before signing.

Witness. When you have both signed, the witness signs two copies (duplicate originals) of the Witness Declaration, which is illustrated on the next page. After this, more audio or video taping is optional. You should have the signatures of both parties and the witness notarized on all documents, so you can either arrange to have a notary present at the signing ceremony or soon after the ceremony go to a notary's office with your witness and sign the documents there. It is best to actually sign in front of the notary, but it is also possible to sign a second time before the notary or to sign an additional document that the notary will provide acknowledging that the signature on the document is yours.

More witnesses? You can use more than one witness, if you want to; just make a separate Declaration for each of them. If you are doing a faith-based agreement, some religions have their own requirements about the number of witnesses and their qualifications. You can add a statement of their qualifications to paragraph 1, if you like. Ask your clergyperson or religious advisor about this if you want your agreement to be binding under religious law as well as state law.

Guest signatures. This is optional, but if you are having family and friends at your signing, you can invite them to share the occasion by signing a declaration recording their participation. Right after the formal Witness Declaration, we've put an example of a Declaration to Bear Witness so you can see what one might look like; customize it any way you like, as its main purpose isn't legal but to recognize the fact that your community is part of your relationship, too. You could make copies of this group declaration after the ceremony and give one to each of your witnesses. Don't forget, your "official" witness(es) must sign and notarize the Witness Declaration form above.

Declaration of Witness to Signing
of Chris and Jamie's Relationship Agreement

I, the undersigned, declare as follows:

1. I am (name), (age) years old, and a (occupation) in (city, state).

2. I am not related to Chris Brown or Jamie Jones.

3. On (date), at approximately (time), I was personally present at (location, city, state) when Chris Brown and Jamie Jones signed their relationship agreement. I was given a copy of the documents they signed, and I was in a position to hear clearly every word spoken and was paying close attention as they each discussed the contents of their agreement.

4. I clearly heard Chris Brown describe in her own words the terms of the agreement and what she was giving up by signing it. She stated that she understood every word of it and was signing of her own free will, in full understanding of the meaning of the terms, and without being influenced by anyone was signing because she thought it was fair and reasonable and in her own best interest to do so.

5. I clearly heard Jamie Jones describe in his own words the terms of the agreement and what he was giving up by signing it. He stated that he understood every word of it and was signing of his own free will, in full understanding of the meaning of the terms, and without being influenced by anyone was signing because he thought it was fair and reasonable and in his own best interest to do so.

6. It appeared to me, and according to my own best judgment, that both parties understood the meaning of their agreement and what they were gaining and giving up by signing it, and that they were each signing it freely, voluntarily and without undue influence because they thought it was fair and reasonable and in their own best interest to do so.

I declare under penalty of perjury under the laws of the State of California that the foregoing is true and correct.

Dated: _____   _____
                                         (signature of witness)

Declaration to Bear Witness to Signing
of Chris and Jamie's Relationship Agreement

We, the undersigned, solemnly declare:

On (date), at (city, state), we were present to bear witness when Chris Brown and Jamie Jones signed their relationship agreement.

By their agreement, Chris and Jamie committed themselves to a lasting relationship, and promised never to take any dispute between them to court. Chris and Jamie explained to us why they were making this commitment, and that they understood the legal meaning of their agreement and any rights they were giving up. They signed it freely and voluntarily.

As their friends, family, and witnesses, we pledge to support Chris and Jamie in helping them keep the commitments they made to each other today. We specifically promise to help them lovingly and respectfully resolve any issues that might arise between them, and to encourage them to use the methods they agreed today to use in case they encounter matters they cannot resolve by themselves. We will encourage them to live together in a relationship of trust, mutual respect, affection and friendship.

In witness of these promises, we sign this declaration on (date), at (city, state).

_____   _____

_____   _____

_____   _____

_____   _____

_____   _____

_____   _____

Duplicate originals. You each get a signed duplicate original of all documents, which you should put in a safe place (section D below). Make two or more copies of each document that you can keep around for reference, but you should each put your copies of the originals in a very safe place.

D. Store documents safely

Your agreement won't mean much if you can't find it later when you want it. "Later" might mean ten or thirty years in the future. This is one of those important documents that you never want to lose. So, first, you should each make two extra copies of your signed originals. Then, put each set of documents in a 9 x 12 envelope. Keep one set at home where it is easy to get at if you want to review it, and put the signed originals in a very safe place.

The ideal place would be a safe deposit box, but that costs a monthly fee forever. Next safest would be a fireproof safe, filing cabinet or document box kept at home; and, finally, any other safe and secure place at home. The second set of copies should be put somewhere else, like the home of a relative or friend, just in case your originals are lost or destroyed by accident.

E. Follow through

After you sign your agreement, you both need to do anything you agreed to do and avoid doing anything not consistent with your agreement. You don't want your agreement to say one thing and your actions later to say something else. This is especially important if you are trying to keep income and debts separate.

Transfers. If your agreement calls for you to change separate property into community property or vice-versa, you will need to actually make the transfers as soon as possible after the agreement becomes effective. If you are not yet married, this means right after your wedding. If you are already married, or don't plan to, it means right after you sign. If you are transferring real estate, you will need an Interspousal Transfer Deed or a Quitclaim Deed, where the owner(s) of property transfer the deed into the name(s) as agreed. Interspousal transfers are not taxable events. You can get these forms from stationery stores or on the Internet, or you can call Couples Helpline and ask them to make up the necessary deeds for you.

Set up accounts. In many situations, you will need to set up both separate and joint accounts for holding funds, and perhaps you will want both joint and separate credit card accounts, too. If you are trying to protect your separate income from your spouse's debts, you will want to close all joint credit card accounts.

Keep separate things separate. If either of you owns separate assets or separate income during marriage, it is essential that you keep that property under separate title and in separate accounts.

- Do not mix community funds with separate funds (defined in chapter 12) in any account, no matter how temporary or how convenient it might seem.
- When applying for joint credit, do not use separate property or a spouse's separate income as a basis.
- When applying for separate credit, make sure the application is in one name only and do not list community assets or income as a basis for the loan.

Wills, estate planning. After you complete your agreement, you might want to look into estate planning documents, such as wills, living trusts, powers of attorney for health care and financial management in case of disability, and so on. Nolo has several fine books and software products to help you with this. Look for them in your local public library or on-line at www.nolo.com.

F.   Periodic reviews

Times change, laws change, your circumstances can change and your relationship can change, too. It only makes sense to take your agreement out every few years and see if it still makes sense in the light of the new you. See if you still want exactly what it says, or if maybe you'd like to change anything. If your agreement has any clauses that expire on a certain date or condition, then it would be smart to take a look at the agreement some time before that date or condition is about to happen so you can see if any action needs to be taken. When anything significant happens—children, change in employment, moving to another state, a big raise—this would be a good time to look back over your agreement. Sit down and talk to each other about the agreement in light of changed circumstances, just like you did when you first made your agreement.

If you agree to change anything about your agreement, you'll need to modify your agreement in writing.

G. How to modify your agreement

Your agreement can only be modified in writing, and you will go through exactly the same steps that you did to make your Couples Contract. This means doing disclosure (chapter 6F), the Explanation of Agreement (chapter 9A), presentation and waiting period (chapter 10B), and signing before a witness (chapter 10C). One big difference is that your modification agreement will probably be a lot easier to write, as you only have to write those clauses that are being changed.

A modification agreement would look something like the example that starts on the next page.

1. Circumstances. Briefly summarize whatever it is that has changed that has caused you to want to modify your agreement. It might be some actual factual difference or just that after living together for some time you now have different goals or ideas about how you want to live.

2. Modification. Modification can mean quite a range of possible changes to your original agreement. As illustrated in the example clauses, you can:

- revoke whole clauses (example 2A below)
- replace specific clauses with new wording (example 2B)
- rephrase a specific clause (example 2C)
- add new agreements (example 2D)

or any combination of these. Use whatever it takes to get the effect you want. Just make sure whatever language you add is perfectly clear, consistent with the rest of your agreement (otherwise make more changes), and not subject to being interpreted in more than one way. See chapter 4D(2) on writing clauses.

Modification of Relationship Agreement

On (date), we, Chris and Jamie, entered into a relationship agreement, a copy of which is attached and incorporated by reference. Our circumstances and goals have changed, so that now we wish to make the specific changes set forth below. In all other regards, we intend for our original agreement to continue in full force and effect.

1. Circumstances

The circumstances that have caused us to want to modify our agreement are (describe briefly, just the high points).

2. Modification

A. We agree to revoke (clause or section numbers to be revoked)

B. We agree to change (clause or section number) of our original agreement to read as follows: (specify)

C. We agree to change (clause or section number) of our original agreement so that (describe the modification, the agreement you now wish to make regarding this clause)

D. We agree to change our original agreement by adding the following new agreements: (specify)

3. Construction

If there should be any conflict or inconsistency between the original agreement and this modification, the provisions and intentions of the modification should control in all respects.

4. Representation and drafting

☐ Chris and Jamie drafted this modification together, jointly.

☐ This modification was primarily drafted by ☐ Chris ☐ Jamie

I, Chris, understand that I have the right to be represented by an independent lawyer in the negotiation and preparation of this modification and I have sufficient

5. Disclosures. If you are not changing any financial relationships, you can get away with using the simple waiver of disclosure illustrated at section 8 in the basic agreement (chapter 5). However, you will want to do the full disclosure shown here if any financial changes are being made in your modification.

H. Portability
—taking your agreement to other states

If you move to another state, your agreement will be interpreted by the courts in that state according to their laws. Of course, your agreement has clause 11D stating that it is to be interpreted according to California law, and clause 10B says that any dispute that you cannot settle will be decided by a California family law attorney acting as arbitrator. Between these two clauses, there's a pretty good chance your document will hold up just as you intended when you signed it. However, there are still uncertainties as to what might happen if one of the spouses decides to attack the agreement, or whether some feature of it runs counter to your new state's public policy laws.

So, if you move to another state, be sure to have your agreement reviewed by an experienced family law attorney in your new state. It's the only safe thing to do.

funds to retain a lawyer for this purpose if I wanted to. Nonetheless, I choose not to be represented. I understand the terms of this agreement and freely and voluntarily choose to sign it without recourse to counsel.

I, Jamie, understand that I have the right to be represented by an independent lawyer in the negotiation and preparation of this agreement and I have sufficient funds to retain a lawyer for this purpose if I wanted to. Nonetheless, I choose not to be represented. I understand the terms of this agreement and freely and voluntarily choose to sign it without recourse to counsel.

5. Disclosures

Each of us has made a full, fair and reasonable disclosure to the other of annual income, all assets owned and all obligations owed on the date such information was presented.

A list of our community income, assets and obligations is set forth in Schedule 1, which is attached to and made part of this agreement.

[Optional]
Attached to Schedule 1 is/are the following additional document(s:)
☐ our joint federal and/or state tax return for years (_years_) ☐ other (_specify_).

A list of Chris's separate income, assets and obligations is set forth in Schedule 2, which is attached to and made part of this agreement.

[Optional]
Attached to Schedule 2 is/are the following additional document(s:)
☐ Chris's separate federal and/or state tax return for years (_years_) ☐ the following appraisals: (name them) ☐ credit report ☐ other (_specify_).

A list of Jamie's income, assets owned and obligations owed by Jamie is set forth in Schedule 3, which is attached to and made part of this agreement.

[Optional]
Attached to Schedule 3 is/are the following additional document(s:)
☐ Jamie's separate federal and/or state tax return for years (_years_) ☐ the following appraisals: (name them) ☐ credit report ☐ other (_specify_).]

We each understand that values set forth in Schedules 1, 2 and 3 are approximate values on the date presented, estimated to the best of our ability, but not necessarily exact.

I, Chris, received a copy of Schedules 1 and 3 [and attached documents named above] on (__date__), and reviewed that information before signing this agreement. I consider this information to be sufficient and waive the right to be given further information.

I, Jamie, received a copy of Schedules 1 and 2 [and attached documents named above] on (__date__), and reviewed that information before signing this agreement. I consider this information to be sufficient and waive the right to be given further information.

Signatures

We have each read this agreement carefully and are signing it freely, voluntarily, and with full understanding of its meaning after having obtained all the advice we each, individually, feel is appropriate.

This agreement was delivered to Chris by Jamie on (__date__)

Dated: _____   _____
                                            Chris Brown

This agreement was delivered to Jamie by Chris on (__date__)

Dated: _____   _____
                                            Jamie Jones

What happens when you say "I do" —general rules

A. Does domestic partnership = marriage?

Marriage has been with us for thousands of years, but domestic partnerships were created only in 2000, primarily for same-sex couples who cannot marry, and, as an afterthought, for retirement-aged couples who don't want to compromise Social Security and other benefits. As of January 1, 2005, registered domestic partners acquired *almost* all the "rights, protections, and benefits, and shall be subject to the same responsibilities, obligations, and duties"[1] that married people derive from California law. The stated purpose for doing this is to

> ". . . move closer to fulfilling the promises of inalienable rights, liberty, and equality contained in . . . the California Constitution by providing all caring and committed couples, regardless of their gender or sexual orientation, the opportunity to obtain essential rights, protections, and benefits and to assume corresponding responsibilities, obligations, and duties and to further the state's interests in promoting stable and lasting family relationships . . . ."[2]

No effect on federal law. Because domestic partnership is the creature of state law, it has no effect whatever on rights, benefits, duties or protections that flow from federal laws, which are considerable: such things as Social Security, tax laws, military benefits, immigration, Medicare, bankruptcy, and innumerable other areas where federal law impacts people's lives.

However, because marriage and domestic partnership are so nearly the same in most regards, as you will see below, it is easier to discuss them together in this chapter and point out differences wherever they occur. So, except where we clearly say otherwise, discussions in this chapter apply to both married couples and registered partners.

Note to domestic partners. Because domestic partnership acquires its rules almost entirely by reference to existing marriage laws that use terms like *spouse, marriage, marital, husband, wife,* and so on, without adaptation to suit domestic partners, we also use similar terms and ask domestic partners to read with the understanding that everything applies to them, too, unless clearly stated otherwise.

---

[1] Family Code § 297.5(a)
[2] Section 1(a) of the California Domestic Partner Rights and Responsibilities Act of 2003

B. The contract that few people read

Most prospective spouses and domestic partners are not aware that their union is, at its core, a *contract*—indeed, California law defines marriage as a "civil contract."[3] The same applies to domestic partnership. When you enter into marriage or domestic partnership, you are agreeing to a large set of rights and duties, but few people read the terms because the provisions are not handed to you in writing. In what other legal arena are contracting parties so much in the dark? Where else are such imposing responsibilities undertaken by oral agreement? There are more rights and more bargaining power in a contract made with a door-to-door salesperson. Prior to getting hitched, if all men and women were required to first read the "contract" and consider their rights and obligations, it would be interesting to see how many would still be willing to say "I do" without some thought, negotiation and planning.

In this part of the book, we discuss what happens when you marry without any written agreement. But, like any other contract, this one can be modified by the parties, and there are big advantages to doing so (chapter 2). In Part Two, we discussed how to make a written agreement that will tailor your union to suit your own preferences and, more important, give yourselves some important advantages.

C. Who can do it

1. Who can get married

California law defines marriage as a civil contract between a man and a woman.[4] In 2004, there were some same-sex marriages in California, but before the year was over, the California Supreme Court ordered the San Francisco County Clerk's office that issued the licenses to refund all license fees and notify the couples that their marriages were void. Still, the Supreme Court probably won't decide for some years whether the California Constitution guarantees the right to marry to same-sex couples. This is an area that you can expect to be in constant flux for the foreseeable future.

Age. California sets 18 as the minimum age for marriage. Even if emancipated, people below 18 need the consent of a parent or guardian *and* a Superior Court judge, who may, and probably will, require marriage counseling before giving consent.[5]

---

[3] Family Code § 300   [4] *Ibid*   [5] Family Code § 301

Family relationship. In California, in-laws and cousins, even first cousins, can marry. Only the following are prohibited: Marriages between parents and children, ancestors and descendants of every degree [this means grandparents and grandchildren, etc.], and between brothers and sisters of the half as well as the whole blood, and between uncles and nieces, or aunts and nephews.[6]

Mental capacity. Insane and severely mentally retarded people are not competent to enter into a contract and thus can't marry. Of course, it is difficult to tell when a person is insane, and courts have held that a person experiencing a lucid interval between periods of insanity can enter into a marriage contract. Certainly the fact that a person has been mentally ill in the past is not a bar to marriage.

Sobriety. A person who is obviously under the influence of a drugs or alcohol will not be issued a marriage license. There are no blood alcohol tests administered; the county clerk has discretion to decide whether a person is drunk or sober.[7]

Physical capacity. The old notion that marriage is a license to have sexual relations aimed at producing children is still with us in law as it is in religion. In theory, each party to a marriage must at least have the physical ability to have intercourse, even though the woman is past childbearing age. A marriage where a person can't have intercourse can be voided (annulled) unless that fact has been completely disclosed and understood by the other person prior to marriage. Frankly, we can't guess how this would work out as a ground for annulling a domestic partnership, so either get a divorce (which is relatively easy) or get an attorney.

Prior marriage still valid. You can be married to only one person at a time. If either party to a marriage was married to someone else when the marriage ceremony was performed, the subsequent marriage is void. This is true *even if neither spouse knew the prior marriage was still valid*. However, if you had reason to think your spouse was dead at the time you remarried, you can choose whether or not to get an annulment if it later turns out your first spouse is still alive.

Married people often file papers to get a divorce or an annulment and think this means they can remarry. Not true—you must wait until the court issues its judgment. California recognizes any divorce or annulment legally obtained in any other state. Divorces from outside of the U.S. will be recognized only if one of the spouses was a resident of the foreign country at the time. If both husband and wife were residents somewhere else at the time, the foreign divorce will *not* be valid in California.[8] If only one spouse gets the foreign divorce, it will probably not stand up if challenged by the

---

[6] Family Code § 2200   [7] Family Code § 352   [8] Family Code § 2091

other spouse. If, however, both spouses act as if the divorce is valid, many courts will prevent them from later contesting the divorce. In some situations, foreign divorces will be recognized to the extent that they end the marriage, but will not be recognized for purposes of child custody, visitation, support or property division. Obviously this is a tricky area of the law and it would be wise to see a lawyer if you have questions.

2. Who can register as domestic partners[9]

Domestic partnership is available only to same-sex couples of any age, or opposite-sex couples where at least one of the partners is at least 62 and also eligible for Social Security old age or disability benefits.

Common residence. The partners must share a common residence. Presumably, this means that they live together, but it is not necessary that the residence be held in both names and it is okay if one or both has additional residences, and it is okay if one leaves the common residence so long as he/she intends to return.

Age. The partners must be at least 18 years of age.

Legally available. Neither partner can be married or in domestic partnership with someone else at the time of registration.

Not too closely related. Domestic partnerships are not allowed between parents and children, ancestors and descendants of every degree [this means grandparents and grandchildren, etc.], or between brothers and sisters of the half as well as the whole blood, or between uncles and nieces, or aunts and nephews.

Competent. Partners must be capable of consent, meaning that severely retarded or insane people are disqualified.

D. How you do it

1. Registering as domestic partners

A domestic partnership is established in California when both persons file a Declaration of Domestic Partnership with the California Secretary of State who should then return a copy to you so you know it was filed. No ceremony or solemnization is required, but partners are free to put on any sort of ceremony they please. These forms are available on-line at www.ss.ca.gov/dpregistry.

---

[9] Family Code § 297 et. seq. (statutes defining registered domestic partnership)

Putative partners. If, for some reason, a couple thought they were registered but were not, or if for some technical reason the partnership was not valid, then the same rules would apply as are discussed in subsection 4 below for putative spouses. If this happens to you, you'll want to consult a family law attorney such as the ones at Divorce Helpline, (800) 359-7004.

2. Getting married

Marriage starts with the issuance of a marriage license followed by solemnization by an authorized person such as a cleric or judge.

Marriage licenses. In California, there are two kinds of marriage license—regular and confidential. To get a regular marriage license, both parties must show up at the county clerk's office and buy a license before marrying. It costs about $40. Both people must state their names, ages and places of residence. The clerk is legally prohibited from asking about race, but he or she can inquire into any of the other requirements discussed above. If either person is under 18, the clerk must also file parental and Superior Court consent forms. The marriage license, when issued, is good for 90 days.

Ceremony and certificate of registry. You must participate in a formal ceremony to become married.

> No particular form for the ceremony of marriage is required, but the parties must declare, in the presence of the person solemnizing the marriage, that they take each other as husband and wife.[10]

A marriage can be solemnized (this is the term used by the Code) by any judge or retired judge, commissioner or retired commissioner or assistant commissioner of a court of record or justice court, a U.S. magistrate or a legislator or member of Congress, or by any priest, minister or rabbi (over 18) of any religion.[11] "Any religion" means just that—a minister of the Universal Life Church, or for that matter the United Evangelical Society of Polar Bear Worshippers, is just as qualified to marry you as the Pope. The person marrying you must fill out a form called the Certificate of Registry of Marriage which will be given to you by the county clerk when you get your marriage license. This form, and a completed copy of the marriage license, must be filed by returning it to the Clerk within thirty days after the marriage ceremony.

---

[10] Family Code § 420   [11] Family Code § 400

Witnesses. California requires one witness to a marriage other than the spouses and the person conducting the ceremony.

3. Confidential marriages

The confidential marriage was created long ago to allow people living in "sin" to get legally married without publicly admitting (by applying for a marriage license) that they weren't married all along. For most people, living together without being married is no longer the shameful thing that it once was, but the law is still with us. The main advantage to a confidential marriage is that you get to keep it quiet—it's not a public record. The County Clerk can authorize certain notaries to issue confidential marriage licenses without requiring the couple to go to the courthouse—many wedding chapels employ a notary who can do this, saving you a little driving.

An unmarried man and an unmarried woman, who have been living together as husband and wife (no specified amount of time is required), neither of whom is under the age of 18, can marry without getting the regular license.[12]

Here's how you do it:

- Both parties appear before the county clerk to obtain a confidential marriage license. You pay a fee, about $40, for the license and other papers you'll need to complete the marriage.
- Get married in the county where the license was issued within 90 days.
- Deliver the license to the person who is marrying you—a judge, priest, rabbi or county clerk; anyone entitled by law to solemnize marriages (see discussion of Ceremony above).
- The person who performs the marriage must return the certificate of confidential marriage to the county clerk, typically by mail, within 30 days after the ceremony.
- The person who performs the marriage must give you a copy of the certificate and give you an application for a certified copy of your certificate.
- Fill out the application, send it to the county clerk and receive back a certified copy of your marriage certificate.

---

[12] Family Code § 500

4. "I *thought* I was married!" —the putative spouse

When a marriage is invalid because some legal requirement has not been met, an *innocent* partner may nevertheless be entitled to the protections of the community property system under what is known as the *putative marriage* doctrine.[13] However, a partner may only be declared a "putative spouse" if he or she had a good faith and objectively reasonable belief that the marriage was *legally* valid. This means you must *really* think you are married.

> ### Example
> George and Barbara got married in 1960. They had a marriage license and a small ceremony in Santa Barbara. George had been married for a few months when he was a teenager, but he never bothered to get a divorce—he just forgot about it. Barbara didn't know about this. Twenty-four years later, in 1994, George died of a heart attack and Hillary showed up to claim George's estate. Since Barbara and George were not legally married—because George had never divorced Hillary—his subsequent marriage was not valid. During all those years of supposed marriage, Barbara was not legally a wife and she is in danger of losing all right to George's estate. However, if she can show that she is entitled to putative spouse status, all property acquired by George and Barbara during their putative marriage will be divided in the same way property is divided at the end of a valid marriage.

If you find yourself in a putative spouse situation, you need to contact a family law attorney in your area to ensure that your rights are protected. It is important to understand the rights of a lawfully married spouse, so read on; the information in this book will help you to better ascertain your rights as a putative spouse.

E. Unions created in other states or countries

1. Out-of-state and foreign marriages

In general, all marriages entered into outside of California that were valid under the laws of the state or country where they were made are valid in California.[14] Under this law, even a marriage entered into with the intent to circumvent California laws will be treated as good here, if it was valid where created.

There is one exception to this rule: marriages performed elsewhere that would be odious in California aren't recognized here. We don't know exactly what "odious"

---

[13] *Marriage of Vryonis* (1988) 202 CA3d 712   [14] Family Code § 308

means, but a woman can't have more than one husband, a man can't have more than one wife and a father can't marry his daughter. Same-sex marriages fall into this category too. Although Canada and Massachusetts have legalized same-sex marriages, those marriages would not be recognized in California, as California limits marriage to a man and a woman marrying each other. Of course, we expect this to be constitutionally challenged, and may ultimately be decided by the US Supreme Court. Stay tuned.

2. Common law marriages—What are they? Are they legal?

In eleven states and the District of Columbia, if you live with a person for a period of time and tell people you are married, you automatically become legally married, even though you never got a marriage license or went through a ceremony. This is called a "common law" marriage.

At press time, common law marriages are permitted in the following states:

Alabama	Kansas	Rhode Island
Colorado	Montana	South Carolina
District of Columbia	Oklahoma	Texas
Iowa	Pennsylvania	Utah

In all other states, including California, there is *no such thing* as a common law marriage. Regardless of how long you live together, or what you intend, the law will *not* recognize your relationship as a common law marriage. But if you formed a valid common law marriage in a state that recognized them at that time, and later you moved to California, you are legally married in California.

Common law marriage is more than just living together. Even in states recognizing common law marriage, living together does not automatically result in marriage. To have a common law marriage, both parties must *intend* to be married.

Conduct showing an intent to be married usually includes using the same last name, holding yourself out to the community as married and filing joint tax returns. The length of time people live together is not in itself normally important, but may be considered insofar as it shows the intent of the parties. Once a common law marriage exists, the marriage can be legally ended only by divorce, annulment or death.

Whether or not you are legally married to your partner becomes an issue when you break up—do you divorce or just split up? Or when one partner dies—who inherits what? Or if a medical emergency should occur—who can authorize medical treatment? It also becomes an issue whenever you deal with government programs, such as Social Security, welfare, and so on.

If you were living with someone in another state, you might wonder if you formed a legal common law marriage. To find out for sure, you will need to do some legal research into the laws of the state you came from. Several states have stopped allowing new common law marriages in the last few years, so it's possible a couple could have a legal common law marriage in a state that is no longer on the list above. Whether you are legally married would depend on what the law of that state was at the time you lived there as husband and wife. You could call a family law attorney from the state where you believe you formed a common law marriage, or you can save some bucks and do the research yourself. Any large county law library or law school library will have laws from all states, although finding the date a state stopped allowing common law marriage might be tricky.

Common law marriage states have no official records of common law marriages (how could they?) but at least one, Texas, permits a couple to file a certificate of common law marriage at the county clerk's office.

Examples

Abigail and Amos started living together in San Jose in 1957. They are still together, never participated in a marriage ceremony and never moved out of California. Are they married? No. They cannot create a common law marriage in California.

Wanda and Walter moved in together in Colorado in 1965 intending to form a common law marriage and have been living together ever since. In 1971 they moved to Los Angeles. Are they married? Yes. California recognizes the marriage as valid, because Colorado permits common law marriages and the marriage took place in Colorado before they moved to California.

If one of you believes that a marriage exists and the other doesn't and you are unable to work it out, you might have to see a lawyer. But remember, anyone can get a divorce in California by simply filing a few papers and, in some situations, making an appearance down at the local courthouse, so it would only make sense to insist that a marriage exists and go through a divorce just to set the record straight and settle any unresolved issues of property, support, or parenting of minor children of the couple.

F. Names

In California, people can use whatever name they like so long as they do not intend to defraud anyone. So, married people are free to keep their own names, use their spouse's or partner's name, hyphenate their names, or choose a completely new name. The key to changing a name is to use the new name consistently. Changing a name by consistent use is called the usage method of name change and is perfectly legal.[15] If you feel the need to have your name(s) changed legally in court, you'll want Nolo's book, *How to Change Your Name in California.*

G. Taxes

Married couples. Under federal and California law filing a joint tax return is permissible, but not required, for married taxpayers. You and your spouse should crunch the numbers and decide how you can save the most money. Consider seeing a tax accountant for expert advice.[16]

Domestic partners. Here is one significant difference between being married and being domestic partners. Under California law, you must file California tax returns in the same manner as you do federal tax returns,[17] and federal law does not recognize domestic partnerships. This means you cannot file a joint return but you must file both state and federal returns either as a single person or Head of Household if you have a qualifying dependent. Moreover, for state tax purposes, earned income cannot be treated as community property but must be claimed entirely by the person who received it.

If you have a registered domestic partnership and have income other than wages and salary, or have deductions you share, such as those connected with a house you own together, see a CPA who specializes in domestic partnerships. You may have some options available to you, such as filing a K-1 partnership return in order to share your tax obligations fairly and minimize the amount of taxes you pay. We expect laws on this to be in flux for some time to come, so it's important you get the most up-to-date help and information every year.

---

[15] Code of Civil Procedure § 1279.5
[16] Internal Revenue Code § 6013
[17] Family Code § 297.5(g)

H. Duty to support

Spouses and domestic partners have a duty to care for and support one another according to the couple's accustomed standard of living. This includes the obligation to pay your spouse's debts for common necessities of life, discussed in chapter 13, as well as the obligation to pay spousal support after the marriage is over, if one spouse is dependent or in need. This obligation is so strong that California law severely restricts a couple's ability to make an agreement before the marriage to change it in any way, and makes it nearly impossible to change during the marriage or while registered. Spouses don't have to ask for it after they split up, but this is one of the aspects of marriage or domestic partnership a couple has the least freedom to change.

I. Medical emergencies and hospitalization —Who can order care? Who can visit?

Every mentally competent adult has the right to make his/her own health care decisions. You can request or refuse treatment, even though your family or doctors disagree about what's best. For example, you have every right to choose acupuncture or naturopathy over surgery and prescription drugs. People with a terminal illness can decide how much life-prolonging medical care they wish to receive. So long as you are able to think clearly and communicate your wishes, there are few legal problems: the patient's choice prevails.

However, sometimes critical decisions must be made when you are not able to participate meaningfully in the decision making—for example, if you were unconscious or no longer able to think clearly or communicate. In these situations, the law provides a specific order of rights in decision making: first, your own written instructions if they exist and can be located; next a spouse; finally, your closest blood relatives. As we all know, people sometimes become estranged from relatives, or you might love them but still have a higher degree of closeness or trust with someone who is not a relative. And, we've all heard of cases where the separated spouse, family and friends are at odds over what should be done. The way to avoid confusion and conflict when minutes are precious is to sign one simple but vitally important document called an Advance Health Care Directive. It has two parts:

(1) A Power of Attorney for Health Care, which allows you to name one or
more people who can make health care decisions if you are not able to,
including the decision to withhold or withdraw life-prolonging procedures.

(2) Instructions for Health Care, which states in advance your wishes regarding how you want to be cared for if you are not able to make decisions yourself, including whether to use life-prolonging procedures.

This form is on the CD that comes with this book.

There's one more step you should take to avoid confusion and conflict: after you finish those documents, sit down with your spouse, relatives, and closest friends and show them the documents, give them a copy, and discuss your ideas for how you'd like to be treated if anything happens. This way, everyone will know what you wanted, whether the document can be found or not.

Visiting. The right to visit a patient in the hospital is another right that comes along with marriage. As hurtful as it might be, if you're not married, the person you have lived with for many years might not be allowed to visit you in the hospital. A health care directive will confer these rights on the person of your choice, as well.

After death. The "next of kin" has the right to decide what happens to a person's remains after death. This includes making decisions about organ donation or other anatomical gifts, as well as deciding where the person will be buried and making other funeral arrangements. These rights can also be given to someone else as part of your Advance Health Care Directive.

J. Perks, privileges and benefits

1. Health insurance

Many employers offer health insurance not only for their employees, but for their immediate families, as well. Sometimes there is a cost for this; sometimes the employer pays it all or heavily subsidizes the cost. California law requires employers and insurance companies to provide the same benefits for registered domestic partners as they do for spouses. If you list someone who does not legally qualify on your policy as your spouse or domestic partner, the insurance company could try to bill you for everything they paid out, even if you paid premiums.

2. Family Leave Act

Employers with 50 or more employees are required to grant leaves of absence of up to four months to employees who have been with the company for at least one year and who need to take time off to care for a newborn or newly adopted baby, or an ill parent, spouse, registered domestic partner or child. When the employee returns, the same or a comparable job must be available. The law also requires that employers let workers on leave continue their health care and retirement benefits, although the employer can insist that the employee on leave pay the group rate.

3. Social Security, welfare and other government benefits

This is one of those areas where marriage and domestic partnership differ a lot. Social Security and all other benefits provided by the federal government will treat domestic partners just like single individuals.

If a couple is married for at least 10 of their working years, and the marriage ends through death or divorce, one spouse may elect to collect Social Security benefits based on either his or her work history or the work history of the former spouse. The benefit based on the former spouse's earnings may be significantly lower than the benefits of the spouse who earned the benefits. If the former spouse is still alive, it is usually 50% of the amount the employed spouse is eligible to receive. If the former spouse is deceased, it may be higher.

On the other hand, if you are receiving Social Security benefits as a widow(er) or former spouse, they will be reduced or eliminated if you remarry before age 60. Changes in the Social Security laws have taken away most of the Social Security incentives for older couples to register a domestic partnership instead of marrying. However, if one of you is collecting or hoping to collect Social Security benefits or pension benefits as a widow(er) or former spouse, we strongly recommend that you consult a certified financial planner before deciding whether to marry or register. For some couples, it could still make a significant financial difference.

4. Pensions and retirement plans

Most pension and retirement plans provide a death benefit to a spouse if the employee dies before retirement. At the time of retirement, the employee usually has to make some irrevocable choices about retirement benefits for the spouse after death of the retiree. These vary greatly, and often there are several options. Generally speaking, though, the employee can receive a higher benefit for the employee's lifetime only, or a lower benefit that will continue (often in a reduced amount) to pay the surviving spouse after the retiree's death. Usually, if the retiree is legally married at the time of retirement, the retiree can't choose the higher benefit with no payments to the surviving spouse unless the spouse consents to this in writing.

For state and local government retirement plans, these rules apply to domestic partners the same as to spouses. Plans provided by the federal government do not provide any benefits to domestic partners. Plans sponsored by private companies are partly governed by federal law and partly by state law. If you are a registered domestic partner, you should check on your specific plan. Since there will be some points at which state and federal laws conflict, we expect to see some court cases and changes before these laws finally stabilize.

5. Will I get any benefits if my partner is killed or injured?

California's wrongful death statute allows spouses, registered domestic partners and a few other close relatives to sue for damages for the death of their loved one through negligence or some other wrongful act. Spouses and domestic partners can also sue for loss of consortium when their partner is injured or disabled and unable to provide the care and companionship he or she usually would. California's workers' compensation laws provide benefits for spouses, domestic partners and dependent children of employees who were injured on the job.

6. Will I inherit from my spouse or partner?

If a married person or registered domestic partner dies without a will, the spouse or partner inherits all the community property and a share—from one-third to all, depending on whether other relatives also survive—of the deceased spouse's separate property. Community property passes to a spouse or partner without going to court by filing of a simple affidavit. If there is not much separate property and all the relatives agree, the separate property can be distributed through a similar procedure.

However, it's wise to do some estate planning ahead of time. For sure, you should make a will. If you have substantial assets, which today can mean that you own real estate, it is often cost-effective to have a living trust into which you put most or all of your property. You keep control during your lifetime, but at death your property passes without probate to named trust beneficiaries. When you make a living trust, you almost always want a "pour-over will" that catches whatever property you did not put into your trust and distributes it to your trust or elsewhere. Living trusts cost more to set up than wills, and require extra paperwork and record keeping, but can be well worth it in the costs and work saved when someone dies. Talk to a lawyer who specializes in estate planning, or go to www.nolo.com to see Nolo's books and software on making your own wills and living trusts.

K. What if we move?

If you move to another state without a relationship agreement, everything changes. Most states don't have community property systems and have completely different property, inheritance and divorce laws. Most don't recognize California domestic partnerships at all. If you split up after you move, domestic partners have an advantage over married couples because they can come back to California, where they know the rules, to dissolve their domestic partnership. For married couples, though, all the planning you've done based on the law alone flies out the window the moment you move to a different state. If you divorce there, everything will be decided by that state's courts (if you don't agree or use ADR) using that state's laws, which may be *very* unlike California's familiar community property system.

Our Couples Contract, along with a good will and possibly a living trust, is an indispensable planning tool for today's mobile couple. Its provisions are designed to keep the system that governs your rights and obligations toward each other as stable as possible, and gives you a method to have any legal problems resolved according to California law, no matter where you may live in the future. The planning you do now will take much of the anxiety out of moving, if ever and whenever that happens. It is possible that your agreement will need some minor modifications if you move to another state, so we still recommend you have a family lawyer in your new state review your relationship agreement and wills and other such documents. Nonetheless, the stability and predictability the Couples Contract offers is greater than anything else available. It is designed to give maximum peace of mind to today's couple, who expect their relationship to last through whatever changes life brings.

Yours, mine and ours —community property

Community property is based on the concept of partnership. Couples joined in marriage are viewed as equal partners in life's adventure, therefore they share equally in whatever either of them earns and acquires during their union, even if one of them never lifts a finger or earns a dime. Community property is a bit of an oddity in the United States, yet it is inherently more fair and equal in its treatment of the parties than the English common law model that is followed in most states.

> **Note to domestic partners**
> Because domestic partnership acquires its rules almost entirely by reference to existing laws that use terms like *spouse, marriage, marital, husband, wife,* and so on, without adaptation to suit domestic partners, we also use similar terms and ask domestic partners to read that language with the understanding that it applies to them, too, unless clearly stated otherwise.

The origins of community property date back to the nomadic Visigoths who brought it to Spain in the 7th century A.D., then to the New World via Spanish explorers who eventually reached California. Based on the recognition that the division of labor between husband and wife was substantially equal, they therefore shared equally in whatever was acquired through their joint efforts. In more recent times, it has been reasoned that the value of taking care of home and children is equal to the value of a salary.

Equal partners have equal rights to manage the community's finances. As the closest kind of partners, the couple owe each other the highest duties of openness, honesty and responsibility in conducting their affairs and in dealing with each other.

In this chapter, we discuss how California community property laws work, with pointers on how you can protect your rights. These laws apply to any couple that does not have an enforceable agreement that modifies the impact of community property laws. Agreements to tailor those rights and duties are discussed in chapter 6. The laws about debts, the negative side of property, are covered separately in chapter 13.

A.   What does "property" include?

In the legal world, "property" includes everything from your tool box to your pension. It includes debts (chapter 13) as well as assets. It can be an idea, a song or a finger painting—anything that has value. So don't confine your concept of the term *property* to cars, boats, houses and furniture.

The estate of a husband and wife (or domestic partners in California) is made up of three possible ownership categories—the community property that they own together and the separate property of each spouse. Community and separate owner-ships can be combined; for example, the family home can be partly husband's separate property, partly wife's separate property, and partly community property. It all depends on when and how the property was acquired, how it was paid for, and any enforceable agreements the couple might have made about it.

B. Separate and community property

Determining whether property is community, separate, or a mix of both, is called *characterization* (section E, below).

Separate property

Separate property is owned by one spouse only. Whether a piece of property is community property, separate property, or a mix of both becomes especially impor-tant when it needs to be divided, as at death or divorce.

Generally, separate property[1] is:

- All property acquired by one spouse *prior* to their union, or acquired during the union with separate funds
- All property given *specifically* to one spouse by gift or inheritance
- All rents or profits from property acquired before the union, or from property acquired after the union with separate funds
- All property *earned* after the couple separates with the intention of divorc-ing.[2] But property acquired during a "trial separation" with the possibility of getting back together, regardless of whether the couple does in fact reunite, is still considered community property[3]

Community property

Community property is anything acquired during the marriage that isn't separate property. Each spouse has an equal right to all of it. The concept is that when people marry, an economic community like a business partnership is formed where both share equally in the accumulation of wealth and debt while they are together.

Example

Harold and Maude met in 1978, began living together in 1980, and got married in 1983. Later, things got rough, so in 1992 they tried living apart on a trial basis. After a

---

[1]Family Code § 770   [2]Family Code § 771   [3]*Marriage of Marsden* (1982) 130 CA3d 426

year apart, they decided to get a divorce. Their income and property ownership would look like this illustration:

Quasi-community property

This refers to any property acquired by a couple who lived outside of California and then moved here. So, all real or personal property that would have been community property had you been living in California when the items, or the funds

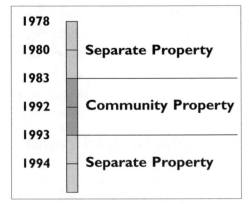

1978	
1980	**Separate Property**
1983	
1992	**Community Property**
1993	
1994	**Separate Property**

with which they were purchased, were acquired is treated the same as community property. However, for probate purposes, quasi-community property does not include real estate located in another state. [4]

Example

Burt earned $10,000 during marriage when he and Loni lived in Florida and he deposited in in a Florida bank. When they move to California, the bank account in Florida is considered quasi-community property, as it would have been community property had Burt and Loni been living in California when Burt earned it.

At divorce, quasi-community property is divided the same as community property but, as a practical matter, California courts may have trouble making orders about quasi-community property still outside the state.

C. Duty of fair dealing and full disclosure

When dealing with community property, spouses owe each other a *fiduciary duty*, which means a very high standard of good faith and fair dealing and a high degree of openness and disclosure, including:

- to provide each other with full access to whatever books and records happen to exist on community transactions or transactions with third persons that involve community property,
- to account for and hold as trustee for the other spouse any benefit or profit derived from investment or use of community property, and
- to give, *on request*, full and true disclosure of virtually everything, including all material facts and information regarding the existence, character and value of all assets and debts that are or may be community property.

---

[4] Family Code § 125; Probate Code § 66

Example

Janis and Tom keep a savings account of community property in Janis's name for community use. If Janis uses it to travel around the world with her lover while Tom believed the money was being saved for a house, Tom could sue Janis for breach of her fiduciary duty of "highest degree of good faith" owed to Tom.

D. Management and control

Spouses have equal rights to manage and control their community property. Either spouse can sell community personal property (other than furnishings or clothing of other family members) without having the written consent of the other spouse, but any such transfer must be for fair and reasonable value. Neither spouse can mortgage or give away community property without the written consent of the other spouse, with the exception of a gift between spouses or by both spouses to a third party. A non-consenting spouse can void an improper transaction if action is taken within one year of transfer of personal property or three years in the case of real property.

Businesses. A spouse who manages a community property business can generally act without the other spouse's consent. However, if the managing spouse intends to sell or give away all or most of the property of the business, he must first receive the non-managing spouse's written consent. For example, a spouse running a couple's business can make day-to-day business decisions, including buying goods for the store, entering into leases, hiring and firing employees and deciding what to sell, without the other's consent.[5] However, the spouse-manager cannot sell the business unless the non-managing spouse consents in writing. All decisions made by the managing spouse *must* be designed to preserve the assets of the community.

Giving away community property. The managing spouse encounters some limitations if he/she tries to give away community property (see section I below).

Deliberate damage. If you're angry at your spouse, don't take it out on the community property. A wife who threw a bottle at their Mercedes was convicted of vandalism, which is defined as maliciously damaging property not your own. The wife argued that she couldn't be guilty of vandalizing her own property, but the court disagreed, emphasizing that because each spouse owns half of the community property, criminal laws protect each owner from "unilateral nonconsensual damage or destruction by the other."[6]

---

[5] Family Code § 1100   [6] *People vs. Kahanic* (1987) 196 CA3d 461

The law that requires each spouse to act with the "highest degree of good faith" toward the other are broad and have teeth that can bite. So if you are thinking of cheating your spouse or hiding assets, or in some other way interfering with your spouse's property rights, we have only this advice—don't!

E. Whose property is it? —characterization

Characterization is the process of determining whether an item of property is a spouse's separate property or the marriage's community property: who owns it—he, she, or we?

Generally, whether a specific item of property is community or separate depends (with a few exceptions) on when it was acquired. Let's look at the most common types of property acquired in the course of a marriage.

1. Income

a. **Earned income** is anything acquired through effort, such as wages, salaries, tips, self-employment income, business profits, and so on.

- Income earned during marriage or during any trial separation is community property. It does not matter when the income is actually received; what matters is when it was *earned*.
- Income earned prior to marriage and after separation is the earning spouse's separate property.

Example
Ozzie and Harriet got married in 1990. In 1989 Ozzie received a $5,000 bonus from his employer, payable as soon as the company had sufficient cash flow. In 1991, the employer sent Ozzie a check for $5,000. Since Ozzie earned the bonus in 1989, prior to his marriage to Harriet, the bonus would be considered his separate property even though he received it during the marriage.

b. **Unearned income** is derived from capital investments and would include interest income, dividends, rents, etc. If a spouse uses more than a little talent or effort to manage the income portfolio or rental property, then some of the unearned income might be considered earned. Unearned income derived from community assets is community property. Unearned income from separate assets is separate property but only so long as it is not mingled with community assets.

Characterization Examples

Harold and Maude met in 1978, began living together in 1980, and got married in 1983. Things got rough after a while, so in 1992 they tried living apart on a trial basis. After about a year, in 1993, they decided to get a divorce. Their divorce becomes final in 1994. Here's how to *characterize* (decide who owns) their property:

In 1980, Harold had an old Jaguar his mother gave him and Maude drove a station wagon that was paid for. They decided to sell both cars in 1981 and use the money to buy a boat, which they put in both their names as joint tenants. They finance the balance over 5 years with a loan from Maude's credit union. They both sign all the loan documents. The boat is half Harold's separate property and half Maude's separate property when they get married in 1983. The boat is worth $10,000 and they owe $4,000 on it.

During their marriage, Maude gets a Social Security check each month, and Harold earns a salary. They keep separate bank accounts, although they have no agreement about whether their income will be community or separate property. Harold makes the boat payments. When the boat is paid for, it is still worth $10,000. The boat is now 30% Maude's separate property, 30% Harold's separate property, and 40% community property, since Harold's community property salary paid 40% of the price.

In 1986, Harold inherits a little money from his favorite uncle. They decide to buy a classic car for $10,000. They make a $1,000 down payment from Harold's inheritance and finance the balance with another 5-year loan from the credit union. Again, they put the title in both names. This time, Maude makes the loan payments. The market for this particular kind of car improves, and when they divorce, they are able to sell it for $15,000. Since they bought the car and put it in both names during the marriage, the car is community property. However, in the divorce settlement Harold is entitled to get back the $1,000 down payment he made from his separate property, and Maude is entitled to get back $9,000 she paid from her Social Security, since it was her separate property. They split the remaining $5,000 equally, as the law requires.

In 1990, Maude grows some flowers in the garden. In June she arranges many of these flowers for her cousin's wedding. Her cousin doesn't know how to thank her. She is a beekeeper, and gives Maude 100 pounds of beeswax. Maude makes candles in the kitchen until Christmas, and sells them at a craft sale for $5,000. The money is community property since it is all the product of Maude's work during the marriage. She should not deposit it in the same account she is using for her Social Security checks, because that would be mixing community and separate property. If she does, it will be difficult to prove when they divorce how much of her checking account is separate property, so it might be treated as if it is all community property.

In 1993, right after they decide to call it quits, Harold finds out he's entitled to a $10,000 bonus from his employer for landing a big account and keeping it for 6 months.

Harold asks his employer to wait until the divorce is final to pay him. Since Harold earned this bonus while he was still married to Maude and while they still thought their separation was temporary, this bonus is community property, no matter when Harold actually receives it. If Harold hides it from Maude in the divorce, and Maude later finds out about it, the court can punish Harold by giving Maude all of the bonus, instead of the half she would have got otherwise.

2. Pensions, retirement benefits, Social Security

"Pension plans" include state, federal and military pensions, IRAs, annuities, Keogh plans, 401(k) funds and employee stock option benefits. In California, pensions and retirement benefits are a property interest—a type of deferred compensation. They are benefits paid to an employee, usually after she retires, for work done years earlier. The portion *earned* during the marriage or domestic partnership is community property and the remainder is the separate property of the employee-spouse.

So the rule is: any pension interest *earned* during marriage is community property and each spouse is entitled to a one-half share.

Primary Social Security benefits are not considered community property, and thus not subject to division by California courts. Social Security is a federal program with its own rules, so contact the Social Security Administration about your rights after divorce. Be aware, however, that if you were married more than ten years you may be able to claim Social Security benefits based on your former spouse's earning history when you reach retirement age.[7] So if your marriage is approaching the ten-year mark, carefully consider whether postponing your divorce will keep you eligible for benefits you will otherwise lose.

However, Social Security based on a former spouse's income cannot be collected while you are married to someone else. If you are receiving Social Security based on a previous marriage and want to remarry, you may want to consider a domestic partnership instead. This is a rare instance where marriage and domestic partnership are different. Social Security is a federal government benefit, and the federal government does not treat domestic partners the same as married people.

Domestic partners. The federal government does not recognize domestic partnerships, so you won't be getting any Social Security benefits based on your partner's work history. But that's not the end of it. Although none of this has been decided by courts yet, we feel confident making a few predictions as to how retirement plans will

---

[7] 42 U.S.C. § 301 et seq. (The Social Security Act)

be treated on dissolution of a domestic partnership. Whenever pension rights are created or governed by federal law, domestic partners will be treated differently than married couples. If the pension is one that comes from the federal government, like railroad retirement, military retirement or pension plans of other government employees, rights of domestic partners will not be honored, so California courts will probably be forced to treat these retirement plans as separate property.

When the pension is a private plan governed by the Employee Retirement Income Security Act (ERISA), a federal law, the pension will be treated as community property, but the court will not be able to order the plan administrator to pay the former domestic partner's share to him or her directly, as they could after the divorce of a married couple. However, the court can order the partner who earned the pension to pay the other a portion of each month's check, or the court can put a value on the pension and award the other partner other community property of equal value.

3. Military retirement and other benefits

For married couples, military and federal pensions are treated like any other pension, unless the military retirement pay was waived in order to receive disability benefits, which are always the separate property of the military spouse.

Spouses of marriages that lasted through ten or more years of military service gain big advantages in the enforcement of pension awards. In addition, spouses of marriages that lasted through twenty years of military service are entitled to commissary and PX benefits. If your marriage is approaching the ten- or twenty-year mark, and your spouse has served in the military during those years, don't rush into divorce until you consider what benefits will be lost.

4. Disability benefits

If disability benefits are intended to replace marital earnings, they are the community property of the marriage. If they are intended to replace the postmarital earnings of the disabled spouse, they are the separate property of the disabled spouse. This is so even when the right to receive those benefits was earned during the marriage. However, if disability benefits are intended to replace a pension interest earned during the marriage, the benefits will be treated as community property.[8] (As mentioned above, this rule does not apply to military disability benefits which are always the separate property of the spouse who served.)

---

[8] *Marriage of Saslow* (1985) 40 C3d 848

5. Other employment benefits

Benefits such as insurance, stock options, profit sharing, and the like can be tricky because of the timing. Anything awarded based on work performed during marriage, even if the benefits are received after separation, are community property. The benefits given to an employee based on work performed *before* the marriage, even if the benefits are received during the marriage, are the separate property of the earner.

6. Workers' compensation

Workers' compensation benefits that are received after separation are the separate property of the injured spouse. Benefits that are received prior to separation are community property.[9]

7. Intellectual property

Intellectual property includes items like books, paintings, software programs, inventions and their related rights, such as patents, trademarks, copyrights, and so on. Often, ownership of the thing itself is one thing and ownership of the right to sell copies of it are another. You can sell the painting once, but you can sell the right to make copies of it for decades. Don't forget to think about both when dealing with this kind of property. Although difficult to value, these items are community property if created, invented or generated (even if not sold) during marriage and prior to separation. Those created, invented or generated prior to marriage (even if sold during marriage) or after separation are the separate property of the creator.

8. Personal injury damages

Personal injury recoveries by a husband or wife from a third party are community property if the injuries occurred during the marriage.[10] But when the couple divorces, what's left of the recovery will be the separate property of the injured spouse,[11] unless the funds were mixed with other community property, or if a judge decides that fairness requires the non-injured spouse to receive some part of the recovery.

Example
While walking across the street, Wilma was hit by a motorist who ran a stop sign. The money that Wilma recovered from the motorist was placed into a bank account she owned jointly with her husband, Herman.

---

[9] *Marriage of Fisk* (1992) 2 CA4th 1698   [10] Family Code § 780   [11] Family Code § 2603

- As long as Wilma and Herman are married, this money is community property. If Wilma should die, the most she could give away in her will is one-half, because Herman owns the other half.
- However, if Herman and Wilma divorce, the money will be given to Wilma, unless the couple mixed the recovery with other community property (in that case the total fund would be divided in half) or a court, after reviewing the economic needs of each party, the time elapsed since the recovery of damages, and other relevant factors, determines that justice requires Herman to receive a share. In that case, the most Herman could get is half, because at divorce, the injured spouse must be given at least half of any recovery.

Sound confusing? It is. In fact, one court has concluded that personal injury damages are a unique beast under California community property laws.

9. Reimbursement

Whenever a personal injury recovery, workers' compensation or disability pay is characterized (or classified) as one spouse's separate property, if community property was spent for medical or other related expenses, the community is entitled to *reimbursement*.[12]

Reimbursement is an important legal concept in the area of marriage and divorce law. It allows a spouse who has paid out money to be reimbursed by the other spouse in certain circumstances. For instance in the example above, if Wilma recovers $10,000 from the accident, and $2,000 of Wilma and Herman's community funds were paid to lawyers who handled the case, upon divorce, if Wilma is given the $10,000 recovery, the judge will also order her to reimburse Herman $1,000 for his half of the community property which was used to pay the lawyers. Why does Wilma only have to reimburse Herman for $1,000, rather than $2,000? Since the lawyers were paid from community funds, Wilma and Herman each owned half of the money spent, so Wilma only needs reimburse Herman for his half.

Reimbursement is a way to make property division fair and equal. It usually comes into play whenever community property or one spouse's separate property has been used to benefit the other spouse alone. A classic example is when community funds are used to pay a child support obligation from a previous marriage. If separate income of the parent was available at the time but not used, then upon divorce the non-parent spouse would be entitled to reimbursement for her half of the community funds that were spent to pay her spouse's support obligation.[13]

---

[12] Family Code § 781   [13] Family Code § 915

10. Gifts and inheritances

Gifts and inheritances made specifically to one spouse or the other, no matter when given, are the separate property of that spouse. Gifts made to both spouses (like wedding gifts) are community property.[14] However, if a gift is given to one spouse in appreciation for something done by that spouse using community labor (anything done by a spouse during marriage is done with community labor), the gift will be considered the community property of the marriage.

Example

Kit and Kat are married. Kit is a carpenter. As a favor for his neighbor, Lula, Kit patched Lula's leaky roof. In appreciation for Kit's help, Lula gave Kit a painting he had often admired in her living room. Even though Lula specifically gave the painting to Kit, it is the community property of the marriage, owned equally by Kit and Kat. This is because Kit did the work for Lula using community labor, which then entitles Kat to half of the proceeds received from Kit's efforts.

11. Family businesses

Characterizing a family business can be tricky. Businesses existing prior to marriage are separate property. However, the community develops an interest in the business to the extent that community labor (a spouse's efforts or skills) went into improving or increasing the value of the business during the marriage. Businesses created during marriage are community property. However, if separate property is invested in it, the investment will be reimbursed if the couple divorces and the business is at that time worth more than the amount invested. If it is worth less than the amount invested, its entire value will be reimbursed, in which case the business is usually treated as separate property by agreement.

What you need to understand is that once you are married, your spouse is entitled to half of anything your talents and labor generate, whether it be a salary, an idea, or a new business.

12. Life insurance proceeds

Life insurance proceeds paid to a spouse during marriage (for example, from the death of a parent, sibling, child, or friend) are the separate property of the beneficiary spouse.[15] Where one spouse dies during marriage and a life insurance policy had been

---

[14] Family Code § 770   [15] Family Code § 770

totally or partially paid for with community property, the portion of the proceeds equal to the percentage of premiums paid with community property are the community property of the marriage. Thus, the surviving spouse may claim one-half of the proceeds even if he (she) wasn't named as a beneficiary.[16]

F. How title to property affects ownership

Title to property is how we designate ownership. For example, the pink slip on your car is the car's title; it tells the world who owns it. Common types of titled assets include houses, boats, cars, stocks, investment accounts and bank accounts. Not all property has a title document; for example, items like jewelry, tools and furniture do not usually have titles.

Married people can hold title as their separate property, joint property or community property, as illustrated in these examples:

Separate property

- Carl Katz, a married man, as his sole and separate property.
- Kittie Katz, a married woman, as her sole and separate property.

Joint property

- Carl Katz and Kittie Katz, as joint tenants.
- Carl Katz and Kittie Katz, as tenants in common.

Community property

- Carl Katz and Kittie Katz, husband and wife, as community property.
- Carl Katz and Kittie Katz, husband and wife, as community property with right of survivorship.

1. Rules affecting title and property ownership

Several rules affect title and property ownership.
- In general, it is *presumed* that a title document accurately reflects the parties' ownership interests. To overcome the presumption that the title instrument is correct, you must show "clear and convincing" evidence of a contrary agreement or understanding.[17]

---

[16] *Pattillo vs. Norris* (1976) 65 CA3d 209
[17] Evidence Code § 662; *Marriage of Weaver* (1990) 224 CA3d 478

For example, if title is in the name of one spouse alone "as separate property," you can try to show, by "clear and convincing" evidence, that it is actually community property. Conversely, if title is in the name of both you and your spouse, you may try to prove that the property is actually your separate property.

- Property acquired *during marriage* which is held in *joint title* form (tenancy in common, joint tenancy, community property or as "husband and wife") is presumed to be community property at divorce, unless a spouse shows in a deed, written agreement or other document that the asset is intended to be the separate property of one spouse.[18]

- If a spouse changes title to property from separate property to any joint-title form during the marriage, the property is considered to have been "acquired" by the couple during marriage and thus presumed to be community property. The original owner spouse, however, may be entitled to *reimbursement* (see discussion of reimbursement above) for the separate property contribution, unless he or she expressly waived (gave up) that right in writing.[19] The following agreement can be used to make such a waiver.

If you don't tailor financial rights in a relationship agreement (chapter 6), it is possible to make a written agreement about a particular piece of property, like this:

Sample waiver agreement

I, [your name], hereby make a gift to the community of [you and your spouse's names], my [item] and waive all rights to be reimbursed for my separate property contribution should we later divorce.

Date: _____   _____
                              Signature

2. Taking title to real estate

The largest purchase most couples make is a house. So, let's go over aspects of the purchase process related to your title options.

When buying a house, you go through a transfer procedure, called "escrow," which is supervised by an escrow agent who computes the various charges and pays expenses of sale. The agent also makes sure that the buyers deposit the purchase

---

[18] Family Code § 2581
[19] Family Code § 2640; *Marriage of Fabian* (1986) 41 C3d 440

money into an account and the sellers deliver a valid deed to the house, naming the buyer as the new owner. In Northern California, escrow is normally handled by a title insurance company; in Southern California, by an escrow company.

During escrow, you'll have to decide how to take title. This subject is covered in more detail in *The Deeds Book*, by Mary Randolph, and *How to Buy a House in California*, by Warner, Serkes and Devine, both published by Nolo Press.

Separate property. If one spouse will own the house separately, title is taken in that person's name alone, and the couple should sign and record, along with the deed, an agreement declaring their intention that one spouse owns the house as his or her separate property. Otherwise, if the couple divorces and disagrees about ownership, a court might characterize the property as community or separate property depending on what funds (community or separate) paid for the mortgage, insurance, improvements and taxes, rather than by whose name is on the deed. Because most couples mix and spend community and separate funds without regard to type, what property was used to make payments won't always be clear. The point to get here is that if you intend the house to be separate property, *make sure that intention is in writing.*

Joint tenancy means that the couple (joint tenants) equally share property ownership and each has the right to use the entire property. If one joint tenant dies, the survivor *automatically* inherits the deceased person's share without a probate hearing (a probate hearing is the procedure for settling a deceased person's estate). When a joint tenant dies, the property passes immediately and directly to the surviving joint tenant, even if there is a will to the contrary. If a joint tenant sells her portion to a third party or unilaterally (without consent of the other joint tenant) changes her own interest to a tenant in common, the joint tenancy ends.

Sometimes, a spouse puts a separate property house into joint tenancy with the other spouse—either as a gift to the spouse, or more usually (and more disturbing) at the request of a lending institution when the house is refinanced. Unless the spouses sign an agreement stating that the property is to remain the separate property of the spouse who originally owned it, it will be considered community property if they divorce. Again, make sure that your intentions are in writing, signed by both you and your spouse. See chapter 6 for sample clauses to clarify and carry out your property ownership intentions.

Tenancy in common means that each spouse owns separately and is entitled to equal use of the property, but they need not own equal shares. Also, if one owner dies, the other does not take her share unless this has been specified in the deceased person's will or, if there is no will, if the survivor is entitled to inherit as a legal heir.

Tenancy in common is normally more appropriate for business partners than for spouses. Spouses who don't want an automatic right of survivorship as in "joint tenancy" should consider the community property alternative discussed below.

Couples who separate and want to continue to own a house together or couples who contribute separate property of the husband and separate property of the wife to a house and want to keep ownership shares clear will find that tenancy in common makes sense.

Community property ownership offers two advantages:
- Avoiding formal probate when a spouse dies; and
- Easy qualification for a federal income tax break.

Probate. When one spouse dies, property held as community property goes directly to the surviving spouse without formal probate, unless the deceased spouse left her one-half community interest to someone other than her spouse. A surviving spouse who inherits community property needs only to file a simple affidavit (available from a title insurance company) with the probate court. This can be done without a lawyer; the survivor avoids lengthy delays in transferring the property (and title), and costly probate fees. However, we think you should consult a lawyer before you do this, because sometimes it's wise to probate an estate that is all community property to protect the surviving spouse from potential lawsuits. See Nolo's book, *How to Probate an Estate*.

Community property with right of survivorship combines some of the advantages of community property with some of the advantages of joint tenancy. The tax advantages of a stepped-up basis are the same as with community property. It passes to the survivor outside probate (saving time and fees) even if a probate is opened to protect the surviving spouse. This is also the most secure form of title because, as community property, neither spouse can sell or give away his or her half during their lifetime unless they both sign the transfer, and the right of survivorship prevents one spouse from leaving his or her half by will to someone other than the other spouse.

Tax advantages. When title is held in community property, a surviving spouse who inherits the property may have a tax advantage that she would not have for property held in tenancy in common or joint tenancy. Because we are talking about a federal tax law, this part does not apply to domestic partners. For married couples, the tax advantage hinges on the *tax basis* of the asset.

A tax basis is basically a dollar amount you spend for an asset, plus the cost of any capital improvement (swimming pool, new kitchen etc.) So if you buy a house for $100,000, the tax basis on that home is $100,000. Why do you care about the tax basis? You care because the IRS cares. The tax basis of an asset is used to determine if you lost or made money when and if you sell the asset. If you made money, the IRS wants to collect capital gain taxes from you. For instance, the rental house you buy in 1990 for $100,000 has a $100,000 tax basis. If you sell the house in 2004 for $150,000, you will have a $50,000 capital gain which might be taxable. (The gain is the difference between the selling price and the original tax basis.) Under the current IRS Code, most people don't have to pay capital gains taxes when they sell their home, but do when they sell a rental house or other property.

Here's how holding title in community property can be a big advantage. On the death of one spouse the surviving spouse receives a "stepped-up" tax basis on the entire property. This means that the surviving spouse can use the fair market value of the house at the time of her spouse's death as a tax basis (called a "stepped-up" basis), should she decide to sell. If title was not held in community property, only the deceased's spouses share of the asset would receive a "stepped-up" basis. Did we lose you? Here's an example to illustrate the concept:

Example

In 1979, John and Yoko, a married couple, buy a rental house for $100,000 and take title as tenants in common, each owning a half interest. In 1984 John is killed. John left Yoko his share of the house in his will. After a long and costly probate, Yoko gets title to the house in her name. Yoko decides to sell the house and return to Japan. She sells it for $200,000. (At the time of John's death, the house was also worth $200,000.) Yoko has a tax basis of $150,000; when she inherited John's half of the house, she also received a "stepped-up" tax basis for his half equal to the fair market value of the house (at John's death, the house was worth $200,000; since he owned half, the "stepped-up" tax basis is $100,000 for his share; Yoko must keep her original basis, half of the value of the house when they purchased it or $50,000—thus her total basis is $150,000). Yoko will have to pay tax on the difference between her total tax basis for the house and what she sold it for, or $50,000 ($200,000–$150,000).

This scenario could have been avoided if John and Yoko had taken title in community property. For tax purposes, a surviving spouse's one-half share of community property is treated in the same way as the property the surviving spouse inherits from the deceased spouse (meaning the surviving spouse's share of community property will also receive a "stepped-up" basis). Thus all community property (the surviving and decedent spouse's shares) receive a new stepped-up basis equal to the fair market value of the home at the time of the deceased spouse's death. Yoko would not owe taxes on $50,000 of capital gain (because she would have a $200,000 basis) if she and John had taken title in community property.

So pay attention to how you take title to an asset and seek expert help if you don't fully understand the various options and their implications.

3. How refinancing can affect title

During the last 20 years or so, when refinancing real estate became a common practice, many married people in California decided to refinance their separate real estate. Many spouses have been told two troublesome things by lenders and mortgage brokers: (1) that the loan application has to be signed by both spouses, and (2) in order to qualify for the loan they want, they have to change title of the real estate from separate to a joint form of title. Too many couples have followed these instructions without thinking about all the important rights they were changing.

Co-signing. If you are not getting the benefit of a loan on your spouse's separate property, why should you agree to share liability for it? It's okay to refuse; your spouse can go to another lender or offer to make you a part-owner of the separate property or compensate you in some other way.

Changing title. We recommend that you do **not** change title without first checking with an attorney and then writing an agreement that states clearly what you are doing. This agreement can be a separate thing or you can add it to your Couples Contract. It's okay to refuse to go along with what the lender says they want, or you can go along and transfer title back again after the loan is complete. However, this leaves the nonowner spouse liable for the loan with nothing to show for it, so it is not a perfect solution. If presented with this choice, you can call Couples Helpline to get some advice and look for alternative solutions.

Example

Chad owned an apartment building before he married Lila. Interest rates have improved, and Chad and Lila would both like to refinance the property to reduce the monthly payments and increase the net rental income each month, after paying the building's expenses. The lender says they can only get the interest rate they want if Lila signs the loan documents and title is changed to a joint form. Chad doesn't want to make an outright gift to Lila of half the property, but he wants Lila to inherit it all if he dies. Lila is willing to sign for the loan if the community receives the benefits of the additional monthly cash flow and she is guaranteed an inheritance.

Sample refinancing agreement

Chad and Lila agree to refinance Chad's rental property at (address). We will both sign the loan application and all other documents, and title will be changed from

Chad's separate property to Chad and Lila, as community property with right of survivorship.

We agree that Chad will continue to pay all expenses connected with the property from the rental income it generates, and if that is not sufficient, from his separate funds. If the property is sold or we ever separate or divorce, this property will be treated as Chad's separate property, and Chad will receive all the proceeds of sale as his separate property. Lila will have no right to any interest in the property and no right to claim any right of reimbursement.

In exchange for Lila's signing the loan documents, Chad will deposit all the net profits from the property in our joint bank account, and Chad will not claim any right of reimbursement. By changing title to community property with right of survivorship, Chad also intends to guarantee that Lila will have the right to the entire property if Chad dies before her.

Date: _____   _____
Signature

An agreement about real estate should be notarized. After refinancing is completed, take it to your county Recorder's office and file it. Before signing this, Lila should carefully read Chapter 13 to make sure she understands her liability for the debt.

G. When separate and community property get mixed —how to keep separate property separate

Whenever you mix separate property with community property, you create a situation that is easy to argue about and difficult to unravel. If it happens, you can only reclaim the separate property if you can trace it; that is, show clearly where it came from and how it was spent. This might require expert evaluation and assistance.

If you have separate property and wish to keep it separate after marriage, do not mix your separate property with the community property and do not use community income or assets to pay for or improve your separate property.

For example, if you have $10,000 in a savings account prior to marriage, and wish to keep that money your separate property after you are married, keep the money in a separate account, in your name only, and don't deposit any money in it during your marriage unless it is also clearly separate, such as a gift to you alone or an inheritance. If you use that $10,000 to buy a house with your spouse, and you want to keep the $10,000 interest separate, draw up a simple agreement stating your intentions.

H. Intentionally changing the character of property —transmutation

Spouses have every right to change the character of their property from separate to community or the other way around, but it must be done in writing.

1. Changing title to property

A *transmutation* is an agreement between spouses to change the character or ownership of an asset. Prior to 1985, a transmutation could be oral, written or inferred from the conduct of the parties. From 1985 on, however, a transmutation must be in writing to be enforceable.[20] (The writing requirement does not apply to personal gifts between spouses, such as clothing or jewelry.)

- If it is an asset with a title document, change the way title is described on the deed or motor vehicle registration, and record the deed with the county recorder's office (for real property); and
- Make a separate written agreement reflecting the change. Drafting this agreement will eliminate the possibility of the ownership being determined by who paid for the property.

Example

Charles and Di wed in 1998. Charles owns substantial property which he acquired prior to marriage, thus it is his separate property. Charles decides that he wants one of his small country estates to be community property, and thus half-owned by Di. He changes the title document to reflect his gift to Di and records it in the county recorder's office. In addition he signs an agreement which states his intention. Charles has effectively *"transmuted"* his separate property to community property.

2. Mixing property

Spouses frequently mix or "commingle" separate property and community property without thinking through how this changes the character of the property. If there is no agreement showing the intent of the spouses, problems arise at death or divorce.

Combining usually takes two forms—separate property used to make permanent improvements on something owned by the community (or vice versa) or community and separate property (or wife's separate and husband's separate property) combined to purchase one item.

---

[20] Family Code §§ 1100, 1101 & 1102

Example

Two years ago Bill got married. Right before the ceremony, he borrowed $10,000 from his mother, signing a note which his future wife, Elaine, didn't sign because she wasn't around. The couple deposited the money, which was to buy land, into a joint bank account. They made many deposits and withdrawals on that account, so the balance fluctuated widely. Eventually, they bought land for $8,000 and put it in both names. Then Elaine filed for divorce and claimed that the $2,000 left in the bank, as well as the land, was community property, but that the $10,000 owed Bill's mother was his separate debt. Bill thinks this is unfair and wants to know if he has a leg to stand on.

Bill might be able to prove that the debt is a community debt or that the land is his separate property—maybe; but only with some difficulty. Bill would be in a far better legal position if either Elaine had signed the original note, or if Elaine and Bill had signed an agreement recognizing that the land was Bill's separate property. Need we say more about the value of doing business in a businesslike way?

I.   Can I sell or give away community property?

Each spouse may give away his or her own separate property without the other's consent. Of course, neither spouse can give away the other's separate property without consent. The rules are different when community property is involved.

1. Giving away community property

Neither spouse can legally make a gift of any community property without the consent of the other. A gift is any transfer of property without the giver getting something of roughly equivalent value in exchange. For instance, a transfer of title to a house in exchange for $1,000 would most likely be considered a gift. Written consent is required for any gift of community property. Money is also community property, so if you make a gift of community cash, the easiest way to show consent is for both spouses to sign the check, even if your bank only requires one signature.

2. Selling community personal property

Either spouse can sell community personal property, except home furnishings and clothing, without the written consent of the other spouse. If one spouse gives away or sells furniture or clothing without the consent of the other, the non-consenting spouse can sue to set aside the transfer. The spouse must sue within three years of the gift or sale of personal community property (furniture or clothing).

3. Selling or giving community real estate

Neither spouse can give, sell, mortgage, lease for more than a year, or otherwise transfer any community real property without the written consent of the other spouse. If one spouse gives away, sells or otherwise transfers any real property, the non-consenting spouse must sue within three years from when the new deed is recorded.

A gift or sale of community property by one spouse can cause problems, especially if the couple later divorces. When people are stressed and upset, they often escalate minor disagreements into something approaching war. The best way to avoid confusion is to make a short agreement when either spouse sells or gives away an item of value and put it in the file where you keep the important papers. You may think that keeping records is too much trouble and that it's easier to trust your spouse. In marriage, as in business, trust is the basic building block of a good relationship. But trust can erode fast if people don't take steps to protect it.

CHAPTER 13

Debts —who owes what

In planning for a long-term relationship, debts can be a matter of more pressing urgency than property. When you marry, you become legally and financially entwined with your partner, so it is important to know how the law applies to debts in your current situation and in the future you're planning to have together. *Don't skip this chapter!*

One or both of you might have debts that you will bring into the relationship. Take a close look, because they might be a vivid clue that you need to discuss your family's lifestyle. They are also an important consideration in shaping your relationship agreement, if you make one. Statistics tell us that many couples consist of a saver and a spender—one who understands that creating credit card debt is one of the worst things you can do, and one who just doesn't get it. Differences over finances are the most common cause of breakups, so this is why sharing information about your debts and spending habits from the beginning can help you plan ways to reduce debt-related stress for years to come. You should try to understand how much debt you each have, how much you are comfortable with, and how you use credit cards—the most expensive of all forms of credit! Talk about how you pay off debts—minimum monthly payments, paying everything in full each month, or somewhere in between.

If one or both of you tends to accumulate debt on credit cards or typically spends more than you earn, you should seriously consider finding a good workshop or counselor who specializes in helping couples control spending. Don't let debt stress or disagreements over spending undermine your relationship.

Once you understand the debts in your life and how you relate to them as a couple, you can decide whether you need to tailor your financial arrangements (chapter 6) to protect yourselves from unnecessary financial stress related to debts.

A. A little bit about debts

A debt is an obligation to pay someone money. It may be a large obligation, such as a home mortgage or monthly rent, or a small obligation, like a monthly newspaper bill. If you don't pay, you usually suffer consequences. At the *minor inconvenience* end of the scale, if you don't pay your magazine subscription, it will be canceled and you'll have to pick one up each month at the news stand. At the *serious trouble* end, if you don't pay your mortgage or rent, your house may be foreclosed or you may be evicted.

Debts can be either secured or unsecured

1. Secured Debts

When a debt is *secured*, this means that an item of property has been put up as *collateral* to guarantee repayment of the debt, which means if you don't pay, the creditor can take the property and sell it. This is what happens when a car is repossessed or a home is foreclosed. However, the creditor does not have to take back the collateral and can try other methods to collect the money you owe. For example, if you still owe $7,500 on your new car loan, but recently wrecked the car, the creditor won't repossess it—creditors want dollars, not dents. Even if they do repossess your car or furniture, they can sell the property for a song and still come after you for the balance due.

Home loans. If the loan is not paid on a home *where the parties reside*, the creditor can foreclose and sell the home, but after the forced sale, the creditor cannot come after you or amounts still due without going through lengthy procedures that are rarely pursued.

When you take out a secured loan, you sign a *security agreement* with the creditor. This agreement specifies precisely what property (collateral) can be taken by the creditor if you default on the loan. The security agreement also creates a *lien*—the creditor's legal right to take possession of the collateral in the event you don't pay. Security agreements are of two kinds:

a. Purchase money. You pledge the property you are in the act of buying—motor vehicles, furniture, large appliances or electronics equipment—as the collateral. This is the most common type of security agreement. Here are some common examples of purchase money security agreements:

- Mortgages (deeds of trust)—loans to buy a house or other real estate. The house or other real estate is collateral for the loan. If you fail to pay, the lender can foreclose.
- Loans for cars, boats, motorcycles, RVs—the vehicle is the collateral.
- Store charges with a security agreement—for example, when you buy furniture or a major appliance, many department or appliance stores require you to sign a security agreement in which you agree that the item purchased is collateral for your repayment. Keep in mind that only a few store charges come with security agreements. Most store purchases are unsecured.

b. Nonpurchase money. You borrow a sum of money and pledge some other piece of property you already own as security. Some common examples of nonpurchase money security agreements include:

- Home equity loans (also called second mortgages) from banks or finance companies—such as loans to make improvements on your house. The house or other real estate is collateral for the loan. If you fail to pay, the lender can foreclose.
- The first mortgage on your home if it has been refinanced.
- Personal loans from finance companies—often your valuable personal property, such as a paid-off motor vehicle, is pledged as collateral.

2. Unsecured Debts

Most debts people incur are unsecured, meaning that there is no collateral. For example, you charge a big flat-screen HDTV on a credit card and they don't ask you to sign a security agreement specifying that the TV is collateral for your repayment. With no collateral, the creditor has nothing to take if you don't pay. This leaves the creditor only one option if she wants to be paid: to sue you, get a judgment for the money you owe and try to collect it. To collect, she can go after your wages, bank account or other property that can be taken to satisfy money judgments. Don't overlook the damage that can be done to a credit report by a creditor who has not been paid. Negative reports to credit agencies can wreck your credit for years to come.

B. Debts from before marriage

Generally, a spouse is not liable for the separate debts his/her partner incurred before marriage.[1] This means that your *separate* property cannot be taken in order to pay a credit card bill your spouse ran up before you were married. *However, all* of the *community property*, including *your* half, can be attached by a creditor to pay your spouse's premarital debts. You can exempt your wages from this rule *if* you deposit them in a separate account and do not mix (*commingle*) them with any other community property. This means your spouse must have *no* access to your separate account.[2]

---

[1] Family Code § 913
[2] Family Code §§ 911, 915; *Marriage of Williams* (1989) 213 CA3d 1239

Because it is possible for a creditor to reach your half of the community property to pay your spouse's premarital debts, this means that if you or your spouse come into the marriage with significant debt, you should discuss setting up a separate account for the non-debtor spouse's earnings and consider writing an agreement like the example at chapter 6D(4) that states your intention to keep earnings separate.

C. Debts during marriage

Here are the rules for who owes what for debts incurred during marriage:

- The *separate property* of one spouse usually cannot be taken by a creditor to pay the *individual* debts of the other spouse. Separate property of one spouse can be taken to pay *joint* debts, and separate property of one spouse is always available to pay his or her own individual debts.

  … There is an exception: the separate property of a spouse can be taken to pay individual debts of the other incurred during marriage *if* the debt is for the "necessaries of life" (e.g. food, clothing, medical care).[3]

  ### Example
  Oliver and Sylvia are both in their 70s. Sylvia owns the home they live in as her separate property. Oliver's faculties have been diminishing lately and Sylvia is concerned that if Oliver gets into a car accident, her house could be sold to pay his debts. If Oliver injures another person or person's property, Sylvia's property is safe from Oliver's creditors, as those debts would not be for Oliver's "necessaries." If Oliver needs medical treatment, however, Sylvia's separate property would be liable, as medical care for Oliver is a "necessary of life."

- *Community property* can be taken by a creditor to pay all debts incurred by either spouse before or during the marriage. "During marriage" does not include the time between separation and divorce.[4]

---

[3] Family Code § 914   [4] Family Code § 910

D. Co-signing for a loan
—can they get my separate property?

Yes! Co-signing any type of loan or credit application with your spouse is the quickest way to make your separate property liable for community debts. If one spouse takes out a loan, or otherwise obtains credit, and the other spouse signs the security agreement or loan, this means that in addition to the couple's community property, the separate property of *both* spouses is liable for the debt. For example, if a wife puts her name on her husband's credit card account, her separate property is liable for any debts he runs up. In other words, money she earned prior to marriage and money she inherits during marriage is liable for the $1,500 he charged on his credit card before buying a one-way ticket to Costa Rica.

E. Tax debts

Taxes, especially federal income taxes, can raise special problems. If one spouse enters the marriage owing taxes, the rule is that the spouse who owes the taxes is liable for the debt and all of her separate property can be taken by the IRS. They can also take *all* community property, including the non-debtor spouse's wages, *if* they are deposited in a joint account. So, if you or your spouse owe a lot of back taxes, set up a separate account for the non-debtor spouse and make an agreement to keep your property and income separate, as described in chapter 6D(4).

If you owe back taxes for a year you were married and filed jointly, even if the bill comes after your divorce is final, both spouses are liable. You *may* be able to reduce or minimize your own liability (this is called the "innocent spouse" rule) if:

- You didn't know, or had no reason to know, of the under-reporting, and you did not benefit from the omitted income; or
- The bill is for omitted income or an illegal deduction, you didn't know or had no reason to know that there was an understatement of your tax liability, and it would be unfair to hold you liable for the taxes owed.

Other new rules may apply. If your joint return is audited or the IRS assesses a deficiency on a joint return after separation, see a good tax accountant.

F.   We can't pay —bankruptcy

For couples overwhelmed by debt, declaring bankruptcy is an option. Married couples can file for bankruptcy jointly or one spouse can file as an individual. In most cases, bankruptcy lets you erase most debts in exchange for giving up "nonexempt" property. Exempt property that you can keep includes household goods and furniture, clothing, some equity in a home, some equity in a car and certain other items.

A few kinds of debts can't be discharged. These include fines, recent tax debts, judgments for fraud and other kinds of intentional wrongdoing, and several kinds of family obligations, such as back child or spousal support and certain other debts owed under a divorce judgment.

Domestic partners, once again, get different treatment. Back spousal support and other obligations owed from a domestic partnership dissolution *are* dischargeable in bankruptcy, even though they would *not* be if the couple had been married. If this happens, though, the court that dissolved your domestic partnership may be able to make a new spousal support order after the bankruptcy is over. Child support is not dischargeable whether the parents were married or not.

Back child or spousal support can *only* be discharged in the following situations:

- Support was owed under a state's general support law rather than a court order. If no court actually ordered the support, the debt is dischargeable. This is true even if the creditor is the welfare department that wants to be reimbursed for benefits that were paid before a court issued a child support order.

- Support was owed under an agreement between unmarried persons. Since we are dealing with federal law here, *unmarried* includes registered domestic partners. If an unmarried couple enters into an agreement that includes support, the debt can be discharged in bankruptcy unless one person won a lawsuit against the other and obtained a court judgment for the support.

- Support was owed someone other than a spouse, ex-spouse or child. If an ex-spouse or child gave (*assigned*, in legal terms) the right to receive the support to someone else—such as a creditor with a judgment against that person—the debt is dischargeable, unless it is owed to the welfare department. When it is owed to the welfare department, the debt is treated the same as when it is owed to the ex-spouse or child—that is, it cannot be discharged in bankruptcy.

If a married couple files for bankruptcy together, they can discharge both their joint and individual debts. If only one files, creditors can go after the other spouse for joint debts (but not for individual debts of the bankrupt spouse) and *all* the community property that is not exempt goes to the creditors. The spouse who doesn't file has a right to designate property he or she thinks should be exempt, but this does not increase the maximum amount of the exemptions. If bankruptcy and divorce come together, it is *very* important that they be carefully coordinated. Expert advice and cooperation between spouses can really pay off here.

There are additional factors to consider before deciding whether one or both spouses should file for bankruptcy; we suggest you thoroughly explore your options. See Nolo's books *How to File for Chapter 7 Bankruptcy* and *Chapter 13 Bankruptcy: Repay Your Debt*, or you may want to seek expert help from a bankruptcy attorney.

Why bankruptcy isn't for everyone. It stays on your credit record for ten years, although in some cases you are able to rebuild your credit and obtain new credit in two or three years after filing. Nonetheless, be sure you understand that bankruptcy is always a possibility (unless you filed within the previous six years) for you and your spouse. If you're overwhelmed by your debt burden, don't immediately count it out. If your spouse assumes a large share of the community debt or owes you a large sum to even up the property division, be on the lookout for any bankruptcy filing, especially if your ex starts to complain loudly about being broke.

G. Debts after divorce or separation

Rule no. 1. How a debt is treated in a divorce will not change the creditor's right to collect from the person(s) responsible when the debt was incurred. If your spouse charged a vacation on a *joint* credit card after separation, the bill will be a *joint* debt in terms of the creditor, but a *separate* debt in terms of a divorce court. This is why **Rule no. 2** is to close all joint accounts immediately after separation.

If there is a divorce or legal separation, each spouse will keep his or her separate debts, and community debts will be divided along with the community property, either by agreement or by a judge. The law calls for the equal division of community property and debts so each spouse gets an equal total as his or her separate property. From this time on, a new creditor of one spouse can no longer take what is now the separate property of the other spouse.[5]

---

[5] Family Code § 910

Nearly all debts incurred during marriage are community debts. Separate debts include:

- Debts incurred before marriage.
- Debts incurred after separation.
- During marriage, if a creditor relied on the separate property of one spouse as collateral, rather than both property and income of that spouse, then the debt is separate, though creditors rarely do this.

Example

Michael had a large stock portfolio before he married Cynthia. He always kept it separate from the community accounts. Occasionally, he borrowed "on margin" to buy more stock. The broker lent him money, holding his stocks as security. The money borrowed on this margin account is Michael's separate debt.

- If the debt is of no benefit to the community, the spouse who benefits by the debt will be solely responsible for its repayment.[6] A community debt must not promote the breakdown of the marriage. For example, if two weeks before separating, one spouse treated her lover to a trip to Hawaii (while claiming to be on a business trip), the spouse who stayed home can argue that the Hawaii trip is the other spouse's separate debt. Compare: a bill for books on a subject only one spouse is interested in is a community debt because it enhances that spouse, which in turn enhances the community. The same can't be said about the Hawaii trip.
- If one spouse is held liable for harm to the other, the debt may be considered a separate debt of the spouse causing the harm and the recovery is the separate property of the injured spouse.

Debts incurred between separation and divorce for necessaries (food, housing, clothing and health care) for a spouse or children are considered community debts, unless there is a support order stating who must pay. A creditor may obtain payment from either spouse. If the wife pays, but the husband incurred the debt, the wife may not be entitled to reimbursement.

Example

George and Fran separated in October and planned to divorce. In December, George was in a car accident, and was billed $250 for fixing the car and $100 toward his medical costs. In March, when George and Fran drafted their divorce agreement, George requested that Fran contribute toward the bills. Fran refused. They took it to

---

[6] Family Code § 2625

court and the judge ordered George to pay the full car bill, but ordered Fran to help with the medical costs—a "necessary" of life.

Remember: dividing debts at divorce does not affect your original relationship with your creditors. Just because Russ agreed to pay back the joint debt to Sears doesn't mean Sears can't go after his ex-wife Mary for the payments if Russ fails to pay. Creditors are not interested in your agreement with your ex-spouse—they are only interested in getting their money.

Make sure your separation agreement doesn't leave you vulnerable. When negotiating a divorce settlement agreement, separated spouses have to keep in mind that even though an ex-spouse is ordered to pay a debt, if he or she has no money, they won't pay and the other may be forced to. If you fear your spouse might not pay debts assigned to him/her, then in your settlement, if there are enough assets in the community, it would be better for you to take on the debts yourself along with a larger share of community assets to balance the extra debt load, or possibly to sell some community property and pay off all the debts right away. It is essential for spouses with overwhelming marital debt to get sound legal advice regarding the best way to handle the situation. If you want to file for bankruptcy, read the section above; be sure you know what's involved, and whether or not it is a good choice in your particular case.

CHAPTER 14

Laws for living together

This chapter is for people who are cohabiting—living together in a couple relationship—but are neither married nor registered domestic partners, and who do not have a written agreement to define their relationship.

A. Why an agreement is essential

Unlike people who are married or registered domestic partners, unmarried couples who live together without an agreement are regarded by the law as two strangers who share a space. You have no clarity as to how you will deal with income, debts, purchases, or any of the things that always come up in any relationship. You have no protections or benefits to fall back on in case of illness, accident or other emergency.

You came together with affection and trust, but without a written agreement, you are living in a state of legal ambiguity, thus subject to misunderstanding which can produce friction, or if upset comes from another quarter, your ambiguous arrangements are subject to reinterpretation through emotional hindsight.

Moral of the story: if you are not married it is *very* important to have a written agreement as to who owns what, who pays which debts, and other financial matters. Oral agreements and understandings are better than nothing, but just barely, as they can be difficult to prove. Clear agreements prevent arguments and lawsuits.

B. How does it start?

People fall in love and start living together. It's so fun and easy that they might forget they are entering into a relationship that has all kinds of ambiguity built in and potential for real trouble if things get strained. They work things out as they go along based on affection, trust, and various oral agreements or understandings about how things will work: how bills get paid, who owns the hi-fi and CDs they buy, and so on.

This is a problem waiting to happen. Oral agreements and understandings are notoriously difficult to prove. Worse, if one person or the other gets angry, the ambiguity is an open invitation for divergent claims as to what they really did or did not agree to. The anger and sense of betrayal escalates and the battle is on.

We recommend a written agreement for every couple living together. In addition to making your relationship clear, you have an opportunity to build in features that can help make your relationship stronger and help you get through snags in communication in the future. This is discussed in chapter 8 in detail.

In this chapter, we discuss the rules for couples who live together without a written agreement.

The *Marvin* case —written, oral or implied contracts will apply

You may have heard about the famous legal battle of *Marvin vs. Marvin*.[1] Lee Marvin and Michele Triola lived together for about seven years, then split up. Michele sued, claiming she and Marvin had agreed orally to share all earnings and assets. She argued that she gave up a singing career to become his housekeeper, cook and companion, and that it would be unfair for Marvin to keep all the assets acquired during their relationship. The California Supreme Court agreed and held that a contract to split assets can be oral or implied by the parties' conduct—another excellent reason to write things down, to make sure that you aren't bound to an agreement you did not quite intend to make. It also means that couples who are not legally married will have their claims against each other decided by principles of standard contract law.

C. Dealings are presumed to be at arm's length

Married couples and domestic partners have a *fiduciary* relationship, which requires a very high standard of fairness and openness in their dealings, but people who live together are treated by law as strangers doing business and are presumed to be dealing at arm's length where one need not be open and forthcoming with the other, so long as there is no outright fraud. A couple can agree in writing to a fiduciary standard for their relationship, as we have you do in the Couples Contract. Otherwise, duties higher than arm's length dealing are not presumed, but must be proven, so the burden is on the party claiming unfair treatment. However, this might not be difficult as a *confidential* relationship—which imposes a fiduciary standard—can arise when one mate gains the confidence of the other and purports to act in the other's best interests, say by undertaking to manage the mate's financial affairs. A fiduciary relationship can also arise if one takes control of the property of the other. For most intimate couples, finding evidence of a confidential relationship shouldn't be difficult. Therefore, committed couples should always act as if a fiduciary standard exists.

---

[1] *Marvin vs. Marvin* (1976) 18 C3d 660

D. Duty of support

Absent a written agreement, there is no duty for one mate to support the other in the present or in the future. However, the *Marvin* case discussed above points out that agreements for support or to share income can be implied from circumstances or conduct, so here, again, it is very important to have a written agreement that makes it clear whether or not a support obligation exists.

E. Property rights

When a couple lives together, California courts apply general contract law to decide legal issues concerning the relationship. If the couple were married, it would be *presumed* that property acquired by either person during the union was owned equally. However, if a couple is only living together, no presumption of equal ownership exists. This means the ownership of all acquired property is ambiguous and open to argument. Moral of the story: if you are not married it is *very* important to have a written agreement as to who owns what, who pays which debts, and other financial matters. Oral agreements and understandings are better than nothing, but just barely, as they can be difficult to prove. Clear agreements prevent arguments and lawsuits.

F. Joint accounts and owning property together

It is often convenient to have a joint account for paying household expenses, but there is some risk involved when you do that. One of you needs to be very good at balancing the statement every month to make sure you can cover your checks. Either of you can use all the money in the account at any time and you are both responsible for any overdrafts and charges. If this is a concern, you can arrange the account so that both signatures are required for withdrawals and checks.

Implied agreement? Remember the *Marvin* case in section B above? An agreement to share earnings can be oral or implied from conduct. A joint account could be one piece of evidence to show such an agreement. So, if you open a joint account or get credit together, it would be better to have a written agreement making it clear that there is no agreement to otherwise share income or to support one another.

Taxes? If one person regularly puts more money into a joint account than the other, the difference can be treated by the IRS as income to the person who put in less.[2] It might seem unlikely that they would ever catch on, but if they did, the rule could be applied and back taxes and penalties assessed. It's possible.

Sharing property. If you decide to buy a house or other large asset with your partner, you should have a written agreement about how you are going to deal with the down payment and all costs of ownership and, especially, how you will deal with the situation when one of you no longer wants to own the property. At least make sure the title and loan documents accurately reflect your ownership interest.

If you separate, you should immediately close all joint bank and credit accounts.

G. Who owes the debts?

Generally, one mate is not responsible for the debts of the other. However, if you co-sign a loan, open a joint bank account or sign a credit agreement with your partner, you are responsible for those accounts. Our advice: unless you have a written agreement, keep your finances separate.

Checking Your Credit

When people live together for a long time, or any amount of time spent sharing credit cards or bank accounts, their credit can get mixed up so that one partner's bad credit can sometimes be attributed to the other. To check this, you can request a copy of your own credit report and check it for errors or outdated information. There are three major credit bureaus that keep national credit records:

- Equifax   (800) 685-1111   www.equifax.com
- Experian   (888) 397-3742   www.experian.com
- Trans Union   (800) 888-4213   www.transunion.com

You are now entitled to one free credit report every year from each of these major credit bureaus. You can contact each bureau individually or apply to all three at once at www.annualcreditreport.com. Either way, you definitely want your report from all three credit bureaus, as their files are not always the same and correcting your records at one organization will not correct them at the other two. If you find an error or outdated information, contact the bureau in writing. They are required by law to investigate and correct errors, so be prepared to provide whatever records you have to prove that there's an error.

[2] Internal Revenue Code § 61(a); Treasury Regulation § 1.61-2(a), (d); *Lucas v. Earl* (1930) 281 U.S. 111

H. Having children together

No one ever doubts who a child's mother is, but with fathers it's not always so easy. By ancient legal tradition (begun centuries before DNA tracing) whenever a married woman has a child, the child is conclusively presumed to be her husband's child.[3] It takes powerful evidence to overcome this presumption. It does not apply to unmarried parents and the presumptions that do apply are much weaker. For children born to an unmarried mother, the paternity of the child is an open question. *Paternity* simply means "fatherhood; the state, fact or condition of being a father." Because so many rights and responsibilities flow from the parent-child relationship, it is important for unmarried partners to clearly establish the paternity of any children born during their cohabitation.

The easiest way to establish legal paternity is to fill out a Declaration of Paternity at the hospital when the child is born. If you didn't do this at the hospital, you can get the forms from the district attorney's office. A man who fills out this form is giving up some of his rights to DNA testing and making it easier for child support to be collected from him. Don't sign it if you are not sure.

On the other hand, signing this form does give the father legal rights to request custody, contest an adoption and establish inheritance rights. Like the decision of whether or not to be legally married, signing this form has legal advantages and disadvantages and should be taken very seriously.

For more about children and parenting, see chapter 15.

I. Can I take my partner's name?

In California, people over the age of eighteen have the right to use any first, last and middle names they like. You have two ways to change your name legally: the *usage* method and by *petitioning the court*. You can take your partner's name by using the new name consistently (the usage method)—no court action is necessary and the change is legally valid.[4] For a more complete discussion and instructions for how to change your name by court petition, see Nolo's *How to Change Your Name in California*.

---

[3] Family Code § 7540   [4] Code of Civil Procedure § 1279.5

J. Medical emergencies

Married couples (and domestic partners while in California) are empowered by law to make medical decisions for each other in situations where the injured or sick spouse has become unable to make his or her own decisions. However, if an unmarried person becomes seriously ill or disabled, even if you have been living together for years, medical authorities will be forced to turn to his or her parents, adult children or siblings to make medical decisions. In fact, an unmarried partner might even have trouble visiting. As we all know, people sometimes become estranged from relatives, or you might love them but still have a higher degree of closeness or trust with someone who is not a relative. Sometimes a separated spouse, family and friends are all at odds over what should be done. The way to avoid confusion and conflict when minutes are precious is to sign one simple but vitally important document called an Advance Health Care Directive. It has two parts:

(1) A Power of Attorney for Health Care, which allows you to name one or more people who can make health care decisions if you are not able to, including the decision to withhold or withdraw life-prolonging procedures.

(2) Instructions for Health Care, which states in advance your wishes regarding how you want to be cared for if you are not able to make decisions yourself, including whether to use life-prolonging procedures.

This form is on the CD that comes with this book.

There's one more step you should take to avoid confusion and conflict: after you finish those documents, sit down with your spouse, relatives, and closest friends and show them the documents, give them a copy, and discuss your ideas for how you'd like to be treated if anything happens. This way, everyone will know what you wanted, whether the document can be found or not.

Visiting. The right to visit a patient in the hospital is another right that comes along with marriage. As hurtful as it might be, if you're not married, the person you have lived with for many years might not be allowed to visit you in the hospital. A health care directive will confer these rights on the person of your choice, as well.

After death. The "next of kin" has the right to decide what happens to a person's remains after death. This includes making decisions about organ donation or other anatomical gifts, as well as deciding where the person will be buried and making other funeral arrangements. These rights can also be given to someone else as part of your Advance Health Care Directive.

K. Health insurance

Health insurance is a contractual benefit, which means that each policy has its own terms and conditions. To determine if your policy will cover your partner, contact the plan administrator. Increasingly companies are allowing unmarried partners to participate in health care plans. But beware! Even if you pay the premiums but are not legally married or registered as domestic partners, coverage can be denied if the policy's terms require that a valid marriage exist before extending coverage.

L. Family Leave Act

Employers with 50 or more employees are required to grant leaves of absence of up to four months to employees who have been with the company for at least one year and who need to take time off to care for a new baby, or an ill parent, spouse, registered domestic partner or child. Unmarried partners have no right to leave to care for an ill mate unless you happen to have an enlightened employer who allows leave for a "significant other." When the employee returns from leave under the Act, the same or a comparable job must be available. The law also requires that employers let workers on leave continue their health care and retirement benefits, although the employer can insist that the employee on leave pay the group rate.

M. Social Security and other government benefits

1. Social Security

Let's take Social Security first. This is one area where the rights of married and unmarried couples are very different. As a partner in an unmarried couple, you are entitled only to whatever benefits you individually earned. This differs importantly from married couples. The spouse of a wage earner who contributed to Social Security is eligible upon retirement to receive benefits based upon their spouse's contribution. A widower or a divorced spouse of a wage earner is also eligible for benefits.

If you and your mate are able (under California law) to get married and you have chosen not to, you should consider that by staying unmarried, the non-wage earner in your relationship will not be entitled to Social Security benefits based on your earnings.

On the other hand, if you are receiving Social Security benefits as a widow(er) or a former spouse, they may be reduced or eliminated if you get married. The Social Security laws sometimes favor those who are married during their working years and unmarried when they need to collect benefits.

2. Welfare

Generally, a person receiving welfare who lives with a partner who is not the child's father can continue to receive support so long as the partner does not contribute to her support or the support of her children. However, if the parent registers a domestic partnership, welfare eligibility would be affected, since registered domestic partners have a duty to support each other. Each welfare office handles cohabitation situations differently, so contact your local office to find out exactly what their guidelines and requirements are so your grant won't be cut off or reduced by living with your partner.

A non-related partner has no duty to contribute to the support of his partner's family. If the mother's grant is reduced or cut off because a non-related partner is living in the house, the mother should seek the help of the nearest Legal Aid office. Look in the white pages of your telephone book for the nearest office.

Welfare laws are in a state of change. Check with your local welfare office or Legal Aid for the most up-to-date information.

3. Other government benefits

The rules concerning medical benefits for old and poor Americans are similar to those for welfare benefits. You can have a live-in partner and still get benefits for you and your children as long as your live-in partner does not contribute to the support of you or your children.

If you are receiving any type of government benefit and plan to begin living with your partner, you would be wise to call the local government office of the benefit program and ask what the restrictions and requirements are for live-in partners, so you can comply with their rules and not risk losing or reducing your benefits.

4. Pensions and retirement plans, military and death benefits

Life insurance policies allow the policy owner to name the person who will receive the benefits upon the death of the insured. This is a contract right, and generally can be assigned to anyone you choose, including your unmarried partner. The same is true of defined contribution retirement plans—funds you pay into and accumulate value through investments you direct, like an IRA or 401(k) plan. If you die, the money in your account is paid to the person you designate. If you are not married, you generally can designate any beneficiary you want. If you want these benefits to go to your partner on your death, fill out the paperwork with your employer, insurance company, bank or broker. Most other kinds of retirement plans only pay death benefits to your spouse, dependent children, and sometimes your registered domestic partner. These include most public and private pension plans that pay benefits based on a formula, rather than on the amount you contributed. Military and other federal government plans won't provide spousal benefits unless you are legally married, which does not include registered domestic partners.

N. Will I inherit from my partner?

If a person who is not married or in a domestic partnership dies without a will, the surviving mate will inherit nothing, as he or she is not considered an heir under the intestate laws that determine who inherits if a person dies without a will. A married spouse or registered domestic partner would automatically inherit from a deceased spouse who dies without a will. Depending on the situation, this can leave the surviving mate in serious financial trouble. If you are involved in a living-together relationship and want your partner to inherit from you, make sure you have a valid will or trust naming him or her as a beneficiary. See Nolo's *Will Book* and *Make Your Own Living Trust*.

O. If my partner is killed or injured, can I get compensation?

California has a wrongful death statute that allows a spouse or registered domestic partner to recover damages for the wrongful death of his or her spouse or partner. However, unmarried persons are not authorized to bring a wrongful death action.[5] Likewise, a spouse or domestic partner might have rights if his/her partner is negligently injured, but unmarried people do not have these rights—if your mate gets injured or killed through someone's negligence, you can't do anything about it.

---

[5] Code of Civil Procedure § 377.60

Examples

Mickey and Minnie, married for 20 years, were at Disneyland riding Space Mountain when the car flew off the track, killing Minnie. Minnie was Mickey's only means of support. Mickey would be allowed to sue Disney for the wrongful death of Minnie.

Daisy and Donald, who lived together for 20 years, were at Disneyland riding Space Mountain in the same car with Mickey and Minnie. Donald was killed and was Daisy's only means of support. Daisy cannot sue Disney under California's wrongful death laws because she and Donald were never married.

Likewise, married persons are also able to recover damages for *loss of consortium* when one spouse is injured or killed. *Consortium* encompasses companionship, love, affection, sex—all the comforts that flow from relationship. The cause of action is *strictly* confined to married partners.[6]

P. Taxes

Nonmarital partners are not allowed to file joint income tax returns. Depending on your income level, this may or may not be a disadvantage. Support or other money transferred between unmarried people might be subject to gift tax if it exceeds the annual $11,000 per person gift tax exclusion, which is limited to $1 million over the giver's lifetime. Any inheritance left to the surviving nonmarital partner worth over $1.5 million will be taxed heavily (up to 55%). $1.5 million may seem like a lot of money, but with the prices of real estate in California, it could be a problem for the survivor. Contrast this with marital partners who can use their *marital deduction* to inherit any sum from their spouse, free of federal taxation. We think all unmarried couples should see a Certified Financial Planner or tax accountant to get some advice and do some planning.

Examples

Bill and Hillary were married for 20 years. Bill left everything he owned to Hillary—primarily a pizza franchise valued at $2 million. Hillary inherits the franchise without incurring any tax liability.

Lucy and Ricky lived together for 20 years, unmarried. Ricky died and left Lucy everything in a will. Ricky owned a home, free and clear, valued at $2 million. Lucy may have to pay many thousands in taxes because she can't claim a *marital deduction*.

---

[6] *Elden vs. Sheldon* (1988) 46 C3d 267

Q. Can a landlord refuse to rent to us?

Landlords are prohibited from discriminating against prospective tenants on the basis of marital status or sexual orientation.[7] The California Supreme Court and federal Ninth Circuit Court disagree about whether this kind of law deprives landlords of freedom of religion.[8] As a result, the law on this is uncertain until both courts agree or the U.S. Supreme Court decides.

R. What if we move?

A few states still make cohabitation illegal for unmarried people. A few refuse to enforce cohabitation agreements on public policy grounds. If you move to another state, be sure to have your relationship agreement reviewed by a family law attorney there; find out if it is valid in your new state and discuss your options if it is not.

*   *   *

So, there you have it—a brief overview of how unmarried relationships differ legally from marriage, a discussion that applies equally whether the relationship is hetero- or homosexual. For more information, we recommend Nolo's books *Living Together: A Guide for Unmarried Couples* and *A Legal Guide for Lesbian & Gay Couples*.

---

[7] Government Code § 12955
[8] *Smith v. Fair Employment & Housing Commission* (1996) 12 C4th 1143; *Smith v. Anchorage Equal Rights Commission* (9th Cir, 1999) 165 F3d 692

CHAPTER 15

Children —having, adopting, raising

A. Paternity —who are the child's parents?

Good news! California does not use *legitimate* and *illegitimate* to describe children. The law now says "the parent and child relationship extends equally to every child and to every parent, regardless of the marital status of the parents."[1] But it is still profoundly important to establish very clearly who a child's biological parents are. Inheritance, child custody, support, visitation, adoption and many other laws specify the rights and duties of parents and children. Then there's the importance of having a coherent medical history.

1. Paternity

While it's normally not difficult to figure out who a child's biological mother is, identifying the father isn't always so easy. California law gives rules to establish whether a parent-child relationship exists.[2] These rules are somewhat complicated, but in a broad sense they provide that a man is *presumed* to be the father of a child in any of the following circumstances:

Circumstance 1. The man is married to the mother when the child is born, or was married to her within 300 days of the child's birth. Even if the man dies, or he and the mother divorce while she is pregnant, he is still presumed to be the father.

Circumstance 2. The man and the mother, before the child's birth, attempted to get married—got a license and had a ceremony—but the marriage wasn't valid for some reason, such as one partner was still married to someone else, *and* the child was born during the attempted marriage period or within 300 days after its termination.

Circumstance 3. After the child's birth, the man and the mother marry (or attempt to marry), even if the marriage is later annulled, *and*

- The man consents to being named father on the birth certificate; *or*
- The man signs a written agreement to support the child or is ordered by a court to do so.

Circumstance 4. The man receives the child into his home and openly holds out the child as his natural child.

---

[1] Family Code § 7602   [2] Family Code §§ 7600–7730 (The Uniform Parentage Act)

These rules now apply equally to registered domestic partners, and we can presume that they are gender neutral (see below), so they may apply to a woman under certain circumstances (see below).

Presumptions can be rebutted. The rules above deal with presumptions, meaning that a certain situation is *presumed* to produce a certain legal conclusion unless rebutted by stronger evidence.[3] In this case, a man who takes a child into his home and says he's the father is legally presumed to be the father, whether or not he is married to the mother. This doesn't mean he actually *is* the father. The mother or another man claiming to be the actual father can *rebut* the presumption by showing clear and convincing evidence that the other man is in fact the child's father.

No presumption. The presumption of paternity will not be allowed in Circumstance 2, 3, or 4 if either of the following is true:

- The child was conceived as a result of rape and the man was convicted for it;
- The child was conceived as a result of "unlawful sexual intercourse," the man was convicted, the mother was under age 15, and the man was over 21.

Conclusive presumption. Finally, there is one situation where the paternity presumptions cannot be rebutted:

The child of a wife cohabiting with her husband, who is not impotent or sterile, is conclusively presumed to be a child of the marriage.[4]

This nonrebuttable presumption has produced some bizarre cases, including some where the racial characteristics of the child were obviously different from those of the mother's husband. For this and other reasons, the legislature modified the presumption to allow certain people—the husband, a man claiming to be the father, or the child through a guardian—to challenge the husband's status as father within two years of the child's birth if DNA tests indicate that the husband is not the father.[5] Advances in genetic testing make it easy to prove or disprove paternity with at least 98% certainty.

However, the court can refuse to allow genetic testing if the mother and her husband are raising the child together, and if the issue is not raised within the two-year period, the presumption can't be rebutted at all.[6] The time is short because courts are concerned to preserve the matrimonial family. In one case, the lover of the child's mother proved with 98% accuracy that he was the father of the child. The California court rejected his claim because the mother was married to another man at the time

[3] *In Re Olivia H.* (1987) 196 CA3d 325 [4] Family Code § 7540
[5] Family Code §§ 7550–7557 [6] *Michelle Marie W. vs. Ronald W.* (1985) 39 CA3d 354

and the court felt the "integrity of the matrimonial family" outweighed any claim to fatherhood by the lover. A very divided United States Supreme Court upheld the decision.[7] More recently, a California court found that the conclusive presumption is unconstitutional when applied to a marital relationship which ended eight days after the child's birth.[8]

This area of law is still changing, but a trend may be emerging. Some recent decisions have found that the legal father is the one who had a parental relationship with the child, if he had ever been married to the mother and the bio-dad did not establish a relationship with the child. A family unit seems important, even if tests prove someone else is the biological father. If the child calls someone "daddy" or "mommy," the court may be inclined to make it legal.

Likewise, recent surrogacy cases looked at the contract to see who the parties intended to be the legal parents and decided the matter accordingly.[9] Expect more developments in this field. Consult a lawyer before you get involved with surrogacy.

Gender neutral. The California Supreme Court is currently considering whether the presumption favoring a man who receives the child into his home (circumstance 4) must be applied in a gender-neutral way, so that a woman (the mother's domestic partner) who receives the child into her home and openly holds out the child as her own is entitled to the same presumption. The appellate court said the child cannot legally have two mothers, but another woman can be the child's legal "second parent" without a second-parent adoption. When the California Supreme Court decides the case, we'll post the decision on our Web site, www.nolocouples.com.

Many legal experts believe that the presumptions related to marriage (circumstance 3 and the conclusive presumption discussed above) will also be applied in a gender-neutral way to a mother's registered domestic partner or to a mother and the woman she has attempted to marry, even though California does not recognize same-sex marriages. Stay tuned.

2. What if the father will not acknowledge paternity?

Whenever there is a paternity issue, the court may on its own motion or at the request of any person whose blood is involved (mother, child, father) order any or all of the parties to submit to DNA tests in order to establish paternity. If a party refuses to submit to the blood tests the court has ordered, that refusal is admissible in evidence

---

[7] *Michael H. vs. Gerald D.* (1989) 491 US 110   [8] *In Re Melissa G.* (1989) 213 CA3d 1082
[9] *Johnson v. Calvert* (1993) 5 C4th 84, *Marriage of Buzzanca* (1998) 61 CA4th 1410

on the paternity issue and the court may resolve the issue against the party who has refused to comply, or enforce the original order for blood tests if the interests of justice require.[10] Paternity disputes can be costly and humiliating. See a specialist attorney or call your local district attorney's office for help.

3. Alternative insemination

When a married woman has a child by alternative (sometimes called "artificial") insemination, and becomes impregnated with semen from someone other than her husband, her husband is nevertheless irrebuttably presumed to be the father and the sperm donor has no rights. The husband's consent to the procedure must be in a writing signed by both him and his wife.[11] The law prefers "intact" families and does not want the donor to come along and disrupt things, nor does it want the husband to fail to support the children. In California, if the insemination procedure for an unmarried woman who does not have a registered domestic partner is performed by a licensed physician, the donor is not considered the father.[12] If a licensed physician is not used, the donor may be considered the father.

4. Surrogacy and in vitro fertilization

In vitro fertilization is the fertilization of a human egg outside the human body. Through this process an egg can be removed from one woman, fertilized in the laboratory with the intended father's sperm, and then implanted in the uterus of a *different* woman, who gives birth to the child. This process allows a woman who is unable to carry a fetus the opportunity to have a child of her own egg.

The legal question for in vitro fertilization is whether the egg donor or the child bearer is the biological mother of the child. The California Supreme Court reasoned[13] that maternity can be established by the act of giving birth *or* by DNA tests.[14] Two biological mothers can be established by such tests, but the court rejected the suggestion that a child may have two natural mothers, so it resolved the conflict by looking to the intent of the surrogacy contract. The court concluded that if the egg donor and the child bearer do not coincide in one woman, the parties' intention, as expressed in the surrogacy contract, will be determinative. This means that the woman who was intended to raise the child as her own, under the terms of the contract, will be considered the child's biological mother under California law.

---

[10] Family Code § 7551   [11] Family Code § 7613(a)   [12] Family Code § 7613
[13] *Johnson vs. Calvert* (1993) 5 C4th 84   [14] Family Code § 7650

Surrogacy. The situation above is to be distinguished from a surrogacy arrangement, where the surrogate provides both the egg and womb. Upon birth of the child, the surrogate mother relinquishes all rights in and responsibilities for the child and turns the child over to the man, whose wife formally adopts the child.

In surrogacy, the surrogate is undeniably the biological mother of the child, but the legal question is whether she can be compelled to perform her contractual promise to consent to the adoption of the child by the intended mother after birth.

You might have heard of the *Case of Baby* M that was big news in the late 1980s. In that case, the surrogate mother refused to give up custody of the child after she was born. The New Jersey Supreme Court ruled that the surrogate contract was unenforceable, declared the surrogate mother the natural mother, and then decided the case as it would any other disputed custody case. Although *Baby* M is not controlling in California, California courts may look to it for guidance in a case where the surrogate mother changes her mind.

If you're planning to have a child by any type of surrogate method, you should definitely see a lawyer who is a specialist in that field.

B. Adoptions

This is a court procedure whereby an adult or a couple assumes a parent-child relationship with the natural child[15] of another. The adopting parent(s) assume(s) full legal responsibility for the child, including the legal duty to support. The natural parent(s), assuming they are alive, are legally eliminated from any relationship with the child. This means that an adopted child inherits from his or her adoptive parents and their family just as if he or she was a natural child, but would not inherit from his or her natural parents should they die without a will.

If a married person wants to adopt, both the husband and wife must consent; one can't adopt without the other. Single-parent adoptions are legally possible and becoming more common, as are adoptions by gay couples. For more information on gay adoptions, see Nolo's *A Legal Guide for Lesbian & Gay Couples.*

Adoption is a weighty step to take. It is a tremendous legal, financial and moral commitment to another human being. Unless you are absolutely sure that you want to raise and support the child, don't adopt. You can divorce a spouse, but you can't divorce a kid. Adoption can be very beneficial for a child because it creates the legal

---

[15] Family Code § 9300 (adoption of one adult by another is also possible)

basis for a stable parent-child relationship. If you're an adult taking care of someone else's child and want some legal recognition, however, weigh an adoption against a guardianship (see Section D below).

Common questions many people have about adoption include:

- "I will be 45 years old next month; am I too old to adopt?"
- "I have a juvenile arrest; does this mean I can't adopt?"
- "My wife is deaf; will they hold that against us?"
- "Ten years ago I placed my own child up for adoption; does this disqualify me from adopting?"

The answer to all these questions is "No," but qualified, because this sort of information and a lot more will be considered in deciding whether or not it is in the best interests of the particular child for you to adopt him or her. Apart from a history of child abuse or molestation, no one fact will either qualify you or disqualify you.

Adoptions of children fall into four categories, which we discuss briefly. For more information, visit your county law library and ask the librarian for assistance.

1. Stepparent adoption

When the parent with custody of a child marries a new spouse, the new spouse (stepparent) has no legal responsibility for the child unless there is a legal stepparent adoption, even though he or she may love the child and perform all the parental duties that a natural parent would normally perform. Stepparent adoptions are the most common type of adoption. You can do one yourself with Nolo's *How to Adopt Your Stepchild in California*.

If a stepparent wants to adopt, and the custodial parent and the child (if he or she is old enough to have an opinion) agree, the next thing to do is deal with the noncustodial parent (the other legal parent). If the parent has died, there is obviously no need to be concerned. Any child adopted by a stepparent after the natural parent dies can still keep any Social Security benefits stemming from the account of the deceased parent.

You may be unsure whether or not the child has a legal father. If the parents were never married, don't assume that the child doesn't. Paternity and fatherhood are covered in Section A, above. If the child has a legal father, or a legal second female parent, he or she must be notified of an adoption and his or her objections (if any) will be considered by the court.[16] Even if there is no presumed father, some effort to locate and get the permission of the biological father is usually required.

---

[16] *Michael U. vs. Jaime B.* (1985) 39 C3d 787

Assuming the child has a legally recognized noncustodial parent, either of the following must happen before an adoption can take place:

- The noncustodial parent must consent to the adoption and sign a consent form before a county clerk or a probation worker if in California, or a notary public if outside California.
- The noncustodial parent must have abandoned the child. This means that he or she has willfully failed to communicate with the child *and* has failed to pay for the care, support and education of the child in question, when able to do so, for a period of one year or more.

If you file a petition in Superior Court for a stepparent adoption, your case will be referred to a county agency to investigate and write a report for the judge. A social worker will visit your home to talk with the natural parent, prospective adoptive parent, and child if he or she is old enough. Don't worry about the visit. The county isn't looking to dig up dirt; it likes stepparent adoptions. The social worker just wants to make sure there's a stable and loving home. Keep in mind that a judge won't approve an adoption if the county submits a negative report.

Let us repeat: don't worry about the social worker's visit. Every family has problems. None of us has a perfect family, even though we often waste a lot of energy trying to convince our neighbors that we do. If something in your life might weigh against you in an adoption, such as a bad conduct discharge from the military or a past drinking or credit problem, it is usually best to be frank with the social worker. She'll probably learn of the skeletons anyway and we have found that old bones don't rattle as much if you bring them out of the closet yourself. After all, in a stepparent adoption you are already living with the child and probably exercising parental authority, so the department has little motive to reject your petition.

Assuming the county report is favorable, the next step is to go to court and have the judge grant her approval. This is pretty much a formality, with handshakes all around, and the adoptive parent assuring the judge that he will assume full legal responsibility for the child and, as well, provide the love and care so necessary to all children. If the child is over 12 years old, he or she must also consent to the adoption.

As part of an adoption proceeding, the child may be given a new name (often the last name of the adopting father). This is not required, however, and the child can keep his or her original surname. Also, the state will issue a new birth certificate with the new name, if desired. If the child was born outside of California, you can probably get the state of birth to issue a new birth certificate. If the child was born outside the United States, however, it is usually impossible.

2. Agency adoption

An agency adoption occurs when a licensed adoption agency places a child in the home of an adopting parent or parents. The agency gets a full relinquishment of the rights from the natural parents before putting the child up for adoption, so there are normally no worries about a natural parent later surfacing to try and claim "his or her child."

Generally, the adoptive parents must be at least 10 years older than the child. There is no upper age limit or rules concerning physical or mental disabilities for the prospective parents, but adoption agencies usually have their own policies. Indeed, as birth control, family size and changing societal attitudes toward "legitimacy" have reduced the pool of children available for adoption, agencies have become very selective in choosing adoptive parents.

Prospective adoptive parents must file a petition in Superior Court and the adoption must be approved by a judge. If the child is over 12, he or she must consent to the adoption. A county social worker will investigate the family (see section 1 above) and submit a report to the judge. The standards applied in agency adoptions are stricter than in stepparent adoptions because, unlike stepparent adoptions, the child has had no relationship with the adoptive parents.

Most reputable adoption agencies charge high fees. Part of this money pays for the investigation to determine whether or not the prospective parents are suitable. Adoption agencies prefer that the adoptive parents retain their own lawyer to prepare and present the necessary paperwork to the judge.

3. County adoption

In a county adoption, children in the care of the county are placed for adoption. In some cases the natural parents consent to the adoption, while in others a judge first terminates parental rights because the parents have abandoned the children or have been found to be unfit parents. Most of these adoptions grow out of foster placements.

Through this program (sometimes called Fost-Adopt), it is now possible for prospective adoptive parents to get on a county list, foster parent and then adopt the child. Keep in mind that the children available through the county program are often not healthy newborns. Many are disabled, abused or emotionally disturbed older children. Many infants coming through the program have been born to drug abusers. They may not be drug-addicted themselves, but the long-term effects of drug addiction at birth are still largely unknown. In addition, Fost-Adopting leaves the adoptive parents vulnerable to the possibility that a reunification will occur. Reunification with the birth parents is presumed to be in the child's best interest for the first 12 to 18 months of the placement. Often, the natural parents rehabilitate themselves sufficiently to regain custody of their children. At the same time, however, if the parents are unable to get their act together, you will be first in line to adopt. Of course, not to be overlooked is the fact that the children in these programs are in desperate need of loving, caring parents. The costs are low, and given that you've already been approved as foster parents, your approval to adopt will be easy.

4. Private adoption

It is possible to adopt a child without going through an adoption agency or the county. These are called "private" or "independent" adoptions. When you read about "baby for sale" scandals, this is the type of adoption involved. Although most private adoptions are carried out honestly and fairly, abuses do crop up now and then. Things have been better in recent years as the state has regulated this area more closely.

When a child is located for private adoption, it is essential that the mother and father sign a consent form. If the identity of the father isn't certain, all possible candidates should sign. Of course, if no one has the foggiest idea who the father is, it is not necessary to get a signature. Even if a parent will not consent to an adoption, the adoption may still be possible if the parent has abandoned the child.[17]

Like other adoptions, private adoptions require that you file a petition with the Superior Court and that a county social worker be appointed to investigate. You will need an attorney's help in preparing the papers, and possibly to advise you on how to deal with the social worker. You can expect a strict investigation. After all, the child is not already in your home, as in the stepparent situation, nor has an agency or the county already investigated you.

You must be 10 years older than the child, but there are no other rules as to mental or physical capability. If you are (or were ever) married, the social worker will want to see your marriage certificate and, if applicable, your final decree of divorce, a certified copy of the child's birth certificate, the marriage and divorce records of the child's natural parents and whatever else the social worker thinks is relevant. It is very important that the social worker recommend the adoption.

If the county approves the adoption and the court grants it, the child is yours. The child will be given your last name if you like and you can have the birth certificate

---

[17] Family Code § 7822

reissued. If you are considering a private adoption, make sure you get expert advice to ensure that your rights are protected and that the adoption is handled correctly.

C. The duty to support children

Parents have a duty to support their children.[18] A child is entitled to support until the child dies, marries, becomes self-supporting or reaches 18. But, so long as the child is in high school full-time and not self-supporting, support will continue to completion of 12th grade or age 19, whichever comes first. If the parents agree in writing, support can be required to age 21 or through college. Support for a disabled minor or adult child who is unable to work extends so long as the disability lasts.

California obligates both the *father and mother* to support their children, but it is a crime only if you *willfully* fail to do so; thus, parents who have no income or savings or can't find work are not guilty of a crime. In determining the ability to support, a court will consider all income—including Social Security, unemployment, pension payments, welfare and other benefits—in deciding if there is enough money to take care of the kids. A nonsupporting parent can be ordered at the request of the custodial parent to submit to a vocational examination to determine his or her ability to work, or be required to submit a list of places he or she has applied for work.[19]

Support is aggressively enforced in court and, if necessary, by government agencies. Nonsupport is a crime, punishable by a jail sentence and a fine,[20] but no particular amount is set by law unless support becomes an issue in a divorce or paternity action, or in an action by the government when the child receives welfare benefits. In court, the amount of child support is very specifically determined by provable facts fed into a formula, and usually calculated with the assistance of child support software. Read more about child support and how to calculate the exact amount the law requires in *How to Do Your Own Divorce in California*, Chapter 5.

It is illegal to abandon or desert your child.[21] Beyond support, parents are obligated to accept their child into their home, or to provide alternative shelter when required to do so by a child protective agency, so when a child is removed from a parent's home, whether for the child's protection or for the child's delinquency, the parents can be ordered to pay for the child's support while outside their care.

---

[18] Family Code § 3900   [19] Family Code § 4505
[20] Penal Code §§ 270, 271(a)   [21] Penal Code § 270.5

D. Guardianship and medical consent

Guardianship

For a variety of reasons, minors may live temporarily or even permanently with adults other than their parents. You may take care of someone else's child—maybe a niece, nephew, grandchild or even a friend's child. Or, you may leave your own child with another adult, perhaps while you are away for an extended period of time.

In California, at least one adult must be legally responsible for a minor. You can use a guardianship to fulfill this requirement. A guardianship legally authorizes an adult other than a legal parent to have custody of, and be responsible for, a minor. The guardian takes care of the minor's physical well-being, provides food and shelter, and attends to the minor's education and health care. In some cases, it also means that the guardian manages the minor's money and property.

Don't confuse guardianship and adoption; they are quite different. When a minor is adopted, the adoptive parent becomes the legal parent of the child. The biological parent loses all parental rights and obligations, including the obligation to support. When a minor has a guardian, the legal relationship between the biological parent and the child remains intact. The biological parent is legally obligated to support the child, and if that parent dies without a will, the child will inherit his or her property.

In California, a *legal* guardianship can be obtained only by:
- Filing legal papers with a court;
- Notifying certain agencies;
- Notifying certain relatives of the minor;
- Appearing before a judge; and
- Being appointed guardian by the court.

In the real world, however, parents make informal arrangements with other adults to care for their children for a specific or even indefinite period of time. Usually these arrangements work just fine, but occasionally situations arise in which the caretaking adult isn't authorized to act—for example, authorizing medical treatment or obtaining benefits for the minor.

An adult taking care of a minor who isn't her child will, sooner or later, need to obtain a legal guardianship. *The Guardianship Book*, published by Nolo Press, gives detailed information on how to obtain a legal guardianship.

Note to stepparents. A stepparent who cares for his stepchild may suddenly find himself lacking the legal authority to seek medical care or to enroll his stepchild in school if someone gets formal. If you're a stepparent, it is imperative that you possess an authorization letter from your spouse like the one on our CD, discussed below.

Medical consent in an emergency

What if you're planning a trip for a relatively short period (let's say up to three months), and can't take your child with you? Or what if you're taking care of a friend's child while she is out of the country on business? Or what if you regularly care for a child (such as a stepchild), but are not in a position to become a legal guardian because the legal parent also cares for the child?

In these situations, it isn't possible or practical to go to court and appoint a legal guardian. But if the minor needs medical treatment or wants to attend a school event and the biological parent can't consent, the caretaking adult must. To facilitate this, the parent and other adult need a document spelling out their arrangement.

On the companion CD you'll find a sample Guardianship Authorization form. If you use it, we suggest you have it notarized. If the caretaking adult and parent anticipate any extraordinary activity for the child (such as taking her out of the country), we suggest you include specific authorization in the document, or have the parent write a letter to the caretaking adult authorizing the extraordinary activity.

Although the sample document uses the word "guardianship," it is not a substitute for a legal guardianship. As stated above, a legal guardianship can only be obtained by going to court.

E. When you must pay for your child's acts

As a general rule, parents are not financially responsible for the acts of their children that cause damage to someone or someone's property. This means that if your child is negligent—for example, trips over her shoelaces and falls on your neighbor's begonia plant—you are not *legally* required to pay for a new begonia even though it might be polite (and worth thousands in good-neighbor relations) to do so.

But (and this is a *big* but) if your child *willfully* damages another's property (little Susie *intentionally* rips up the begonias) you will be responsible for up to $25,000 for each intentional act.[22] And if your child (or a child you are legally responsible for) uses paint or a similar product to deface another's property, you will also be on the

---

[22] Civil Code § 1714.1

hook for court costs and attorney's fees, in addition to the $25,000.[23] If the child causes injury to a person, damages are limited to that person's medical, dental and hospital expenses. Parents! Check your liability insurance!

The parent or guardian having control of the child is liable. If both parents have custody and control, each parent is liable for the full $25,000. A parent without physical custody, who is not exercising actual control over the child when the willful act occurs, cannot be held liable.[24]

What is a "willful" act as opposed to a "negligent" one? "Willful misconduct" is pretty much figured case by case. Most accidental or clumsy acts by children won't constitute willful misconduct, but if the act is semi-delinquent, and especially if the parents knew about the behavior and didn't stop it, liability is likely to be found.[25]

Guns raise the ante of liability and responsibility (not just legally). Any injury caused by a child less than 18 years old with a gun that a parent let the child have, *or left where she could get it,* can cost the parent up to $30,000 for the death or injury of one person or his property, or $60,000 for the deaths of or injuries to more than one person and the owner of the gun can be charged with a felony.[26] If you have a gun, take this advice to heart: get a lock and make sure your children cannot get to it.

School, library and store-related damages raise different liability. Parents may be liable up to $10,000 for the willful misconduct of their children that results in:

- Injury to school employees or other pupils;
- Damage to school property; or
- Damage to personal property belonging to school employees.[27]

The parent or guardian having legal custody of a child who steals merchandise from merchants or books or materials from libraries may be liable for the retail value of the merchandise or fair market value of the books or materials, up to $500.[28]

Cities across the nation are enacting laws to make parents clean up the graffiti their children cover our buildings with. So, keep an eye on your children, or you may find yourself with a scrub-brush in hand and minus some cash in your wallet.

---

[23] Civil Code § 1714.1(b)   [24] *Robertson vs. Wentz* (1986) 187 CA3d 1281
[25] *Reida vs. Lund* (1971) 18 CA3d 698   [26] Civil Code § 1714.3; Penal Code §§ 12035, 12036
[27] Education Code § 48904   [28] Penal Code § 490.5

F.   Delinquents

Parents are required to keep their children within their control. This doesn't mean you must know where your kids are every minute and account for their every action, but it does mean that if your daughter is picked up by the police for tossing a brick into a bicycle shop window, she may be declared "beyond parental control." Not good, because if a child is "beyond parental control" Child Protective Services (CPS) might try to have the child removed from the parental home. If your child is taken away, he or she will be placed in a juvenile detention center.

The Juvenile Court also has the authority to exercise informal probation when it appears that a child is headed for trouble. This will only be done with the cooperation of the parent and child. The CPS worker will attempt to help the parent and the child work through their problems in a positive way, perhaps by getting them involved in community programs. The time to use this program—which bypasses all the court hearings, lawyers, formal reports and reunification plans—is before, not after, real trouble develops.

We don't have space to explain all the juvenile laws. To look up the laws yourself, go to your county law library or to the main (or a large) branch of your public library. Ask a librarian to help you find the Welfare and Institutions Code, which contains most laws pertaining to minors and their welfare. You can find codes on the Internet at www.leginfo.ca.gov/calaw.html.

G.   Neglect, abuse and losing children to foster care

Supporting a child is not enough. Parents must also refrain from abusing or neglecting their children. Generally, child abuse is broadly defined by statute to include a parent's failure to provide adequate shelter, food, clothing, medical treatment, etc. The government has a significant interest in protecting children, and so the legislature has enacted severe criminal penalties for child abuse. Practically speaking, child protective workers give broad latitude to how parents raise their children and won't interfere unless they receive a report indicating abuse, neglect or lack of parental control.

If a child is abused or neglected, the Child Protective Services (CPS) of the California Department of Social Services (DSS) may try to have the kids removed from the home through a dependency hearing; parents are entitled to have an attorney appointed to represent them. The CPS worker will try to work out an arrangement for reunification at a prehearing conference. A reunification arrange-ment usually requires the parents to attend parenting classes and some kind of therapy sessions. If the parent agrees to the arrangement, he, she or they must sign a reunification plan. If the parents and CPS can't negotiate an agreement, or the parents want to dispute charges, the parents can request a formal hearing before a Juvenile Court judge.

If the children are taken away, they may be placed with other relatives or put into foster homes.[29] During this period, the parents will want to act quickly to get their children back and do whatever the court has ordered as condition for reunification. For the first 12 months of separation, the court presumes it is in the children's best interest to be reunited with their parents. Between 12 and 18 months, the presump-tion decreases. At 18 months, the court presumes that "stability" is in the children's best interest—stability is defined as staying in the foster placement. If reunification is not progressing at the end of the 12- or 18-month period, the judge will make an order of permanent foster care or guardianship (in which case the parents will have the right to stay in touch with the children), or adoption (in which case parental rights are terminated).

When children are in foster care, DSS often seeks reimbursement of the foster care costs and legal fees from parents. Usually, DSS won't pursue parents on welfare, but will try for some reimbursement if the parents have any non-welfare income.

The incidence of child abuse in this country is horrifying. Abused children are often the voices never heard. As a parent you are entrusted with the care and welfare of your child. If you unable to deal with the stresses and difficulties of parenthood and find yourself treating your children badly, please realize that there are many good programs available which can help you and perhaps save your children.

For more information or help contact:

California Youth Crisis Line
(800) 843-5200
or find a local number for many kinds of help at
http://suicidehotlines.com/california.html

---

[29] Welfare and Institutions Code § 202 states that when a child is removed from his or her home, the state must give the child a home as good as the one the natural parents should provide. Sad to say, however, standards of care in some foster homes and juvenile centers in California are miser-able. We have seen situations where a child is taken out of an admittedly bad home and then placed in a worse one.

H. Emancipation —when a minor is no longer minor

An emancipated minor is a person under age 18 who is considered legally to be an adult. To become emancipated, a minor must:

- Enter into a valid marriage, whether or not the marriage is terminated by a dissolution;
- Be on active duty with the U.S. military; or
- Be declared an emancipated minor by a court.[30]

To obtain a court order, the minor must file a petition showing that he or she is at least 14 years old, manages his or her own financial affairs, and lives apart from his or her parent or guardian with that person's "consent or acquiescence." A judge will then decide whether or not to declare the minor emancipated.

Once a minor is emancipated, he or she has most of the same rights as an adult, such as the rights to:

- Consent to medical treatment;
- Enter into binding contracts;
- Buy and sell real estate;
- Sue and be sued;
- Make a will or a trust;
- Establish his or her own residency; and
- Apply for welfare.[31]

If the law establishes an age different from 18 for certain activities (such as driving, which is 16, and drinking, which is 21), an emancipated minor must wait until he or she reaches that age before legally engaging in the activity.

---

[30] Family Code §§ 7110–7122   [31] Family Code § 7050

Domestic violence

Domestic violence is the leading cause of injury to women, causing more injuries than muggings, stranger rapes, and car accidents combined.

It is tragic that so many couples who once blissfully bonded together (formally or informally) come to violent blows. Although family abuse is certainly not a recent phenomenon, public recognition and concern over the seriousness of the problem is.

Acts of domestic violence occur in households of every race, income level, and education. Everyone from doctors to ministers batter. It is primarily a crime against women and children—but not always.

Words, fists, guns and knives are all used as weapons. None are more hurtful than the other because it is not the bruises and broken bones that paralyze victims; rather, it is the damage done to self-esteem, self-respect and sense of worth that leaves victims damaged and helpless.

Every situation, though different, is strikingly similar. And only one thing needs to happen in every case for the abuse to stop—the person being abused needs to decide that she will not allow it to happen anymore. Once that commitment is made, financial, legal and emotional help are available to assist you through the process. You can't expect the abuser to the stop the violence—*you* must stop it, by regaining your power and making decisions which will protect yourself and your children.

A. When to get help

Domestic violence is defined as emotional, physical or sexual harm, or credible threat of immediate harm to someone in a family, household or dating relationship. Victims of domestic violence can get immediate court orders to keep the abuser out of the house and other places where the victims routinely go (work, school, day care, etc.), and to prevent future harassment. The California legislature has attempted to address the problem of domestic violence by enacting a number of laws that allow victims to obtain appropriate court relief—which often means instant relief.[1]

Often, the hardest part of getting help is recognizing and accepting the fact that you need it. If you are in an abusive situation, you need help—there is no shame in being a victim of domestic violence; the shame belongs to the abuser.

In this chapter we will give you an overview of the kinds of protections available and where and how to get them.

[1] Family Code §§ 6240–6388

B. What kind of protection is available?

Here's the good news—restraining orders work. If you are in a violent situation, get a restraining order so the police have something to work with in protecting you. The police want to help you, but you have to help yourself first.

Current domestic violence laws are far-reaching when compared to those of only a few years ago. They provide relatively simple procedures a person can follow, either with or without an attorney, to prevent further violence to her and her family. There is no filing fee to obtain a restraining order and it is something you can do yourself.

You can get instructions for how to get a restraining order at your county clerk's office or at the California Courts Web site at www.courtinfo.ca.gov. Click on "forms" at the top of the page, then select "Domestic Violence" from the menu. The forms and information are available in English and several other languages.

Caution! If it is possible that your computer might be monitored by your abuser, you can't be 100% sure you have cleared all traces of the Web sites you have visited. If using the Internet might put you in danger, call one of the toll-free numbers at the end of this chapter or in the front of your phone book. If your phone stores numbers or has a redial feature, be sure to clear it out after you call, or use a friend's phone or a pay phone. If you're in immediate danger, you should not hesitate to dial 911.

1. Types of relief

The purpose of the domestic violence laws[2] is to prevent a recurrence of domestic violence and to assure a period of separation for the persons involved. To facilitate these goals, a court is authorized to issue emergency protective orders *ex parte*, meaning, where only one party tells her side of the story to the judge. These are called Temporary Restraining Orders (TRO). The TRO can:

- Legally restrain the abuser from "contacting, molesting, attacking, striking, threatening, sexually assaulting, battering, or disturbing the peace" of the other household members specified in the order.
- Order the abuser to leave the home, regardless of whether he is the legal owner or renter, and not return to the home unless it is necessary to recover clothing and personal things.
- Order the abuser to keep away from certain places, things or people.
- Determine temporary child custody and visitation rights in both marital and nonmarital situations.

---

[2] Domestic Violence Prevention Act; Family Code §§ 6200 et seq.

In addition, the court has the authority in a TRO to:

- Restrain the abuser from disposing of real or personal property; and
- Determine the temporary use of real or personal property and payment of certain kinds of debts.

A judge can also issue the above orders by telephone when court is not in session.[3] A law enforcement officer (policeman, sheriff or even Department of Parks and Recreation officer) must request the order, based on his or her belief that the adult or child is in danger of domestic violence. The officer gets the order orally, writes it down, and then serves it on the party to be restrained. The orders last a few days after being issued, so you need to go to court for a regular TRO and a hearing date as soon as possible. The regular TRO will last until both sides have had a chance to express themselves at a hearing. After the hearing, the court is authorized to make orders that can continue in effect for up to three years and may include any of the following:

- Any of the six "ex parte" orders listed above; and
- An order for child support;
- An order that the abuser pay any household member for any loss (like wages) or out-of-pocket expenses (such as medical costs or temporary housing) incurred because of the violence;
- An order requiring all household members to participate in counseling where the parties agree, intend or continue to live with each other; and
- An order for the payment of attorney fees and costs to the prevailing party.

The court can issue these more permanent orders without first issuing a TRO if one party sets a hearing and formally notifies the other of the day, time, location and issues. This ensures that each party has an opportunity to present his or her views.

Remember—temporary restraining orders work. If you are in a violent situation, get one. It sends an important message to the abuser that you won't tolerate any more abuse and that society stands behind your decision to have it stop.

Resist mutual restraining orders. Some judges like to issue temporary restraining orders against both parties when one party requests protection against domestic violence. You should protest this practice, which equates your conduct with the abuser's, and remind the judge that the law allows mutual restraining orders only if both parties appear and show evidence justifying the mutual orders.[4]

---

[3] Family Code §§ 6241, 6250   [4] Family Code §§ 6320, 6305

2. How do I get a restraining order?

How to get a restraining order is explained in material available at your county clerk's office or on-line at www.courtinfo.ca.gov/selfhelp/protection/dv/. Help is also available from domestic abuse centers found in most communities. Most telephone books have a local domestic violence hotline number listed in the front with other emergency numbers and information. You can also call the Legal Aid office in your area (you will find them listed in the white pages) and ask for contacts and references. The police are required to keep a list of local shelters and programs to assist people facing domestic violence. Call and ask for referrals from their list. Although all these agencies may have names that indicate they are for women, they must provide services to abused men also if they receive government funding.

3. How long does it take?

Emergency or ex parte orders are usually issued immediately upon filing properly completed paperwork—three forms: *Application and Declaration for Order, Order to Show Cause*, and *Temporary Restraining Order*—with the county clerk's office in the Superior Court. When the judge grants your ex parte temporary restraining order, a hearing will be scheduled within 21 days so that the other person can tell his side of the story. The exact procedure for getting the judge's signature and hearing varies from county to county. The Superior Court clerk's office or a local women's support center will have this information.

A restraining order granted at this hearing can last up to three years unless the court shortens or lengthens the time or unless both parties agree to an extension.

4. Will I have to go to court?

Yes, you will have to attend a hearing, which will usually take place in a courtroom open to the public. This can be very intimidating for an abuse victim, who must confront the abuser in public. Fortunately, most court personnel are sensitive to this and try to make you feel as secure as possible, and you have the right to have a "support person" be with you at the table during the hearing and accompany you to mediation if there is a custody or visitation dispute.[5]

---

[5] Family Code § 6303

When your case is called, you have to explain why the abuser should be restrained. This will usually be the same explanation you gave in the *Declaration* that accompanied your *Application* for the TRO, but you may also introduce additional facts. Once you complete your presentation, the defendant has a right to tell his side. No matter how much you believe he is lying, you must prevent yourself from reacting while he is testifying. You will be given a chance to speak again when he is finished.

Both you and the abuser have a right to ask each other questions (cross-examination). If you become extremely upset by this process (many people do), take time to compose yourself—ask the court for a recess if necessary. If you feel you are being mistreated, say so. The judge will lean over backward to protect you.

When both you and the abuser have been heard, the judge will ordinarily decide the case right there, usually in favor of the victim, and extend the TRO (now called a temporary or preliminary injunction) to last up to 3 years. Or, the judge may modify the terms of the TRO in accordance with the testimony. Judges almost never remove all restraints in the face of testimony showing that domestic violence has occurred.

5. What if he violates the order?

If the abuser knowingly and willfully violates a court order, he has committed a crime, punishable by imprisonment and/or a large fine.[6] Each county handles this situation differently, so call your local police department to find out their policy. Possession of firearms by anyone who has been convicted of a domestic violence crime is a federal offense under the Federal Violence Against Women Act.

C. Mate rape

The essential guilt of rape consists in the outrage to the person and feelings of the victim. Any sexual penetration, however slight, is sufficient to complete the crime.[7]

Society is beginning to change its notion of rape from that of a sexual act to that of a violent act. As in so many other instances where there is an evolution in societal values, laws concerning rape have been amended to reflect the change. For example, in many states, cross-examination of a rape victim on her previous sexual history is forbidden, and definitions of rape have been modified to be gender-neutral so that both males and females can be victims of rape.

---

[6] Penal Code §§ 273.5, 273.6   [7] Penal Code § 263

Get real protection!
Over 85% of restraining orders work, but a piece of paper that says you are protected is not the same as real physical protection. If you fear for your physical safety, a secret change in physical location is likely to be of more immediate help than a restraining order. Only you know what your spouse or partner is capable of. Don't leave yourself or your children exposed to real physical danger.

In California, spousal rape is a crime.[8] Previously, courts and legislatures were reluctant to deviate from the ancient rule that a husband was immune from the crime of raping his wife. But, in the wake of growing concern over the large number of married women in this country subjected to abuse by their husbands, and recognizing that rape is a violent act, the crime of rape in California is now defined to include:

- The act of sexual intercourse when a wife resists, but her resistance is overcome by force or violence; or
- The act of sexual intercourse when a wife is afraid to resist because of her husband's threats of great and immediate bodily harm.

There can be no arrest or prosecution for spousal rape, however, unless the violation is reported to the proper authorities within 90 days. This 90-day reporting requirement appears to have been included because of the fear on the part of lawmakers that charges of rape would be used months later as a weapon in divorce.[9]

D. Recoveries for injuries

In California, one spouse can sue the other for injuries inflicted deliberately or as the result of negligence, just as if the spouse were a stranger. If you have an abuser spouse who has regular income, property (like his share of the family home), or liability insurance, you should seriously consider a suit for damages.

Personal injury damages recovered by one spouse for an injury inflicted by the other spouse are separate property of the injured spouse. This is the rule whether the injury occurs prior to marriage, during marriage, prior to permanent separation or after permanent separation.

---

[8] Penal Code § 262   [9] Penal Code § 262

E. Common questions

1. If I call the police, what will happen to my partner?

Your safety and the safety of your children must be your primary concern. Having said that, if your spouse has violated a restraining order in force or has otherwise battered or harassed you,[10] and the police are called, here's what will happen. A statement will be taken from you, and your spouse (or whoever the abuser is) will be arrested and taken to the police station. Depending on his record and the circumstances, he may or may not be granted bail (if he was already on probation for another violation, he will be kept in jail for at least 48 hours).[11] The District Attorney's office will decide whether there is enough evidence to press charges and will usually want you to testify against your spouse.

What about firearms? A sheriff or police officer may, at the scene of an incident of domestic violence involving a threat to human life or a physical assault, take temporary custody of any firearm in plain sight or discovered in the course of a search consented to by one of the occupants of the residence. A gun or other firearm so seized cannot be released for at least 48 hours, but must be released within 72 hours. Also, a person subject to a restraining order may be ordered to refrain from owning, possessing or purchasing a firearm while the protective order is in effect.[12]

2. I have no money—where can I go?

Many times a woman and her children are in immediate physical danger and common sense dictates that they get away from the physical presence of the abuser (or potential abuser) as quickly as possible. In the past, one reason women failed to do this is that they had no place to run. Consequently, California has enacted legislation that provides funding for shelters for women and children in this situation. The locations of the shelters are not made public in order to protect the victims and staff. Battered women's shelters unfortunately pass in and out of existence frequently. To locate a battered women's shelter or program near you, call one of the organizations listed at the end of this chapter, or in the emergency section at the front of your local phone book.

---

[10] Penal Code § 646.9(d)   [11] Penal Code § 243(e)   [12] Penal Code § 12021(g)

The police have an obligation to provide a written notice to victims of domestic violence that informs them:[13]

- How to obtain information about available shelters;
- How to obtain information about other domestic violence services in the community;
- That the victim has the right to press charges, that is, ask the district attorney to file a criminal complaint against the abuser; and
- That the victim has the right to petition the civil court for various protective orders.

If you have children. A battered woman who takes her kids into hiding is not guilty of child concealment or kidnapping if her case fits one of these two situations:

- She gets protective orders first, authorizing her to take custody of the children and denying the abuser visitation. Emergency orders are available by telephone with the aid of a law enforcement officer where the parent and child are in imminent danger.
- She has "good cause" to take the kids and run—a reasonable belief that it is necessary to protect the child.[14] But you must file a report with the law enforcement agency where the child had been living within a reasonable time (your address will remain confidential).

If you do run off with the children, we strongly recommend that you get a court order either before you go or very soon afterward.

Before a court will permit the abuser to visit with the children (when the danger is likely only to the spouse), it is first *required* to consider whether the circumstances require that visitation be supervised (where third persons are present), or whether visitation should be suspended or denied entirely. If visitation is permitted, the court is *required* to specify the time, day, place and the manner of transfer of children for visitation purposes, in order to ensure the safety of all family members.[15]

3. What should I do?

If you are in an abusive situation, start gathering information about who can help you and where to go for help. If you are in immediate danger, call 911. Call any of the organizations listed at the end of this chapter; call your local police department; call a local shelter. They will help you end the abuse in a safe manner. Do not allow domestic violence to be your children's inheritance or your legacy.

---

[13] Penal Code § 13701; Family Code § 6389   [14] Penal Code § 277   [15] Family Code §§ 3031, 6323

You are not alone, and there is help available. We repeat: the hardest part is recognizing and accepting that you need help.

F.   Nonviolent emergencies

Some situations faced by divorcing or quarreling couples do not involve violence or the need for temporary custody arrangements, but they still call for emergency orders from a judge. Nonviolent emergencies include:

- **Child-snatching within state.** You have come home from work to find that your spouse has left and taken the children to another place in California.
- **Child-snatching to another state.** You and your spouse had worked out a custody and visitation schedule but, over the weekend when she had the kids, she left California and said you'll never see them again.
- **Left high and dry.** You don't work outside the home (and didn't during the marriage). Now that you've separated, he refuses to support you, has closed the joint accounts, and you have no other source of income.
- **Children need support.** Although you are able to meet most of the children's financial needs, you can't meet them all. Your spouse, from whom you're separated, refuses to provide any assistance.
- **Assets need protection.** Your spouse left last night; you have good reason to believe that she is going to empty the community bank accounts and that she will cash in other community assets.
- **Foreclosure** of your home is threatened. Your spouse left about three weeks ago and refuses to contribute toward the mortgage or other monthly bills. You're afraid the bank is going to start foreclosure proceedings pretty soon.

Even if your situation is not precisely one of these just listed, if you're experiencing a domestic emergency of some similarly pressing type, you may be a prime candidate for an ex parte or other type of temporary protective order. As a reminder, an ex parte order is issued by a judge at your request without the other person (party) being present. In this section, as in section B, we give you an overview of when and how these orders can be obtained, but for detailed instructions, you will want to ask your County Clerk's Office for material on domestic violence.

1. I need help today! —*ex parte* orders

Ex parte means without the other party being present. You can go in immediately for an ex parte order in these three situations.

- Child-snatching within state
- Child-snatching to another state
- Assets need protection

It may also be appropriate if foreclosure of your home is threatened. Here's a brief description of how ex parte orders are obtained in these situations.

You fill out two forms (*Order to Show Cause and Temporary Restraining Order* and *Application and Declaration for Order*), available from the county clerk. If the request is to keep your spouse from emptying the bank accounts or taking other community property, another form called a *Property Declaration* is also completed. If custody is involved, a *Declaration Under Uniform Child Custody Jurisdiction and Enforcement Act (UCCJEA)* must be filled out. If the child has been taken out of state, you will need a lawyer.

You deliver the filled-out forms to the judge for her signature. If a foreclosure of your home is threatened, the other side must be notified before delivering the forms to the judge. A telephone call is enough. Child-snatching or asset protection would not require this prior notice, as they fall within exceptions to the notice requirement. Notice is not necessary when it would be futile to do so or unduly burdensome under the circumstances, or when it would defeat the purpose of the order.

When the judge signs the papers, she grants a temporary order which usually lasts only a few weeks. She also schedules a hearing to be held within 20 days. At that time, the issues raised in the ex parte order are addressed by both sides.

The emergency or ex parte order is not enforceable until it is *properly* served on your spouse. If your spouse has taken off with the kids and you don't know where she's gone, the district attorney's office may be able to help.

After the papers have been served, there is an enforceable order. If there's a violation of the order before the scheduled hearing, the court has the power to declare your spouse in contempt of court and, depending on the violation, throw him in jail. At the hearing, the judge will decide whether to make the ex parte order remain effective. Chances are that if the other party has done something fairly nasty and the judge fears he or she will do it again, the judge will make the order permanent.

2. I need help soon—non–ex parte orders

Non–ex parte orders should be sought in these situations at what's called an Order to Show Cause hearing:

- Left high and dry;
- Children need support; or
- Foreclosure of your home is threatened.

Briefly, here is how it works:

You fill out two forms (called *Order to Show Cause* and *Application and Declaration for Order*). If the request is for support, payment of debts, or any other financial issue, an additional form (called an *Income and Expense Declaration*), with its attachments, also must be completed.

The next step is to call the Clerk to set up a hearing date. Then, as with the ex parte order, the *Order to Show Cause* must be delivered to the judge for her signature. No notice to the other side is necessary because he is just being ordered to appear in the courtroom and tell his story.

The papers are then filed at the courthouse and served on your spouse. A hearing is held at the time and place indicated in the papers and both sides have an opportunity to tell their story. The judge then determines whether the requested order should be granted.

G. Organizations that help you get out of a bad situation

Remember, only you can stop the violence. A lot of help is available if you will just call on it.

To find a local women's center or shelter or support group, look in the emergency information section in the front of a major local phone directory, or call your local police department, Legal Aid office, or district attorney's office. If you belong to a religious group, talk to your minister, priest or rabbi. If you are too embarrassed to talk to your own minister, go to the competition.

You can also call on one of these organizations. They may have information on groups near you.

National Domestic Violence Hotline
(800) 799-SAFE (799-7233)

This service maintains 24-hour hotlines.

California Coalition Against Domestic Violence
(800) 524-4765
web site: www.caadv.org

Serves as an information and referral center for grass roots shelters and service programs assisting battered women and their children.

Woman, Inc.
(415) 864-4722

National Domestic Violence Hotline
(800) 799-SAFE (799-7233)

The two services above maintain 24-hour hotlines.

Battered Women's Justice Project
(800) 903-0111

Focuses on battered women and the criminal justice system; supplies information to advocates and attorneys.

CHAPTER 17

How to reduce pain and cost when it's over

This book is about lasting relationships and how to preserve them, but sometimes they can't be saved. Breaking up[1] is almost always painful, but the essential thing is to avoid *unnecessary* pain and cost, much of which can be avoided or minimized if you are careful. It is essential to avoid words and actions that escalate from hurt, fear, and anger to hostility, lawyers, courts, and huge expense. That would be very hard on you, on your kids if you have any, and devastating to your pocketbook. There are ways to go about breaking up that will give you the best chance for a smoother trip through one of life's most difficult passages. This is an exceedingly sensitive time when it doesn't take much to stir things up. Fortunately, because we go through this with other couples a few thousand times a year, we know exactly what you can do, and the kinds of things you must avoid, to make breaking up as smooth as possible.

A. Alternatives if you're not sure

If one of you decides it is definitely over, then it is definitely over for both. You can't make an unwilling person stay. But, if you are both open to the possibility of at least trying to save your relationship, there are steps you can take and people who can help you. If you signed a Couples Contract, you have already committed yourselves to making use of these resources in case of trouble in the relationship.

Conciliation or counseling. Sometimes the intervention of a third party can help a great deal, especially when it is difficult for you to talk to each other about your problems. Consider getting help from a marriage or couples counselor, religious advisor, conciliator or other trained and certified professional. John Gottman's bestseller, *The Seven Principles for Making Marriage Work*, points out that building up the positive features of your relationship is even more important than resolving conflicts (see chapter 2C), and many couples counselors now work from this perspective.

Trial Separation. A trial separation can provide a cooling-off period that helps to settle your emotions and clear your thinking. It gives you a comfortable situation from which to think about and work on reconciliation. If you are concerned about your spouse mismanaging community funds or assets, a trial separation may not be a good idea unless you can make arrangements that will put that worry to rest. You also

---

[1] For couples who are not married, breaking up presents much the same challenges. In this discussion, if you replace *divorce* with *breakup* and *spouse* with *partner,* it will work the same for you.

have to make practical arrangements for paying bills for both spouses and parenting if you have children. Legally, however, there is nothing you need to do—just go ahead and arrange your trial separation, and good luck.

Divorce counseling is also widely available and we highly recommend it, especially if you have children. In this case, the idea is not to get back together, but to separate decently.

B. If you decide to separate —setting the tone

If you decide to separate, don't do one more thing or say one more word to your spouse until you've read the rest of this chapter. The way you announce the decision, or respond to it, will make a huge difference in the way things unwind.

The most common cause of conflict in separation and divorce is lack of mutuality in the decision—in other words, both spouses haven't accepted the idea that you're breaking up. Ideally, the decision would be arrived at together, but in most cases one spouse decides alone after taking time to think about it, get advice from friends or professionals, process emotions, and make plans.

Once the decision is made, it is presented to the other spouse as a done deal and the sooner the better. Opportunities to solve problems and possibly save the relationship have been lost. What's worse, a long, hard divorce is more likely because the first spouse is ready to break up right away while the other spouse is upset and still working through denial and resistance. This person hasn't had time to process the reality and will be in some kind of emotional upset, in no way ready to discuss details or work out accommodations.

This is not a good time to push along on the breakup, even though the first spouse is ready and highly motivated to do so. Moving along too quickly at this point is the root cause of a lot of trouble to follow.

Advice for the first to decide. You are in a unique and powerful position to affect the future tone of the divorce. By being abrupt and insensitive, you can almost guarantee a bitter, expensive divorce. If you want to encourage a sane resolution of divorce issues, be patient, be sensitive, but most of all, slow down. Give your spouse time to process the changes. Stay positive and as close to your spouse as possible. You can express caring and concern while being firm in your decision. Work with your spouse until you can both accept the fact that going your separate ways is inevitable, and you can both focus on moving forward.

C. Can you stop a divorce?

Yes, and no. If you both agree you want to work on your relationship and try for a reconciliation, the two of you together can stop the divorce any time, right up to the day the judgment becomes final. But after a divorce petition is filed in court, there is no way to stop a divorce by contesting it. A court will not consider whether there are really "irreconcilable differences." If one spouse says there are irreconcilable differences and the other says there aren't, that's an irreconcilable difference. If you think you can work things out, try to persuade your spouse, not a lawyer or judge. Of course, you want a fair deal on the terms, but if you simply try to obstruct a divorce, you only guarantee that some attorneys will make a lot of money and you will end up hurting yourself and your children for no gain.

D. The five causes of conflict [2]

To reduce conflict, you have to avoid or overcome the forces that create it. There are four or five in every case:

1. Emotional upset and conflict. This is about high levels of anger, hurt, blame, and guilt—a very normal part of divorce. If one or both spouses is upset, you can't negotiate, have reasonable discussions or make sound decisions. Complex and volatile emotions become externalized—attached to things or to the children. When emotions are high, reason is at its lowest and will not be very effective *at that time*.

2. Insecurity, fear, lack of confidence, unequal bargaining power. You can't negotiate if either spouse feels incompetent, afraid, or that the other spouse has some big advantage. Divorce is tremendously undermining; it tends to multiply any lack of self-confidence and self-esteem. Also, there are often very real causes for insecurity: lack of skill and experience at dealing with business and negotiation, and lack of complete information and knowledge about the process and the marital affairs. It doesn't matter if insecurity is real or reasonable; it *is* real if it *feels* real.

3. Ignorance and misinformation. Ignorance about the legal system and how it works can make you feel uncertain, insecure and incompetent. You feel as if you don't know what you are doing . . . and you are right! Misinformation is when the things you think you know are not correct. Misinformation comes from friends, television,

---

[2] Sections D through L are summaries of material discussed at greater length in Nolo's award-winning book, *Divorce Solutions: How to Make Any Divorce Better*.

movies, even from lawyers who are not family law specialists. It can distort your expectations about your rights and what's fair. It's hard to negotiate with someone who has mistaken ideas about what the rules are. Fortunately, both conditions can be easily fixed with *reliable* information.

4. The legal system and lawyers. The legal system is one of the most insidious contributors to conflict and expense in divorce cases. The legal system is by nature *adversarial*; it is based on the principle of conflict; one side struggles against the other, trying to win. If you retain an attorney to "take" your case, you will probably be dragged into the legal system and this is not what you want in a divorce. Lawyers cannot help you talk to your spouse rationally or overcome the emotional upset, but are rather likely to reinforce it.

In all but the most conflicted divorces, you want to avoid the legal system as much as possible and—with the help of your Couples Contract, Nolo's books and other services—you can. Unless you are facing immediate threat of harm to yourself, your children or your property, it would be better if you do not *retain* an attorney. Read *How to Do Your Own Divorce* first.

5. Real disagreement. These are the real issues that you want to deal with rationally and negotiate with your spouse. Real disagreement is based on the fact that the spouses now have different needs and interests. After dealing with the first four obstacles, these real issues may turn out to be minor, but even if they are serious, at least they can be negotiated rationally.

The solutions are in your hands. Apart from the legal system—which you can avoid—all obstacles to your agreement are personal, between you and your spouse and between you and yourself. The solutions to your problems are entirely in your own hands and the legal system has little to offer compared with the potential for harm, and especially compared with all the things you can do for yourself outside the legal system.

Take care. Pay special attention to emotional upset and especially insecurity and fear. These are the forces that drive people into a lawyer's office. You want to avoid doing anything that might increase the upset and fear of either spouse.

- The upset person is saying, "I can't stand this, I won't take it anymore! I'm going to get a lawyer!"
- The insecure person is saying, "I can't understand all this, I can't deal with it, I can't deal with my spouse. I want to be safe. I need someone to help me. I'm going to get a lawyer."

This is how cases get dragged into unnecessary legal conflict.

E.   How to reduce conflict

Once breaking up becomes a reality, there are very practical and effective things you can do to deal with the forces that create conflict. They might not all be of use in every case, so just use what applies to you.

1.   **Make some "new life" resolutions.** Start thinking of yourself as a whole and separate person. You may feel wounded, but you are healing and becoming whole and complete. Keep that picture in mind. Pain and confusion are part of healing. Let go of old attachments, old dreams, old patterns that don't work; this is your chance to build new ones. Decide you will not be a victim of your spouse or the system or yourself. You will not try to change or control your spouse—that's all over now, it doesn't work, it's contrary to the meaning of divorce. Concentrate on yourself, especially on your own actions. You can do something about what your spouse does by changing what you do. Take responsibility for yourself: if anyone hurts or upsets you, try to understand how you let them do that. Try to become quiet and calm. Keep your life as simple as possible.

2.   **Insulate and protect your children.** Involving children will harm them and upset the parents. Keep children well away from the divorce. Tell them the truth in simple terms they can understand, but otherwise, don't discuss the divorce in front of them. Don't pass messages through them. Don't let them hear your arguments or hear you criticize their other parent. Let them know you both love them and will always be their mother and father, no matter what happens between you. Help them understand that loving their other parent is not a betrayal of you; they shouldn't have to choose sides. Help them establish a new pattern of stability so they feel safe, and help them have as much contact as possible with both parents.

3.   **Get safe, stable and secure, just for a while.** Your first and most important job is to do *whatever* you have to do to arrange short-term safety, stability, and security for yourself, the children, and your spouse—in that order. This doesn't mean forever, just for a month or a few months at a time. Don't be concerned yet about the long term or the final outcome, and we're talking about minimum conditions here, not your old standard of living. Don't even try to do anything else until minimum conditions are met. You can't negotiate if you don't know where you will live or how you will eat, or if you are afraid for your safety or if you think your house is about to be foreclosed or your car repossessed. You can't negotiate if your spouse is not in a safe and stable situation, too.

If you can't get both spouses stabilized, the fear and the upset level will go up and even if you can stay out of court by relying on your agreement to arbitrate, the process will get more complicated and expensive. Your case might even get dragged into the legal system at an early stage, despite your agreement to use mediation and arbitration (ADR), if one of you, out of desperation, creates an emergency situation before ADR gets started. These legal procedures are tremendously upsetting and *very* expensive, on the order of tens of thousands of dollars for each side. To avoid this kind of outcome, you have to help each other even if you don't feel like it.

4. Agree on temporary arrangements. It takes a long time for things to settle down and for the spouses to work out a final agreement. Meanwhile, you have to arrange for the support of two households on the same old income, the parenting of minor children, making payments on mortgages and debts, and so on. Ideally, arrangements for such things will be set out in writing.

If you can work out your own temporary arrangements during separation, neither spouse will need an attorney to get temporary court orders. Start by agreeing that you want a fair result and will both act fairly. Agree to communicate before doing anything that will affect the other spouse or the estate or the children. Agree on a mediator or conciliator and meet with him or her as soon as possible. The goal here is to avoid surprises and upset. Among other things, that includes closing joint accounts or starting legal actions.

5. Slow down, take some time. If you can make your situation safe and stable for a while, you don't have to be in a hurry. Think of divorce as an illness or an accident; it really is a kind of injury, and it takes time to heal. You have to go slow and easy. Some very important work goes on during this slowdown. You work on reducing emotional upset—this takes time. You work on mutual acceptance—this takes time. You work to help both spouses become confident, stable, secure. Use this time to get reliable information and advice; find out what the rules are; line up the mediation/arbitration services you agreed to use in your Couples Contract.

6. Get information and advice. First, organize your facts, records and documents. You'll want lists of assets, deeds, statements, account numbers, income and expense information, tax returns and wage stubs. Get information from your records and from your accountant, from recent tax returns, and from your spouse. Spouses should have a full and open exchange of information; it helps to build trust and confidence—and it's the law, so you might as well just go ahead and do it. If information is not exchanged freely outside of the legal system, you will probably end up in court with attorneys doing very expensive discovery work.

Learn the rules as they apply to your case. Read Nolo's best-sellers, *Divorce Solutions: How to Make Any Divorce Better* and *How to Do Your Own Divorce*. Make sure your spouse has a copy of these books, then maybe you can discuss some of the issues and ideas in them.

Be *very* careful where you get advice. Friends and relatives will want to help, but while emotional support is welcome, when they offer legal and financial advice, *don't take it*—the price is too high if they're wrong. They mean well, but probably don't know what they're talking about. Don't take advice from paralegals or forms typing services; they're not trained for it. You can call Divorce Helpline attorneys (section I) for practical, settlement-oriented advice.

7. Focus on needs and interests; don't take positions yet. A position is a stand on a final outcome: "I want the house sold and the children every weekend." In the beginning, there's too much upset and too little information to decide what you want for an outcome and, besides, positions are a setup for an argument: the other side either agrees or disagrees. It's better to think and talk in terms of needs and interests. These are more basic concerns: "I want what's fair and what the rules say is mine; I need to be secure and have enough to live on; I want to know what I can count on for living expenses; I want maximum contact with my children; I need to get out of debt, especially on the credit cards; I want an end to argument and upset." Put this way, these are goals that you and your spouse can discuss together.

8. Stick with short-term solutions. Concentrate on short-term solutions to immediate problems, like keeping two separate households afloat for a few months; keeping mortgages paid and cars from being repossessed; keeping children protected, secure, stable, in contact with both parents. These are things you can possibly work on together.

9. Minimize legal activity. You want to avoid any legal activity unless it is necessary—zero is best, or the minimum required to protect yourself or just get your case started, but do nothing else until you've arranged mediation and arbitration. Ideally, you will avoid retaining an attorney and you won't give your spouse any reason to retain an attorney.

10. Get help if you need it. For yourself or your children, consider counseling or therapy. For help with talking to your spouse, consider couples counseling or go see a mediator. These low-conflict professionals can help with emotional issues, defusing upset or, in the case of the mediator, with making temporary arrangements.

F.   What divorce is really about

To get a divorce, you have to settle these issues:
- How to divide whatever property and debts have accumulated during the marriage; and
- If there will be spousal support; and, if so, how much and for how long.

If you have minor children, you must also decide:
- How parents will share the care and duties of raising the children; and
- How much will be paid for child support.

As far as the law is concerned, this is what a divorce is about—property, children and support. That's it and that's all. If you can't settle these issues between you, a third person—judge or arbitrator—who doesn't know you or your family, will take as little time as possible to make the decisions for you. Whether you do it yourself or an attorney does it for you, you still have to gather your own facts and make your own decisions as to what you want to do, so you might as well do most or all of it yourself.

California laws are so detailed that in most situations, one can predict with reasonable certainty what a judge or arbitrator will decide, so there is little to be gained from going through costly litigation or arbitration. Any problem you have has almost certainly been legislated and litigated already. This makes it possible and attractive for couples to settle their issues through negotiation or mediation rather than arbitration or court. Family resources should be split between the partners to a marriage rather than the partners in a law firm.

G. When the date of separation matters

In some cases, the date you separate can be important, as it affects the character of both income and liability for debts. In most cases, it won't particularly matter whether separation was one date or another, so you can just pick a date that seems about right; but there are times when it can mean a great deal, as where a large debt was incurred or a big chunk of money earned near the end of the relationship.

The date of separation is whenever you can prove that one spouse intended to make a complete, final break (not just a temporary separation), with *simultaneous* conduct furthering that intent. Living physically apart is mandatory, which generally means a separate residence. It is possible to "live apart" in the same house, but this must be shown by clear, unambiguous conduct. Living physically apart does not, by itself, determine the matter because one can live apart without intending a final break. Courts consider evidence of all conduct and circumstances.

Let's suppose the wife earned a large commission on April 1. And say that on January 15 she had said, "I'm leaving you for good and this isn't like the other times I said it; this time I really mean it," and the couple stopped sleeping together from that time on, but it took until April 15 for her to actually move out. The husband thinks the date of separation was April 15 so therefore the commission is community property and he should get half. The wife thinks the separation was on January 15 and her earnings thereafter are entirely her own. Here's another case. Does the wife have to pay half of a loan the husband took out two months before she moved out when six months ago he had announced (again) his intention of divorcing her and she believed him so she started sleeping with another guy? It's often hard to say exactly when the separation actually took place. In the examples, any lawyer would be happy to argue either side, assuming the couple can't work it out. This is when you need to weigh the cost of fighting against the amount at stake. We think you should mediate before you arbitrate, as you agreed to do if you made a Couples Contract.

Spouses who separate and then reconcile several times may have more than one period during their marriage where property acquired is the separate property of one spouse rather than the community property of the marriage.[3]

H. Should you do your own divorce?

Yes! You *can* do your own divorce. Since Nolo's *How to Do Your Own Divorce* was first published, millions of Californians just like you have done their divorces without retaining lawyers, so you can almost certainly do it too. *How to Do Your Own Divorce* tells you what the rules are and how things are normally done. It helps you make your decisions, then shows you how to get your case through the courts.

You *should* do your own divorce. The legal process—and the way attorneys work in it—tends to cause trouble, raise the level of conflict and greatly increase your expense. Whether using mediation/arbitration, or going straight to court, no one should *retain* an attorney in any divorce case unless it is absolutely necessary. This does not mean you can't get advice and information from an attorney, just that you should not retain one to *take* your case and try to do it for you.

---

[3] *Pattillo vs. Norris* (1976) 65 CA3d 209

There are a few cases where you should *not* do your own divorce. You should retain an attorney if there is an immediate threat of harm to you or your children, or if your spouse is trying to transfer valuable assets. You may need help if your spouse is on *active* military duty and will not sign a waiver.

I. Who can help?

Nolo books. *Divorce Solutions: How to Make Any Divorce Better* gives you practical advice about getting through the emotional, practical and financial obstacles that you face. It's about how to deal with your spouse, how to negotiate, and how to keep your divorce sane. *How to Do Your Own Divorce* is about the laws of property, children and support. It tells you about the rules and what judges normally do, then shows you how to fill out the forms to get a divorce. These best-sellers may save you tens of thousands of dollars and lots of pain. Get a copy of each book and copies for your spouse, too. Shared information works better. It will be the best money you ever spent.

Friends, relatives and "common knowledge" are the worst and most expensive sources of legal advice. Use friends for moral support, but when they give you advice, just say "thank you," but do *not* take it seriously without checking with a reliable source. If you didn't get it from a *current* Nolo book or a family law specialist attorney in California, *don't trust it!* Just because you like or trust someone doesn't make them right. Bad advice can cost you dearly—perhaps for the rest of your life.

Legal Document Assistants (LDAs) used to call themselves "paralegals" but that was changed by law in 2000. LDAs act, basically, as a typing service for people doing their own divorces. You tell them exactly what you want and they type up the forms and handle the secretarial work. We introduced this innovation in legal service in 1972 and LDAs have since changed the face of the legal map. Their rates are generally $300 to $800 for doing your basic paperwork.

It is very important for you to understand the limitations of LDAs. Some are trained, but no training or other qualifications are necessary—anyone can do it. You *can't* get reliable legal advice from LDAs, nor can they safely prepare your marital settlement agreement (MSA) unless you have a *very* simple case, very little property and use the MSA in Nolo's *How to Do Your Own Divorce.*

There are many good LDAs out there, but be careful who you hire—just as when hiring a lawyer or a mechanic. Ask how long they have been in business and be sure to check references. If you know *exactly* what you want and have no legal questions, no problems, and no MSA beyond the one in *How to Do Your Own Divorce*, then using an experienced and reliable LDA is a very good way to get your paperwork done.

Lawyers who specialize in divorce know a lot, but because of the way the system works and the way lawyers work, they will almost certainly cause you unnecessary conflict and expense. Do not retain an attorney unless there's no other choice. Getting information and advice from attorneys is tricky, too, because they don't want to help you help yourself; they want to take your case and represent you.

Attorneys will frequently do the first interview for a fairly small fee, but too often they spend that time convincing you that you need them to handle your case. Hourly rates can run over $400, but $190–$250 per hour is average. Most attorneys require a retainer, about $5,000 is typical, but the amount doesn't matter because the final bill will almost certainly be much higher. Few attorneys will give you a fixed figure for the whole job. You are doing *very* well if you end up spending less than $2,500 *per spouse* on the *simplest* case; the average in LA and Orange counties when both spouses are represented is over $18,000 *per spouse!*

Divorce Helpline was created to change the way attorneys practice in divorce cases, to provide expert support for people who are doing their own divorces.

Divorce Helpline attorneys work exclusively on solving problems and settling divorces. We will not litigate or represent people—we don't believe in it. Instead, we serve as your guide and assistant. Divorce Helpline attorneys are trained in mediation and communication, and are good at solving problems in a practical way. We have to be, because—unlike other attorneys—we earn *less* if you can't settle your case. If you can't settle, we refer you to a litigating attorney in your area and give a refund for any work that was not completed due to your unresolved conflict.

Divorce Helpline can do a much better job for you when we do the *whole* case— the paperwork and the marital settlement agreement—as well as giving you advice. That way we have *all* the information, not just the small bit you are asking about. When we do the whole case, we often find issues, problems to solve and ways to save money that people didn't know to ask about. If you are using mediation and arbitration, Divorce Helpline does that, too, as well as the paperwork to file in court. Divorce Helpline attorneys charge $1,995 for a complete divorce package, which includes an attorney-drafted marital settlement agreement. If you use a lot of counseling and other services, it is possible to run up a bill as high as $2,500—your *total* cost for *both* spouses, but the higher cost is not typical.

J. Children of divorce

Fighting over your kids—custody, visitation, parenting—is the worst possible thing that can happen to you or your kids. It's always ugly. Studies show that harm to children is more closely related to conflict *after* the divorce. Everyone has conflict before and during a divorce, but if you want to help your children, get finished with the conflict and resolve it as soon as possible, at least within yourself.

Children need their relationship with both parents. There is a bonding that can never be replaced by a surrogate parent or stepparent. To protect the essential parent-child relationship, you have to insulate children from your own conflict with their other parent. The divorce is not their problem; it's yours. Being a bad wife or husband does not make your spouse a bad parent. So, don't hold the children hostage—they are not pawns or bartering pieces in your game. In the area of custody and visitation, don't bargain with your spouse on any other basis than what will give your children the most stability and the best contact with both parents.

The worst thing for the child of a broken home is feeling responsible for the breakup and feeling that loving one parent is a betrayal of the other. These feelings cause children intense stress and insecurity. To protect your child from almost unbearable pain, don't say anything bad about the other parent in front of the child; don't undermine or interfere in any way with the child's relationship with or love for the other parent; don't put the child in a position of having to take sides. Do encourage every possible kind of constructive relationship your child can have with your ex-mate. Let the children know that you are happy when they have a good, loving time with their other parent.

Kids can really get on your nerves at times and single parenting is enough to overwhelm any normal person. You are not Superman or Wonder Woman and kids are not designed to be raised by one lone person. You need help and support and you need time off from the kids. Make a point of getting help from family, friends and the many parent support groups and family service agencies throughout California. Get referrals to groups in your area through temples, churches or social service agencies.

K. Ten ways to divide property without a fight

If dividing your property is a problem, here are ten ways it can be done without a fight. Even if you agreed to use mediation/arbitration in your Couples Contract, the more things you can work out on your own, the better. Just talk it over and agree to use a method that you can both accept. This list was originally developed by Judge Robert K. Garth of Riverside, California.

1. Barter. Each party takes certain items of property in exchange for other items. For instance, the car and furniture in exchange for the truck and tools. Let's make a deal!

2. Choose items alternately. The spouses take turns selecting items from a list of all the marital property, without regard for the value of items selected.

3. One divides, the other chooses. One spouse divides all the marital property into two parts and the other spouse gets the choice of parts.

4. One values, the other chooses. One spouse places a value on each item of marital property and the other spouse gets the choice of items up to an agreed share of the total value.

5. Appraisal and alternate selection. A third person (such as an appraiser) agreed upon by the parties places a value on contested items of marital property and the parties choose alternately until one spouse has chosen items worth his or her share of the marital property.

6. Sale. Some or all of the marital property is sold and the proceeds divided.

7. Secret bids. The spouses place secret bids on each item of marital property and the one who bids highest for an item gets it. Where one receives items that exceed his or her share of the total value, there will be an equalization payment to the other spouse.

8. Private auction. The spouses openly bid against each other on each item of marital property. If one spouse gets more than their share, an equalization payment can be made.

9. Arbitration. The spouses select an arbitrator who will decide the matter of valuation and division after hearing from both spouses and considering all evidence.

10. Mediation. The spouses select a mediator who works to help them reach an agreement on matters of valuation and division.

L. How to negotiate with your spouse

1. Get information and advice. Use the Nolo Press books, *How to Do Your Own Divorce* and *Divorce Solutions: How to Make Any Divorce Better.* Give your spouse these books. Call Divorce Helpline and talk to one of our consulting attorneys who will help you develop options. The toll-free number is (800) 359-7004.

2. **Be prepared.** Get the facts about your assets, debts, incomes and expenses and help your spouse get the facts, too. Make sure you understand the rules that apply to your facts.

3. **Be businesslike**

- Keep business and personal matters separate.
- Meet in a neutral place where you can be free of interruptions.
- Make appointments to meet; be on time; make an agenda ahead of time.
- Be polite and insist on reasonable manners in return. If things become unbusinesslike, ask to set another date to continue the discussion.

4. **Problem solving.** Approach your negotiations as problem-solving sessions—something you work on together.

5. **Balance the negotiating power**

- If you feel insecure, become informed, be well prepared, use an agenda, get advice and guidance from Divorce Helpline. Don't feel pressured into responses or arguments; state your ideas, listen to your spouse, think it over until the next meeting. Then get advice if you want it. Don't continue if you aren't calm or if the meeting doesn't stay businesslike. Consider using professional mediation.
- If you are the more confident spouse, help build your spouse's confidence so he or she can negotiate confidently. Share all information openly. Be a super listener. Restate what your spouse says to show you've heard it. Don't respond immediately, but take time to think about what you've heard. Tone yourself back: state your points clearly but don't try to persuade or repeat yourself. Listen, listen, listen.

6. **State issues in a constructive way.** Instead of, "I want the house," say, "The house is very important to me because . . . ." The second statement encourages discussion and negotiation.

7. **Build agreement.** Start with the facts and don't go forward until you both agree to the facts about your property, income, expenses, and debts. Write down the facts you agree on and those you don't. Do research and exchange documents to resolve differences. Compromise. Make a list of issues you agree on. Try to refine the issues you do not agree on and make them more clear and precise.

8. **Be patient and persistent.** It takes time for people to accept new ideas and adjust their thinking. Don't be in a hurry; don't be surprised at upsets and reversals. Things will almost always resolve themselves later.

9. Get help. If you think your case is blowing up, don't give up. This is exactly the time to call Divorce Helpline. Helping people negotiate and settle differences is what we do best. It goes much better if we get involved with your case as early as possible, but it's never too late to try.

10. Mediation. When you and your spouse have come to an impasse on an issue or a group of issues and need a guide to help you find your way, a good mediator may be the right prescription. You can call Divorce Helpline for mediation. They work with you in person if you are convenient to San Jose, Walnut Creek, Sacramento, or Santa Cruz. More frequently, they do mediation by telephone. When you look for a professional mediator, choose one who is also a family law attorney. Non-attorney mediators do not feel comfortable with the legal issues in a divorce. The best way to find a mediator is by recommendation from someone you trust.

Mediation is not marriage counseling and is not used to get back together with your spouse, although if this is something you might be open to, you should tell your mediator and ask his or her attitude about working with couples in that situation. You should look at mediation as a positive step taken to resolve your disagreements that will help direct you and your spouse toward a fair settlement.

M. Last words

Hard times or difficult problems do not necessarily mean your relationship is over. Before you make up your mind about separation or divorce, go back and read chapters 1–3 again. Talk over the process you went through when deciding to make a life together and crafting your Couples Contract, if you made one. Recall your promises and intentions back then and what you agreed to. Remember your dream for a lasting relationship together.

Statistics tell us that two-thirds of all couples who stayed together through a very unhappy marriage reported five years later that their marriages were happy. Even if you've discussed the possibility of separation or divorce, your relationship may not be over. Consider your options and get help from your community and professionals. Consider resources like Retrouvaille (www.retrouvaille.org), that specialize in helping couples deal with severely troubled relationships.

You began your relationship making plans and choices together. Even though not all relationships last a lifetime, many do, so yours can. The choices are still yours. Take every opportunity to realize your commitments and hopes. No matter what, we wish you the very best!

Nolo Supplementary Family Arbitration Rules

Arbitration rules have been published by many organizations that provide arbitration services, such as the American Arbitration Association, Peacemaker Ministries, and the Beth Din of America. Arbitration rules that apply in cases in which the parties have not specified rules have been enacted by law in many states, including California, found in the California Code of Civil Procedure §§ 1280 to 1294.2.

These rules have in general been adopted with business disputes in mind and therefore do not provide for the kinds of temporary, preliminary or interim measures that are often necessary in family disputes or circumstances of marital separation. They also do not provide for the kinds of post-judgment relief and modifications that are sometimes necessary in family disputes.

To fill this gap, we created the Nolo Supplementary Family Arbitration Rules, which are intended to supplement any set of arbitration rules a couple might adopt, in order to deal with situations not anticipated by most sets of arbitration rules currently published by recognized organizations.

Exhibit A
Nolo Supplementary Family Arbitration Rules
Nolo Press Occidental • www.nolocouples.com

1. Scope and application

Any dispute subject to arbitration pursuant to a prenuptial, postnuptial, living together, marital settlement agreement, couples contract or relationship agreement that refers to these rules shall be governed by the arbitration rules named in the agreement or otherwise by the parties in writing, except that interim and post-judgment matters shall be governed by the following supplementary rules:

2. Interim relief and interim measures

(a) In the case of an arbitration where arbitrators have not yet been appointed, or where the arbitrators are unavailable, a party may seek interim relief directly from a court as provided in subsection (c) of this section. Enforcement shall be granted as provided by the law applicable to the type of interim relief sought.

(b) In all other cases, including cases of modification of interim relief obtained directly from a court prior to commencement of the arbitration or under subsection (a) of this section, a party shall seek interim measures as described in subsection (d) of this section from the arbitrators. A party has no right to seek interim relief from a court, except that a party to an arbitration governed by this Article may request from the court enforcement of the arbitrators' order granting interim measures and review or modification of any interim measures governing child support or child custody.

(c) In connection with an agreement to arbitrate or a pending arbitration, the court may grant under subsection (a) of this section any temporary or *pendente lite* orders a court is permitted by state law to make during the pendency of a family law proceeding, including but not limited to:

(1) A temporary restraining order or preliminary injunction;

(2) An order for temporary child custody and visitation while the arbitration is pending or until a judgment may be entered on the arbitration award;

(3) An order for temporary support of any party or child of the parties while the arbitration is pending or until a judgment may be entered on the arbitration award;

(4) An order for temporary possession and control of real or personal property of the parties;

(5) An order for the immediate sale of any asset of the parties;

(6) An order for payment of debts and obligations of the parties;

(7) Any other order necessary to ensure preservation or availability of assets or documents, the destruction or absence of which would likely prejudice the conduct or effectiveness of the arbitration.

(d) The arbitrators may, at a party's request, order any party to take any interim measures of protection that the arbitrators consider necessary in respect to the subject matter of the dispute, including interim measures analogous to interim relief specified in subsection (c) of this section. The arbitrators may require any party to provide appropriate security in connection with interim measures.

(e) In considering a request for interim relief or enforcement of interim relief, any finding of fact of the arbitrators in the proceeding shall be binding on the court, including any finding regarding the probable validity of the claim that is the subject of the interim relief sought or granted, except that the court may review any findings of fact or modify any interim measures governing child support or child custody.

(f) Where the arbitrators have not ruled on an objection to their jurisdiction, the findings of the arbitrators shall not be binding on the court until the court has made an independent finding as to the arbitrators' jurisdiction. If the court rules that the arbitrators do not have jurisdiction, the application for interim relief shall be denied.

(g) Availability of interim relief or interim measures under this section may be limited by the parties' prior written agreement, except for relief whose purpose is to provide immediate, emergency relief or protection, or relief directly related to the welfare of a child.

(h) Arbitrators who have cause to suspect that any child is abused or neglected shall report the case of that child to the appropriate child protection authorities of the county where the child resides or, if the child resides out-of-state, of the county where the arbitration is conducted.

(i) A party seeking interim measures, or any other proceeding before the arbitrators, shall proceed in accordance with the agreement to arbitrate. If the agreement to arbitrate does not provide for a method of seeking interim measures, or for other proceedings before the arbitrators, the party shall request interim measures or a hearing by notifying the arbitrators and all other parties of the request. The arbitrators shall notify the parties of the date, time, and place of the hearing.

3. Post-judgment modification and other relief

(a) In the case of any dispute which may arise after the conclusion of the original arbitration proceedings or after a court has entered a judgment between the parties, requests for modification or set-aside of any matter subject to post-judgment modification or set-aside under the California Family Code or Code of Civil Procedure, shall be subject to arbitration to the extent and in the same manner and to the same extent as the arbitration of a prejudgment dispute between the parties.

(b) Where arbitrators have not yet been appointed, or where the arbitrators are unavailable, a party may seek post-judgment modification relief directly from a court as provided in subsection (d) of this section. Enforcement shall be granted as provided by the law applicable to the type of post-judgment relief sought. A party may not seek directly from a court a set-aside of a judgment based on an arbitration award under California Family Code §§ 2120-2129 or any similar statute or rule. The arbitrators shall have exclusive jurisdiction over such matters, except that a party to an arbitration governed by this Article may request from the court enforcement of the arbitrators' order granting such post-judgment measures.

(c) In all other cases a party shall seek post-judgment measures as described in subsection (e) of this section from the arbitrators. A party has no right to seek post-judgment relief from a court, except that a party to an arbitration governed by this Article may request from the court enforcement of the arbitrators' order granting post-judgment measures and review or modification of any post-judgment measures governing child support or child custody.

(d) In connection with an agreement to arbitrate or a pending arbitration, the court may grant under subsection (b) of this section any orders a court is permitted by state law to make upon a showing of changed circumstances after entry of judgment in a family law proceeding, including but not limited to:

(1) A restraining order or injunction;

(2) An order for modification of child custody and visitation;

(3) An order for modification of support of any party or child of the parties after judgment;

(4) Any other order necessary to ensure preservation or availability of assets or documents, the destruction or absence of which would likely prejudice the conduct or effectiveness of the arbitration.

(e) The arbitrators may, at a party's request, make any post-judgment orders the arbitrators consider necessary in respect to the subject matter of the dispute, including post-judgment measures analogous to post-judgment relief specified in subsection (d) of this section. The arbitrators may require any party to provide appropriate security in connection with post-judgment measures.

(f) In considering a request for post-judgment relief or enforcement of post-judgment relief, any finding of fact of the arbitrators in the proceeding shall be binding on the court, including any finding regarding the probable validity of the claim that is the subject of the post-judgment relief sought or granted, except that the court may review any findings of fact or modify any post-judgment measures governing child support or child custody.

(g) Where the arbitrators have not ruled on an objection to their jurisdiction, the findings of the arbitrators shall not be binding on the court until the court has made an independent finding as to the arbitrators' jurisdiction. If the court rules that the arbitrators do not have jurisdiction, the application for post-judgment relief shall be denied.

(h) Availability of post-judgment relief or post-judgment measures under this section may be limited by the parties' prior written agreement, except for relief whose purpose is to provide immediate, emergency relief or protection, or relief directly related to the welfare of a child.

(i) Arbitrators who have cause to suspect that any child is abused or neglected shall report the case of that child to the appropriate child protection authorities of the county where the child resides or, if the child resides out-of-state, of the county where the arbitration is conducted.

(j) A party seeking post-judgment measures, or any other proceeding before the arbitrators, shall proceed in accordance with the agreement to arbitrate. If the agreement to arbitrate does not provide for a method of seeking post-judgment measures, or for other proceedings before the arbitrators, the party shall request post-judgment measures or a hearing by notifying the arbitrators and all other parties of the request. The arbitrators shall notify the parties of the date, time, and place of the hearing.

Relationship Resources*

Relationship

A Couple's Guide to Communication, John Gottman, Cliff Notarius, Jonni Gonso, & Howard Markman

The Couple Communication Program: www.couplecommunication.com

The Couple's Survival Workbook, David Olsen and Douglas Stephens

The Divorce Remedy: The Proven 7-Step Program for Saving Your Marriage, Michele Weiner Davis

Fighting for Your Marriage, Howard J. Markman, Scott M. Stanley, Susan L. Blumberg

The Five Love Languages, Gary Chapman

Getting the Love You Want, Harville Hendrix

The Gottman Institute: www.gottman.com

How to Get the Most From Couples Therapy, Peter Pearson (on CD, Resources folder)

Love Knots: How to Untangle Those Everyday Frustrations, Lori H. Gordon

Marriage Encounter: www.marriage-encounter.org

Passage to Intimacy: Gordon and Frandsen

Reconcilable Differences, Andrew Christensen & Neil S. Jacobson

The Relationship Cure, John Gottman

Retrouvaille: A Lifeline for Married Couples www.retrouvaille.org

The Seven Principles for a Making Marriage Work: A Practical Guide, John Gottman & Nan Silver

Smart Marriages: www.smartmarriages.com

Tell Me No Lies: How to Face the Truth and Build a Loving Marriage, Bader and Pearson

Why Am I Afraid to Tell You Who I Am? John Powell

Why Marriages Succeed or Fail…and How You Can Make Yours Last, John Gottman

You Just Don't Understand, Deborah Tannen

Financial and estate planning

Debtors Anonymous: www.debtorsanonymous.org

Just Give Me the Answers, Sheryl Garrett et. al.

Legal Affairs, Frederick Hertz

Smart Couples Finish Rich, David Bach

Unmarried America: www.UnmarriedAmerica.org

(continued)

*Reported to us as recommended to their own clients by practicing professionals

Financial (continued)

Unmarried to Each Other, Dorian Solot and Marshall Miller

The Wealthy Spirit, Chellie Campbell

Your Money or Your Life, Joe Dominguez and Vicki Robin

Faith

Beth Din of America: www.bethdin.org

Marriage Encounter: www.marriage-encounter.org

Peacemaker Ministries & Christian Conciliation: www.hispeace.org

Retrouvaille: A Lifeline for Married Couples www.retrouvaille.org

Index

"They've done the nearly impossible! This brilliant book helps couples craft an agreement based on mutual respect, affection, and friendship. Their flexible and clarifying approach to committed relationships is a gift to couples everywhere. I can't think of a better antidote to the potential carnage that comes from an unexpected or unwanted ending of a relationship. Just the process of creating a Couples Contract has the potential to strengthen your relationship. Give yourself a gift and read through this book."

— Peter Pearson, PhD, Menlo Park, cofounder of The Couples Institute

"*Legal Essentials for California Couples* contains crucial information that every couple needs. Anyone who counsels couples, including psychologists, physicians, marriage counselors, and financial advisors, will find this book an indispensable reference."

— Jonathan Rich, PhD, Irvine, author of *The Couple's Guide to Love and Money*

"This book reveals a void that exists between legal books and relationship counseling books, and then fills it. I would like to see this book in the hands of every couple. It will prevent many breakups, divorces, and children growing up in one-parent families."

— Sylvia Weishaus, PhD, Sherman Oaks, co-founder of Making Marriage Work

"Your book is really terrific! I think every couple should have it."

— Nancy J. Ross, San Jose, couples counselor, cofounder of
CollaborativeDivorce.com

"It's a great tool! I will recommend it to all my couples."

— Pamela Adams, MA, MFT, Carlsbad, couples counselor

"Your book is a breath of fresh air blowing to the center of our lives. Every couple would benefit from a relationship agreement. In our work we see couples all the time who could be so much more fulfilled without unresolved financial issues."

— J. Jeffrey Lambert, CFP, Sacramento, Lighthouse Financial Services

"What a breakthrough! As a minister, psychologist, and founder of the largest church-based counseling organization in California, I highly recommend this book to all couples to get them on the right footing for a lifelong relationship."

— Dr. Peter Robbins, La Mirada, Turning Point Counseling

"Sherman and Cameron have provided a wonderful resource for couples, an invitation for couples to consciously and carefully examine the 'contract' they are really signing in marriage. In an era where more then 50% of marriages end in divorce, this book should be required reading, as it could effectively prevent tremendous pain later in the relationship."

— David Olsen, PhD, coauthor of *The Couples Survival Workbook*

"This is extremely important information for couples. In mediation, we so often see people who *could* have prevented conflict if they had only made some decisions at the beginning, when their relationship was good. This will be an important guide to prevent problems."
— Robin Seigel, San Diego, National Conflict Resolution Center

"This book is a rich resource for California couples. With a written relationship agreement at its core, it provides strong, clear and specific advice, and much more. It is a wake-up call to all [couples] to be proactive in defining the terms of their union. The book also gives therapists a clear, goal-directed way to bring up challenging issues with loving partners who may be uneasy discussing anxiety-creating issues. No therapist should be without a copy of this resource. In fact, I will keep extra copies on hand to give to my clients."
— Ellyn Bader, PhD, Menlo Park, cofounder of The Couples Institute

"I am very impressed with the sensitivity, comprehensiveness, thoughtfulness, practicality of content, plus user-friendly organization of your book. The Couples Contract provides couples with a road map on how to establish, maintain and sustain a loving, respectful lifelong relationship, even when they hit the inevitable bumps in the road."
— Dr. Mackenzie Brooks, PhD, couples coach, counselor, trainer, teacher

"Extraordinary! Every financial professional should have a copy of this book to better understand legal aspects of relationship for California couples. The financial and legal understandings presented make it a "must read." This book is easy to read and very down to earth. I highly recommend it."
— Mary Dee Dickerson, PhD, CFP, San Diego, author of *Grow Your Goals*

"I find this book exceedingly useful and informative."
— Mahmoud Abdel-Baset, PhD, Islamic Center of Southern California

"[Your book] will be a real service to couples. I intend to use it as a text in my graduate Family Mediation course. I recommend the book for any couple. Congratulations!"
— Prof. Duane Ruth-Heffelbower, MDiv, JD, Fresno Pacific University

As a pastoral counselor, I found your relationship agreement to be a great step in the right ection."
— Peter Agnew, MA, Long Beach, pastoral counselor, director Restored Hope

Couples Contract is an important tool to help couples build a solid foundation for a onship with better odds of succeeding. Marriage counselors could do their clients a real by encouraging them to read this book and craft a relationship agreement. This will y protect them financially and legally, but it is a beautiful step toward creating a more nd trusting relationship with a chance of lasting."
— Catherine Auman, LMFT, San Francisco